D1065465

THE CROSS

THE CROSS

HISTORY, ART, AND CONTROVERSY

Robin M. Jensen

HARVARD UNIVERSITY PRESS

Cambridge, Massachusetts, and London, England

2017

Printed in the United States of America
First printing

Library of Congress Cataloging-in-Publication Data

Names: Jensen, Robin Margaret, author.
Title: The cross : history, art, and controversy /
Robin M. Jensen.
Description: Cambridge, Massachusetts : Harvard University Press, 2017. |
Includes bibliographical references and index.
Identifiers: LCCN 2016040930 | ISBN 9780674088801 (alk. paper)
Subjects: LCSH: Crosses—History. | Crosses in art. |
Holy Cross—History. | Holy Cross in art.
Classification: LCC BV160 .J46 2017 | DDC 246/.558—dc23
LC record available at https://lccn.loc.gov/2016040930

Contents

Preface

AMONG the memorials surrounding the September 11 attacks on New York's World Trade Center is a large object known as the Ground Zero Cross. Discovered in the wreckage of one of the twin towers by a worker, Frank Silecchia, it was to many eyes simply a couple of intersecting steel beams that happened to take the shape of a cross. Others, however, regarded the structure's survival as symbolic—a symbol of consolation, hope, and healing. Many believed it to be a miraculous and divinely granted sign that God had not abandoned his people. However they perceived it, visitors began to attach messages and prayers to the cross; they left mementos and photos of lost loved ones. It became simultaneously a tourist attraction and a pilgrimage site. Some view this cross as a holy relic.

During the process of debris removal, Silecchia and others sought permission to rescue the cross, and with the permission of New York's mayor, Rudy Giuliani, they moved and reinstalled it on a mound of rubble at the edge of the site, where it became a shrine of sorts. A Catholic priest, Father Brian Jordan, sprinkled it with holy water and declared, "Behold the glory of the cross at Ground Zero. This is our symbol of hope, our symbol of faith, our symbol of healing." Father Jordan said Mass at the foot of the cross each subsequent Sunday, drawing large crowds. On Good Friday in 2002, Jordan led a congregation of workers in reciting the stations of the cross. The Ground Zero Cross remained at the site until construction of the new World Trade Center began, and it was temporarily moved into the adjacent St. Peter's Roman Catholic Church, at Father Jordan's behest. After the completion of the National

September 11 Memorial and Museum, the cross was moved once again and is displayed there among other artifacts of the catastrophe.

The inclusion of the Ground Zero Cross in any official memorial of September 11 was almost immediately controversial. An organized group of atheists protested, arguing that it was inappropriate to use public funds to construct (or preserve) a sectarian monument. Their spokesperson, Ellen Johnson, pointed out that many of the victims of the disaster were non-Christians and described the cross as an advertisement for one religion over others. Once plans for the museum were announced and it was evident that the cross was to be included, the American Atheists filed a lawsuit, contending that this was a violation of the First Amendment prohibition of the establishment of religion and New York State's civil rights legislation. The directors of the museum responded by requesting the court to dismiss the lawsuit, arguing that the museum—an independent, nonprofit organization—viewed the cross as a historic artifact whose display was not intended to endorse any particular religion. In 2014 the Second Circuit Court denied the atheists' suit and ruled for the museum, adding that the exhibit was aimed at neither converting nor discriminating against non-Christians.

Today, the Ground Zero Cross not only survives in the site's museum, it has been widely replicated. A copy was set up at the gravesite of Father Mychal Judge, Order of Friars Minor, a New York City Fire Department chaplain who as one of the first responders to the disaster was killed by falling debris from the strike on the second tower. Another replica was constructed from salvaged steel and installed at the New York headquarters of the Franciscan Society of the Atonement. Gift shops in the museum and nearby stalls sell posters, lapel pins, rosaries, and other artifacts with depictions of the cross. Troops wore replica pendants into battle in Iraq.[1] Although the recent and relatively brief story of the Ground Zero Cross hardly compares to the sweeping and incredibly complex narrative of Jesus's cross, it can serve as just one among countless examples of how the Christian cross has been simultaneously a historical artifact, a symbol of a religion, an agent of miracles, a recipient of devotion, an infinitely reproducible image, and a narrator of its unique and tragic legend. Where some see a sign of hope, healing, or the comforting assurance of divine love, others see an emblem of exclusion, intolerance, or domination.

Preface

For nearly two millennia, the cross has been an instantly recognizable and defining symbol of the Christian faith. However, it also appears in secular as well as religious contexts, from centuries' worth of masterpieces to cheap costume jewelry, from grand cathedrals to highway billboards. It may seem so commonplace or even so exalted that one could forget its origins in a horrible form of execution. Yet, sometime in the first or second century, this dreadful device paradoxically became the identifying badge of an emerging religious movement. Assigned a potent, positive meaning, the cross largely overcame its negative connotations, and the visual depiction of a dreadful object was reimagined and transformed from a totem of ignominious suffering into a trophy of triumphant victory.

For all these reasons and more, the cross's story is neither simple nor straightforward. Embedded in the vast history of Christianity, this multifaceted symbol is implicated in almost every aspect of that much larger narrative. Whether as sign, artifact, instrument, or character, the cross has been cast into a myriad of roles. No single book could encompass more than a fraction of its saga, nor is it possible to completely separate historical facts from legends. This volume represents a modest attempt to cover some ground and to lead readers more or less chronologically through some of the highlights (and lowlights) of the history of this epic symbol, from its earliest days to the present time. Illustrations are meant to balance the words with powerful images that not only supplement the text but also provide their own kind of powerful witness to the narrative. Suggested additional readings for each chapter, which can be found at the end of the book, direct still-interested readers to more detailed and scholarly studies.

Writing this book has been a learning exercise. Throughout, I have been indebted to the fine scholarship of colleagues, most of whom I have only met through their publications. Even though I have tried to be sparing with endnotes, I hope I have given them all due credit. In any case, I must acknowledge that without their work, I would not have been able to complete mine. Many other individuals have also helped me with this project. They include the generous friends and the staff members at institutions who have provided me with the photographs that fill these pages with examples of visual art and artifacts. John Granger Cook, Giuseppe Camodeca, Annewies van den Hoek, John Herrmann, Donnel O'Flynn, Joe Zias, Yves Gunzenreiner, Jaime Lara, and

Jeffrey Spier have been extremely kind. They, along with the staff members at the University of Notre Dame's Snite Museum, the Yale University Art Gallery, the Dumbarton Oaks Museum, and the British Library deserve a shoutout. I appreciate the Metropolitan Museum of Art in New York City and the Walters Museum in Baltimore for their generous policy on open access for images. I am especially grateful to my long-term conversation partners Felicity Harley McGowan and Steven Fine, whose studies of the iconography of the crucifixion and the menorah, respectively, have been invaluable in my thinking about this topic. Students, family, and friends performed heroic and sometimes time-crunching feats of proofreading, copyediting, and indexing. Among them are Zachary Gresham, Robert McFadden, Theodore Harwood, and Madeleine Fentress Teh. I am indebted to the Institute for Scholarship in the Liberal Arts, College of Arts and Letters, University of Notre Dame for generously providing a subvention to assist in the costs of production and additional funding to pay for professional indexing. I also must thank my editors at Harvard University Press, Sharmila Sen and Heather Hughes, for their guidance, patience, and steadfast encouragement throughout.

Finally, I want to acknowledge the twenty-three students who enrolled in my Spring 2016 course, The Cross. The opportunity to try out drafts of my chapters and to test my organization of materials and concepts was helpfully supplemented by their weekly discussion questions and research papers. Their contributions to the course sometimes prompted me to include topics that I had overlooked or to develop ideas that I had initially skimmed over. The perfect focus group and sounding board, they were a joy to teach but they also taught me, and so I dedicate this book to them.

I

Scandalum Crucis

The Curse of the Cross

> They proclaim our madness to consist in the fact that we give to a crucified man a place, second to the unchangeable and eternal God, the Creator of all; for they do not discern the mystery that is herein, to which as we make it plain to you, we pray you to give heed.
>
> —Justin Martyr

At the heart of the story of the Christian cross is the narrative of Christ's crucifixion. For Christians, the cross's meaning is embedded in this narrative and testifies to it. Thus, the cross's tale begins with the event of Christ's crucifixion, as it was both reported and interpreted by the earliest textual and material sources. These witnesses reveal that adherents to the Jesus movement had to wrestle with a nearly incomprehensible fact: that the savior and Son of God died in an ignominious and excruciating way. The earliest written accounts show that his followers were initially confused and frightened even though they were soon reassured by the empty tomb and Christ's reappearance on the road or in an upper room. However, even believing in Jesus's resurrection did not erase their need to understand why God would have let the beloved Son suffer such a death. With insight, they converted an ostensible stumbling block into a symbol of divine love and defeat of evil. In so doing, they also transformed the figure of the cross from a badge of dishonor into sign of victory.

One of the best examples of this appears in a very early Christian document, St. Paul's letter to the Philippians, in which the author inserted an ancient summary of belief about Christ. It declares that Jesus, though in the form of God, humbled himself and became obedient unto death, adding the phrase "even death upon a cross" (*thanatou de staurou*—Phil. 2:8). By including this specific reference to the form of his death, the writer recognizes that Jesus's crucifixion had to have been troubling, while asserting that it was both purposeful and momentous. The next line explains, "Therefore, God has highly exalted him and bestowed on him the name that is above every name," so that all creation should bow before him and confess that he is Lord (Phil. 2:9–10). Thus, from earliest times, Jesus's death unquestionably was perceived as a paradoxical juxtaposition of degradation and elevation. It was at once the most intense expression of his obedience and humility and the clearest indication of God's approval and his glorious identity. Through the centuries, artists have illustrated this glorification by showing the elevation of the cross itself, borne up to heaven by angels, while still accompanied with the instruments of his Passion. Saints, prophets, patriarchs, and angels alike gaze up in awe.

Post–New Testament documents show that Christ's death on the cross continued to pose problems for early Christian missionaries, who undertook both to explain and to defend it as part of the divine plan and not a simple accident of history. Their case for the defense required creative rhetorical strategies, aimed at the objections of their opponents but perhaps also at assuaging their own doubts. Crucifixion was an intentionally brutal and humiliating form of capital punishment, meted out to thieves, rebellious slaves, leaders of insurrection, and army deserters. Jews, awaiting a kingly messiah, saw death by crucifixion as cursed and contradictory to their expectations; pagans could not fathom a crucified god. The former found it incomprehensible, the latter ludicrous. They could not accept that a messianic savior or someone the gods favored would undergo such humiliation; it was contrary to logic and scandalous to entertain. Thus, certain early Christian groups revised the story to remove the troubling elements and to allow Jesus to escape death altogether. Those who maintained the narrative of suffering acknowledged the cross's confounding nature yet then sought to demonstrate its providential purpose. Further, they attempted to show that the cross was not only foreshadowed in sacred texts but also perceived everywhere in the external, secular world. Once recognized as universally evident in both scripture and nature, its power and promise could not be gainsaid. Instead of a mere instrument employed by

1.1 Luigi Gregori, *Exaltation of the Holy Cross*, ceiling of the Lady Chapel, Basilica of the Sacred Heart, University of Notre Dame, ca. 1891.

secular executioners, the cross was assigned a role in God's plan for human redemption.

The Cross in the Pauline Epistles

The Pauline epistles are, arguably, the oldest testimonies to the place of the cross in Christian theology. In addition to incorporating what is likely an ancient statement of faith (the so-called Philippians hymn), St. Paul portrays his adversaries as enemies of Christ's cross (Phil. 3:18). Here he may refer to those who did not assign value to Christ's suffering and death by crucifixion, or to those who denied it, or, more likely, to those who remained loyal after believing that their messiah had ostensibly been proven to be a fraud. Paul's words reveal that Jesus's manner of death was a matter of controversy while simultaneously reinforcing its significance. What matters is not simply that Jesus died but *how* he died. Paul places the event of the crucifixion at the center of his theology, neither denying it nor trying to explain it away, rather facing it head on and fundamentally affirming it as a central mystery of the faith. Jesus's crucifixion was an inescapable fact and, for Paul, it must therefore have a profound meaning. Thus the crucifixion became, for Paul, the primary proof of Jesus as Son of God and the central event in salvation history, and he came to be regarded, over time, as arguably the most vehement and eloquent expositor of the crucifixion's significance.

Despite his manifest attachment, Paul refers neither to the cross nor to Christ's crucifixion in what scholars believe to be his earliest surviving letter, 1 Thessalonians. Although he mentions Jesus's death (and resurrection) several times in this letter, he never brings up the manner of his death nor emphasizes his suffering. Paul's focus on the mode of Christ's execution emerges most fully in his letter to the Galatians, where he mentions both the cross and crucifixion in seven different places. In one of these passages, Paul implies that the manner of Jesus's death may even have been publically exhibited, "O foolish Galatians! Who has bewitched you, before whose eyes Jesus Christ was publicly portrayed as crucified?" (Gal. 3:1). This could refer to especially evocative preaching or even an actual visual display. He goes on to concede that, on the basis of Deuteronomy 21:23, Christ's death could be understood as cursed

1.2 Bible from northeastern France, last quarter of the thirteenth century. At the beginning of Epistle to the Philippians, Paul is pictured holding the epistle from which Christ's cross emerges.

(Gal. 3:13).[1] In another passage (Gal. 5:11), Paul acknowledges the fact that Christ's death on the cross was an obstacle to belief in Jesus as Messiah.

In his first letter to the Corinthians, Paul employs the cross in a more metaphorical sense. In his introductory remarks, Paul explains that he was not called to baptize new Christians but to proclaim the Gospel, so that "the cross of Christ might not be emptied of its power" (1 Cor. 1:18). In the next line, he grants the irony of this symbol and admits that it will be incomprehensible to those who are not being saved. He explains that those who count themselves wise or who seek more positive signs will judge any celebration of cross or crucifixion to be a kind of madness. He concludes this thought by confirming that he preaches

Christ crucified as a "stumbling block to Jews and folly to Gentiles" (1 Cor. 1:20–23). Later, he again stresses his decision that nothing was more important to know than Jesus Christ and him crucified (1 Cor. 2:1–2).

Without doubt, early Christians had to overcome the perception that they were attempting to turn a horrible ending into a happy triumph. Crucifixion was a particularly scandalous death; it should have been a shattering defeat rather than a brilliant coup for the followers of a crucified leader. These oldest Christian writings recognize this conundrum. This theme appears again in the Epistle to the Hebrews, which attests that Jesus endured the cross while disregarding its paradoxical shame (Heb. 12:2). The influence of Paul's statement on the next generation is evident in an epistle written by Ignatius of Antioch (ca. 35–107 CE), "My spirit is a humble sacrifice to the cross, which is a stumbling block to unbelievers but salvation and eternal life to us."[2]

Yet, despite Paul's emphasis on belief in Christ crucified, he never emphasizes his suffering. He speaks of the atoning or reconciling blood that Jesus shed (Rom. 3:25, 5:9; cf. Eph. 1:7, 2:13; Col. 1:2), yet avoids any mention of Christ's pain or bodily torment. Rather, it is only the Epistle to the Hebrews that attends in any detail to Jesus's physical agony (Heb. 5:7–9). Nevertheless, Paul's words in 1 Corinthians and Galatians show that he clearly regarded Christ's crucifixion as core to Christian faith and identity. This is clearest, perhaps, in his concluding words in his Epistle to the Galatians, "But far be it from me to glory except in the cross of our Lord Jesus Christ, by which the world has been crucified to me and I to the world. For neither circumcision counts for anything, nor uncircumcision, but a new creation" (Gal. 6:14).

The Cross in the Gospels

Each of the four New Testament Gospels provides a relatively lengthy account of Jesus's arrest, trial, death, and burial, and each contains certain distinct elements. Scholars assume that some oral traditions circulated before the compilation of these four accounts and that some common source or mutual influence can be discerned among the synoptic Gospels. For example, Matthew, Mark, and Luke all report that Simon of Cyrene was ordered to carry Jesus's cross to Golgotha, the site of execution, which suggests that Jesus was too debilitated to bear it himself, possibly from the flogging he received before setting out (Matt. 27:26; Mark 15:15; John 19:1). Nevertheless, allowing (or obliging) someone other than the condemned to carry his cross likely would have been contrary to usual Roman practice.[3]

Once at Golgotha, Jesus apparently was stripped of his garments, since Matthew, Mark, and John mention soldiers casting lots for them (a reference to Pss. 22:18). Historians believe that crucifixion victims were typically stripped and that Jesus likely would have been crucified naked or possibly wearing only a loincloth *(subligaculum)* for the sake of Jewish spectators who would have taken nakedness as an affront, if not also to Jesus's own modesty.[4] Although some early Christian writers, including Melito of Sardis, describe Christ as naked upon the cross, later tradition visualizes him wearing either a loincloth or a knee-length knotted or draped cloth *(perizoma)*.[5]

Matthew, Mark, and John (but not Luke) mention Jesus's being offered a drink of wine mixed with a bitter substance, gall or myrrh, which might have been either an analgesic or a poison meant to speed death. However, this drink also is an explicit reference to Psalms 69:21, and so is given as an instance of Jesus fulfilling scripture (cf. John 19:28–30). While Matthew's and Mark's Gospels imply that this was a form of mockery, and Mark further claims that Jesus refused the mixture (Mark 15:23), John's Gospel has Jesus appear to request it with the words "I thirst" (John 19:28). Though the Gospels do not identify the one who held up the wine-soaked sponge, tradition came to name him Stephaton, and from the early Middle Ages onward, visual art pairs him with the lance bearer, who similarly received a legendary name, Longinus.

Although each Gospel offers many of these details, none describe the actual form of Jesus's cross or the way he was suspended upon it. Presumably, his crucifixion would have been similar to other ancient crucifixions, obviating any need for a detailed description. Despite traditional visual representations of nails as the instruments of crucifixion, the Gospel accounts do not actually describe Jesus being nailed to the cross. The first mention of nails is in the story of Doubting Thomas, who asks to see the "mark of the nails in his hands" (John 20:25). Although this may be a mistranslation (the Greek word *cheir* may also be translated as "wrist"), it is possible Jesus was nailed to his cross as well as being tied. The earliest Christian writings, including a mention of nails being removed from his hands in the apocryphal *Gospel of Peter,* support the claim that he was "truly nailed."[6]

John's Gospel alone mentions soldiers arriving before sunset to break the victims' legs (John 19:31–33). This would hasten death by reducing the body's ability to support its weight. As they find Jesus already dead, they do not perform this act upon him (fulfilling the words of Pss. 34:21). Similarly, John's is the only Gospel to mention a soldier piercing Jesus's side. The blood and water described as flowing from the wound could have been a result of the suffocation caused by hanging: water having filled Christ's lungs. It is also possible the Gospel includes this less as a nugget of medical information than as a sign of Jesus's filling the sacrificial role of the paschal lamb while also alluding to him as the source of living water.[7]

All four Gospels specify that a plaque (or "title") was placed upon the cross, naming Jesus as "King of the Jews" (Matt. 32:37; Mark 15:26; Luke 23:38). According to the Fourth Gospel, this title was ordered by Pontius Pilate and inscribed in Hebrew, Latin, and Greek (John 19:19–20). While such a multilingual inscription would have been exceptional in these circumstances, scant documentary evidence attests that printed accusations of the victim's offenses were often hung around their necks, probably to add to their public humiliation and to serve as admonition to others.[8] The question of its historicity aside, the title comes to be one of the most important Christian relics, and it shows up in nearly every artistic rendering of the crucifixion.

Crucifixion in the Ancient World

Despite their lack of detail and somewhat varied descriptions, the Gospels' accounts of Jesus's crucifixion accord reasonably well what is known about crucifixion in antiquity. As a degrading, slow, and especially painful form of execution, Romans almost never imposed crucifixion upon their citizens but rather inflicted it on individuals considered to be undeserving of more humane forms of capital punishment (thieves, slaves, or traitors).[9]

Romans, however, were not the first to practice crucifixion. Historians have found literary evidence for its use among Assyrians, Phoenicians, and Persians.[10] Romans also could have borrowed this form of execution from the Carthaginians, having come into contact with it during the Punic Wars. Famous instances of mass crucifixions of Jews include the Hasmonean king Alexander Jannaeus's execution of eight hundred Jewish rebels in the first century

BCE, according to first-century Jewish historian Josephus.[11] Josephus also records that when Publius Quinctilius Varus was governor of Syria in 4 BCE, he quelled a revolt in Jerusalem by crucifying two thousand of its inhabitants,[12] and that Emperor Titus executed as many as five hundred Jews a day for several months following the siege of Jerusalem in 70 CE.[13]

Rome did not inflict crucifixion solely upon condemned prisoners of vassal nations. In the first century BCE, the orator Cicero defended the senator Gaius Rabirius against the charge of treason. Those found guilty could be sentenced to death by being hanged from an "unfortunate tree" *(arbor infelix)*. In his speech for the defense, Cicero referred to the repulsion that Romans felt toward such a death, and why Roman citizens may have been spared it:

> But the executioner, the veiling of the head, and the very word "cross" *(nomen ipsum crucis)* should be far removed not only from the person of a Roman citizen but from his thoughts, his eyes and his ears. For it is not only the actual occurrence of these things or the endurance of them, but liability to them, the expectation, nay the mere mention of them, that is unworthy of a Roman citizen and a free man.[14]

Despite the traditional depiction of Jesus's cross as an intersection of a vertical post extending above an intersecting horizontal beam, the word for "cross" in the Greek New Testament, *stauros* (Latin = *crux*) did not necessarily imply such an object. Historically, both Greek and Latin words simply referred to an upright stake to which those condemned to death might be bound or tied until they suffocated to death. The conventional picture of a Latin cross *(crux immissa)* has been challenged over the centuries as some scholars and even Christian communities have argued instead that Christ died on a T-shaped cross *(crux comissa)* or even upon a single vertical stake *(crux simplex)*.[15]

Ancient textual evidence suggests that crosses probably took different forms. Josephus reports that the Romans fixed their prisoners to the cross in a variety of positions. Titus's soldiers, he says, nailed their victims to the cross in different postures. Sometimes only the upright post would be used, with the prisoners' hands nailed or tied directly above their heads.[16] Seneca the Younger, a source for some detailed information on crucifixion in the mid-first century, commented that sometimes individuals were crucified upside down, while others were impaled by a stake through their genitals or extended by the arms upon the horizontal crossbeam.[17] He asks whether anyone might be found who would prefer crucifixion—which, he says, involves being fastened "to that accursed tree" *(ad illud infelix lignum)* and slowly wasting away in protracted agony—to any other form of death.[18]

Contrary to traditional depictions of Jesus carrying his cross to Golgotha, most historians believe that victims probably carried only the crossbeam *(patibulum)* to the place of execution. The beam would then have been fixed to the vertical post *(stipes)*, which had already been set into the ground. Also contrary to popular representations of Jesus's crucifixion, it was far more common (and more practical) for Romans to tie the victim's wrists to the crossbeam with ropes. Nailing through the palms would have been useless as a means of fixing a person to the cross, as the structure of muscle and bone is too fragile to support the body's weight.[19] Thus, at the site, the condemned's hands or wrists would be tied or nailed (or both) to the crossbeam, which would be hoisted up by two-pronged pitchforks *(furcillae)* and inserted into a slot at the top of the upright. Once raised up, the victim's feet could be bound or nailed.

Sometimes a footrest *(suppendaneum)* or a small seat *(sedile)* would be attached to the post. These additions, rather than offering some relief to the dying, actually prolonged their suffering by lengthening the time that it would take them to die—from several hours to as many as three or four days—which is why it is unlikely that they would have been used in Jesus's crucifixion, even though they often appear in the visual art of later centuries.

Romans normally carried out crucifixion outside of the city walls, which is consistent with Jesus's crucifixion outside Jerusalem's walls at Golgotha, the place of the skull. However, crucifixions also became an occasional part of public games, intended to be a kind of gruesome entertainment along with the deaths of those condemned to the beasts. In other circumstances, soldiers would have been assigned to accompany the condemned, to carry out the execution, and to observe the death. Most scholars think that victims were initially flogged, probably to weaken them so that their deaths would be relatively swift once they were fastened to the cross.[20]

In his commentary on the Gospel of John, Augustine of Hippo explains why Jesus had to die on the cross, and then goes on to review the reasons why this death was especially painful:

> Among all the different kinds of death, nothing is like this. In fact, the most painful suffering is called "excruciating" *(cruciatus)* from the word "cross" *(crux)*. Those crucified, hanging on a tree, fixed by nails to the wood by both feet and hands, die a prolonged death. For to be crucified is not only to be killed, but to be alive for a while on the cross, not because the victim wishes it, but so death might be protracted and the suffering extended.[21]

Visual and Physical Evidence for Ancient Crucifixion

Rare physical evidence for nailing the feet has survived from antiquity; a skeleton discovered in a Jewish tomb from the first century was identified from an accompanying inscription as "one hanged with his knees apart." A nail had pierced the man's right heel bone, causing archeologists to surmise that, in this instance at least, each of the victim's feet were pierced through the heel by nails.[22]

Ancient visual depictions of crucifixion include two non-Christian graffiti. Not surprisingly, both of these are crude and underscore the humiliation of this type of execution. One of these graffiti, quite firmly dated to the second century, appears to depict a crucified woman who may have been executed as part of a gladiator show that took place in the Italian city of Cumae.[23] This graffito, found on a shop wall in nearby Puteoli, may even have been an advertisement for the games, as it was found amidst images of other kinds of spectacles, including some beast fighters. In detail, it shows someone tied by the arms and hanging from a T-shaped cross. At the upper left, the name Alkimilla is etched, which historians have taken to identify the crucified individual as female. The victim's body is presented frontally. Her knees are bent and her legs straddle the stake, although she is tied to it at the ankles. She appears to be nude, and a series of horizontal lines across her upper torso either indicate ribs or marks from flaying or scourging.

A more famous example of these crucifixion graffiti is the so-called Palatine graffito. This is also dated—with less certainty—to the second century. It was discovered in the 1860s on the Palatine Hill near the Circus Maximus in a room that has been identified variously as a section of soldiers' barracks, servants' quarters, or a school for imperial pages. Now housed in the Palatine

1.3 Heel bone (right calcaneum) with crucifixion nail from the first-century tomb of Yohanan after reconstruction, with mock-up.

Museum, it depicts a crudely drawn crucified figure. Seen from behind, the victim appears to have a donkey's head turned in profile and gazing down and to the left at a smaller figure who appears to be saluting it. The inscription, *"Alexamenos sebete theon,"* may be translated as "Alexamenos worships [his] god."

This graffito has traditionally been interpreted as a pagan caricature intended to mock the Christian worship of a crucified deity. It also corresponds to evi-

1.4 Crucifixion graffito, west wall, taberna 5, Puteoli.

1.5 Alexamenos graffito, from the Palatine Hill area, Rome.

dence that Jews and Christians were accused of worshipping the head of an ass or a donkey god. Josephus, as well as the early second-century Christian writers Tertullian of Carthage and Marcus Minucius Felix, records such rumors.[24] Tertullian (160–220) specifically identifies the Latin author Cornelius Tacitus as one of the primary sources for the calumny.[25] Tertullian also recounts an instance of a Carthaginian Jew (who was also a gladiator) displaying a cartoon of a man with the ears of an ass and one hoofed foot, carrying a book and wearing a toga. The caption below this image reads "Onocoetes," which, though difficult to translate, could mean "offspring of an ass," implying that Christians worshiped an ass.[26]

Minucius Felix (d. ca. 250), another North African, also attests to the slander of the ass-headed god. In the words of his pagan interlocutor Caecilius, Christians supposedly venerated the most degenerate of animals, an ass, for reasons that seem unfathomable yet well suited to adherents of a religious sect that also worships a man punished by crucifixion. Thus, he says, they worship the kind of god they deserve. Defensively, Marcus records himself as responding that the story is merely based on hearsay and that no one would be stupid enough to worship such an object.[27]

Pagan Assessments of Jesus's Crucifixion

As the Palatine graffito demonstrates, the scandal of the cross that the Apostle Paul acknowledged did not ebb as Christianity spread beyond the region of its origins. Paul's "enemies" of Christ's cross (Phil. 3:18) would have included those who found the cross an impediment to their conversion. By the second century, traditional Roman polytheists clearly found the idea of a crucified god ridiculous if not abhorrent. Their perspective was understandable. How could any powerful and immortal god be subject to a humiliating and painful death? How could anyone believe that a crucified man should be a god? Why would any religion make a virtue out of innocent suffering? Answering this was the work of a group of early Christian apologists, among them the well-traveled and literate writer Justin, a Judaean-born Gentile who moved to Rome at some point following his conversion to Christianity. At Rome, he became an instructor of Christian philosophy and ended his life as a martyr during the reign of the emperors Marcus Aurelius and Lucius Verus (ca. 165).

Justin specifically took on the problem of explaining the crucifixion in his *First Apology*, written around 150. He allows similarities between Jesus and certain Roman gods—for example, Asclepius and Bacchus, who suffered death and were raised to heaven. Yet, he insists, none were crucified because none of them would have dared to imitate the manner of Jesus's death, nor could any non-Christian appreciate the importance of the cross as a figure, insofar as it had been foreordained as a great sign of Christ's power and rule in ways that only the initiated would recognize and understand.[28] To those who could perceive its significance, however, the cross as the Christ's distinctive symbol was visible everywhere. It appeared in the masts of ships and the shape of a plough, in the banners of armies, and even in the human form itself.[29] Nothing, he says, could have existed without the form of the cross.[30]

Another early Christian writer, Origen of Alexandria (184–254), recorded a debate with a pagan named Celsus, who charged that Jesus was nothing more than an ordinary thief or a magician.[31] In response to Celsus's assertion that Christians perversely deemed Jesus to be the Son of God just because he was crucified, Origen explains that it was not the manner of his death that showed forth his divinity but the fact that he willingly suffered it for the sake of the human race, as one who was good, wise, and perfect. He insists that the prophets foretold Christ's sufferings and that Christ not only willingly embraced them but regarded them as the first blow in a cosmic conflict between good and evil. Origen also denies that Christians are superstitious about the cross, although he acknowledges that they venerate it. Furthermore, he points out that pagans had long venerated other objects that began with an armature in this shape, misconstruing effigies of the gods for the one object that was truly worthy of adoration.[32]

Origen's African contemporary, Tertullian, also addresses the rumors that Christians adored crosses or could be described as a priesthood of the cross. He points out that pagans also regard such figures as worthy of honor insofar as images of their gods (Athenian Pallas or Pharian Ceres, for example) often were formed from cross-shaped wood. Similarly, he suggests that they adore the trophies they set up to celebrate military victories and sarcastically commends them for at least clothing the cross-shaped armatures that serve as their basic structure. At least, he adds, the Christian cross does not imperfectly imitate a human figure but is merely a simple cross. Idolaters worship deities derived from shapes modeled on the cross while Christians worship a god who is whole and complete unto himself.[33]

Although these defenders all aimed at showing that Christian practices were not substantially different from pagan ones, they also reveal that early Christians did, in fact, venerate plain crosses. Like Justin, Tertullian also pointed out the ubiquity of crosses in the world, from military banners to the human form itself, standing erect with its arms outstretched.[34] These objects are not accidentally similar to the cross; they are, in fact, testimonies to its transcendent truth—a truth made obvious to any who would simply open their eyes to see.

Marcus Minucius Felix was similarly conscious that pagans found the Christian attachment to crosses incomprehensible and even depraved. In an invented dialogue between a Christian and a pagan, the latter even declares that Christians worship what they themselves deserve: the cross. In response, the Christian protagonist falls back on a trope already used by Justin and familiar to Tertullian, that because the sign of the cross can be seen everywhere in the world, from ships' masts to yokes to trophies of military victory, it must be fundamental to nature. Yet, the speaker adds, Christians do not worship crosses in themselves, whereas pagans consecrate figures of the gods that are based on this shape and made likewise of wood.[35]

Undoubtedly, pagans regarded Jesus's death by crucifixion as a folly. Augustine reports that the third-century philosopher Porphyry counseled the pagan husband of a Christian wife to seek the advice of Apollo. Through his oracle, the god replies that the husband probably will find it easier to write upon water or to fly like a bird than to dissuade his foolish wife from her commitment to a dead deity who was condemned by right-minded judges and who suffered an offensive and humiliating execution.[36]

Jewish Objections to a Crucified Messiah

Although for different reasons, the assertion of a crucified messiah disturbed Jews no less than the idea of a crucified god dumbfounded pagans. According to Jewish expectations, the Messiah was to be a reigning king in the line of David, someone who would bring peace, freedom, and prosperity to Israel. They certainly did not expect or hope for an itinerant teacher and healer who would be ignominiously executed by the hated Roman occupiers. Jews, of course, also had a lasting and deeply painful memory of the crucifixions under the Hasmonean ruler Jannaeus and the Syrian governor Varus. Based on these horrid cases, scholars have suggested that Jews themselves repudiated crucifixion as a form of punishment because they saw it as a kind of taboo.[37]

Beyond simply finding this kind of capital punishment generally repellant, Jews had a particular objection based in their sacred text: a key passage from scripture asserts, "A hanged man is accursed by God" (Deut. 21:22–23). This was the kind of death assigned to Haman in the Book of Esther (Esth. 8:7); it was likely the very stumbling block to which Paul referred (1 Cor. 1:23). In his letter to the Galatians, Paul actually refers to this ominous scripture, even directly quoting it: "Christ redeemed us from the curse of the law, having become a curse for us—for it is written, 'Cursed be everyone who hangs on a tree' " (Gal. 3:13). Here Paul introduces another curse—the curse of the law—which, he argues, is reversed by the fact that Christ took on the curse of being hung upon a tree.

Other New Testament texts allude to this curse, indicating that it must have been cited in general debate. For example, when the high priest questions the apostles' teaching in Acts 5, Peter responds, "The God of our fathers raised Jesus whom you killed by hanging him on a tree" (Acts 5:30). A similar phrase comes up again in the Book of Acts (Acts 10:39–40). Other references to Jesus as being hung on a tree, but without mention of the curse, occur in Acts (13:29) and in the first epistle of Peter (1 Pet. 2:24). Although this kind of execution might refer to any kind of death by hanging, it also appears to be an alternative way of speaking about crucifixion, in particular the kind of execution that would have invoked the Deuteronomic curse.[38]

Scholars have argued about why death by suspension was specifically cursed. Answers vary, depending on whether one consults later rabbinic laws or tries to recreate the historical context of passages in Deuteronomy or the New Testament.[39] It may be that the type of crime that prompted this penalty was especially repugnant or involved especially heinous religious infractions such as blasphemy or idolatry. In any case, Paul and the other New Testament authors must have known, of course, about the Jews whom the Roman general Varus crucified in 4 BCE. Depending on the date of their writing, they also could have been aware of the crucifixions that then took place under Titus. And yet, Jews never emphasized this particular form of Jewish suffering or martyrdom, perhaps because of its associations with this curse—or more likely—because of the cross's adoption as the preeminent Christian symbol.

The problem of this curse, raised by Paul, continued to plague Christians who were in dialogue with contemporary Jews. Justin Martyr constructed a dialogue with a Jew named Trypho in which he worked to overcome the implications of Jesus's particular form of death. According to Justin, Trypho accepts that the scriptures attest that the Messiah had to suffer, but refuses to allow that the anointed one could ever die in a manner that was cursed under the law.[40] To overcome his objections, Justin offers a long series of instances in which the cross or crucifixion was signified in the Hebrew scriptures, including Moses's raised hands during the battle with Amelek (Exod. 17:11), Moses's lifting up a bronze serpent upon a pole (Num. 21:9), and the passage from Psalm 22:16–18 that has the speaker describing his pierced hands and feet and enemies casting lots for his garments.[41] The Fourth Gospel already had cited the figure of the serpent pole as prophetic, quoting Jesus as saying, "Just as Moses lifted up the snake in the wilderness, so must the Son of Man be lifted up" (John 3:14). Justin also argued that the Passover Lamb pointed to the crucifixion of Jesus as the Lamb of God, like that sacrificial animal supposedly roasted on a cross-shaped spit.[42] Justin thus argues that Trypho's own tradition and sacred texts jointly demonstrate the truth of Christian teaching about Jesus's crucifixion.

Tertullian offers many of these same proof texts as a counterpoint to Jewish claims that Jesus could not be the Messiah as he was hung upon a tree.[43] Initially admitting that Jews could have reasonable doubts about this—that God would have exposed the Divine Son to that kind of death—Tertullian insists that God intended Jesus to die in this way precisely because it was cursed. The curse, however, could only be attributed to those who deserved to die in this way by the fact of their own guilt. Because Christ was innocent, he did not die in this manner for the sake of his own sins but so that the mystery of his Passion to which the prophets had referred in adumbrations or figures might be fully revealed. He adds that so great a mystery could not be made obvious, that it necessarily had to be set forth in symbols only. Tertullian's list of figures includes many of those cited by Justin, including Moses's brazen serpent. He adds a few others, including the image of Isaac carrying the wood of his own sacrifice and Moses's rod that struck the rock to produce water in the wilderness.[44] Therefore, Tertullian says, despite all its troubling associations, the cross upholds the whole structure of heaven and undergirds the earth. It is the source and guide of human salvation.

Notwithstanding their rejection of a crucified Messiah, later Jewish sources never denied that Jesus the man was crucified. The sentence to crucify him even was deemed defensible, insofar as it was in fulfillment of the law. Texts found in the Talmud demonstrate that Jews of subsequent centuries believed that Jesus was fairly tried and justifiably executed for apostasy, sorcery, and blasphemy.[45]

The amount of Jewish *"adversus Christianos"* literature is paltry in comparison with the amount of anti-Jewish writings by Christians from the early Christian era onward. Yet extant documents from the Middle Ages show that Jews did argue that if Jesus was crucified, then, based on Deuteronomy 21:23, his death was cursed.[46] Moreover, according to a medieval Jewish source, the *Toledot Yeshu* ("The Story of Jesus"), the reason that Jews sought to have Jesus's body taken down off the cross before the Passover could begin (John 19:31) was to follow the law requiring that criminals executed and hung from a tree must be buried on the same day (Deut. 21:22–23).[47]

Gnostic and Manichaean Reconstructions

Many early Christians also rejected the idea that the Son of God could truly suffer physical torment and bodily death. Rather, they believed that Christ would have escaped actual crucifixion either by suffering only in his human nature or by being replaced by a proxy (such as Simon of Cyrene) or an imposter. Some type of denial of Christ's actual crucifixion or bodily suffering—along with his real human incarnation—was widespread among groups that were ultimately marginalized and denounced as heretical sects. Their teachings varied widely, but they typically have been grouped together as gnostics. Their ideas are often referred to by the more general or inclusive label "docetism," which is a term derived from the Greek word *dokein,* meaning "to seem." As a descriptive term, this refers to a belief either that a divine Christ could only appear to be have been born, suffered, and died (that he could not truly do so in an ordinary human body), or that his death on the cross was a means of differentiating his divine being from his human nature. Such views were not limited to groups we might call gnostics in a restrictive sense, but rather may have been held fairly broadly by many different kinds of self-identified followers of Christ. Both Irenaeus of Lyons and Hippolytus of Rome refer to these theological views, yet evidently their proponents had already been circulating these teachings from the beginning of the Christian movement, at least judging from certain passages in the New Testament that condemned them (2 John 7 and others).[48]

The texts that make up the gnostic Nag Hammadi Library, discovered in Upper Egypt in 1945, are a trove of information about the teachings of some of these groups and suggest that they were not necessarily outliers. In some of these noncanonical texts, Jesus looks down upon the scene of the crucifixion and alerts some of his disciples that he is not actually the one whom they see dying upon the cross. In others, the resurrection takes place at the same time as the crucifixion, so that Christ seems to evade death, even while still on the cross. In most instances, Jesus is exempted from mortality and physical pain. In others, like the Valentinian *Gospel of Truth,* Jesus accepts his suffering with the understanding that his death will be the source of life for many and his being nailed to the cross is a means of imparting instruction in saving secret knowledge of the divine being within oneself.[49]

For example, the gnostic *Apocalypse of Peter* describes what Peter actually sees as he witnesses Jesus's crucifixion. Rather than follow the Passion narrative of the canonical Gospels, this document claims that the true, spiritual Christ is unharmed. Instead, only the "fleshly part" is tortured and shamed. Jesus appears to Peter as two persons: one who dies on the cross, the other who stands by glad and laughing. Jesus explains that the one who laughs is the true, living Christ; the other is the substitute, the one who came in his likeness. The text goes on to insist that those who sought his death were ignorant because the flesh is of no value. Equally useless is worshiping a dead man. Only the spiritual Christ can be a savior.[50]

Similarly, the *Acts of John* relates how John met Christ while the crucifixion was happening. Christ explains that he is not the one being pierced with lances while on a wooden cross, that to believe this is to be misled by what others say, and that such a death is unworthy of him.[51] Another example, the *Gospel of Philip,* interprets Christ's words from the cross, "My God, my God, why have you forsaken me," as a demonstration of this departure of the heavenly Christ from the human Jesus.[52]

Most ancient gnostics seem to have held a docetic view of Christ, typically of a savior whom they identify with a heavenly being from the realm of light. In some gnostic systems this heavenly being descended upon Jesus at his baptism and departed from him as he died upon the cross. Human salvation was understood to be a release of fragments of this light, trapped in the earthly, material world and in certain human bodies. This release was aided by a savior figure who was not ensnared by any corporeal reality.

Augustine of Hippo includes Manichaeans in this group, as some of them, like many gnostics, believed that Jesus did not have a mortal body and that his death was only an appearance.[53] Manichaeism, a religious movement founded by the prophet Mani (216–276), was characterized by its dualistic teachings that proposed the cosmos was engaged in a struggle between forces of good and evil. The Manichaean Jesus had several distinct aspects, among them a messianic figure who had a human form and only appeared to suffer and die on the cross. This suffering was associated with the suffering of every human soul that is attached to physical matter. Thus Jesus's suffering was a kind of release from this bondage, a spiritual deliverance that ultimately can be attained by adherents of the sect as their souls are enabled to enter the realm of light. They were therefore deeply attached to accounts of Christ's crucifixion and composed discourses and hymns in its honor.[54]

According to Augustine of Hippo, a one-time adherent, Manichaeans also had an interesting teaching about a cross of light. Augustine reports that they taught peculiar doctrines about *Jesus Patibilis* ("Suffering Jesus") and the *Crux Lucis* or *Crux Luminis* ("Cross of Light," "Luminous Cross").[55] Augustine explains that in the Manichaean system, this cross of light represents fragments of the divine nature that have become entrapped in human bodies or elsewhere in creation, particularly in vegetables or fruits. These fragments then feel acute pain when they are cut, cooked, chewed, or digested.[56] Jesus's crucifixion was analogous to this, insofar as his suffering uniquely revealed the luminous cross.[57] Studies in later (eighth–eleventh century) Manichaean art from Central Asia have pointed out a great many cross symbols, probably having some reference to this cosmic cross of light.[58]

The humiliating and agonizing death of their proclaimed Messiah and Savior God presented a challenge to early Christians, who had to explain it to Jews and Gentiles alike—if not also to themselves. In spite—or perhaps because—of this, Christians duly identified pre-Christian scriptures that prophesied the crucifixion, sought to comprehend its divine purpose, and found significance and meaning in what was at least initially a confounding historical event. In their accounts of Jesus's preaching, the synoptic Gospels also cite Jesus's admonition that his followers should "take up the cross," ostensibly a prediction of their own suffering and self-sacrifice (Mark 8:24 and parallels).

1.6 Leaf from a Beatus manuscript, "The Lamb at the Foot of the Cross Flanked by Two Angels," ca. 1180, Spanish.

Despite their unwavering trust that the crucifixion had some divine purpose, early Christians found themselves trying to explain an almost incomprehensible paradox. For that reason, some denied that it actually happened, at least to the Savior. Others turned the cross into a radiant symbol of liberation from the unfortunate entrapment of souls into bodily existence. For them, Christ's escape from this mortal state was evidence of his divinity, and the realization of its possibilities could be extended to those who comprehended its truth.

In the end, the cross—rather than the empty tomb—became the universal symbol of the Christian faith. Yet, while this figure remained inextricably linked to the story of Jesus's death by crucifixion with its potentially scandalous associations, it was gradually reimagined and transformed into a providential symbol of redemption to be embraced and celebrated instead of a reminder of an unfortunate scandal to be either rationalized or rejected. In this way, it became both a figure of sacrifice and of triumph.

This combination of dark past and bright future comes through in a twelfth-century illumination of an Apocalypse commentary by Beatus of Liébana. Here a slender golden cross stands against a lapis blue sky with the Greek letters alpha and omega hanging from its two arms. Underneath the cross, two angels flank the Lamb of God within a green field. The image comes from the Book of Revelation, which describes the reign of the Lamb, the descent of the New Creation, and the end of human suffering. However, the illumination also depicts the lance and the vinegar-soaked sponge from the Passion story. These two implements pierce the Lamb's back, perhaps to remind viewer that the cross is at once a symbol of glory and a memorial of Christ's suffering.

2

Signum Crucis

The Sign of the Son of Man

> Then shall appear the sign of the Son of Man in Heaven, that is, the cross being brighter than the sun, since this last will be darkened, and hide himself, and that will appear when it would not appear, unless it were far brighter than the beams of the sun.
>
> —John Chrysostom

The apostle Paul's acknowledgment that the crucifixion was neither a scandal nor a stumbling block to those who understood its divine purpose is amplified by other New Testament passages that describe Jesus's crucifixion as a victory over human sin, corrupt earthly authorities, and evil cosmic forces. For example, the letter to the Colossians proclaims, "God made [you] alive together with him, having forgiven us all our trespasses, having canceled the bond which stood against us with its legal demands; this he set aside, nailing it to the cross" (Col. 2:13–14). In exultant tones, the author continues, "He disarmed the principalities and powers and made a public example of them, triumphing over them in it [the cross]" (Col. 2:15). Thus the cross became a kind of talisman, a protective shield, a symbol of deliverance, and even a trophy.

In the Fourth Gospel, Jesus tells the Pharisee Nicodemus that the Son of Man's elevation can be compared to Moses raising the serpent in the wilderness: so "that whoever believes in him may have eternal life" (John 3:14–15). Nicodemus might not have realized that Jesus's comparison of his being raised up to that of the miraculous bronze serpent that healed the Israelites from

2.1 Moses raising the brazen serpent, from Peter Lombard's *Commentaries on the Psalms and St. Paul.*

poisonous snakebites (Num. 21:9) referred to the way that he would die. Rather, Nicodemus would have concluded that Jesus's elevation would bring about a salvific remedy for death. However, the early Church understood the figure of the serpent on the cross to signify Christ's being lifted on the cross, which the Gospel of John regards as a sign of his glorification, not of his humiliation (John 12:32, 17:4–5). The typological juxtaposition of the brazen serpent of Numbers with the depiction of the crucifixion appears frequently in Christian art, as in this twelfth-century illuminated manuscript of Peter Lombard's *Commentaries on the Psalms and St. Paul.*

Although the figure of the cross was inseparable from the story of Christ's Passion, early Christian writers came to identity it with the "sign of the Son of

Man" mentioned in the Gospel of Matthew—the sign that was to precede the Son when he returns on clouds of heaven at the end of time (Matt. 24:29–24:31).[1] Exegetes, like Cyril of Jerusalem (bishop from ca. 350–386), understood that this "sign" was a luminous cross that would announce Christ's imminent return at the end of time. He likened it to the royal standards that preceded the king's ceremonial entrance to a city.[2] Other commentators saw the cross's very shape as cosmically significant; it pointed in all four cardinal directions and encompassed all dimensions of time and space. Moreover, it was more than a mere sign: it was a potent indicator of God's power and intention to destroy evil, sin, and death.

The faithful saw this sign everywhere in their world, from builders' tools to ships' masts. This confirmed its universality as well as its constancy. Applied to persons, it became an indelible—but invisible—mark on the foreheads of those initiated into their community and identified them as belonging to the flock of the Good Shepherd who would find and claim them. It offered them protection from evil spirits, warded off danger or disease, reminded them of their baptismal oaths, and was their surety of safe passage from this world into the next at the end of life.

The Cosmic Cross in Apocryphal Literature

The apocryphal *Gospel of Peter* provides a somewhat different account of Christ's crucifixion than appears in the New Testament Gospels. Most scholars date the document to the latter half of the second century because it is cited in the works of Origen of Alexandria (184–254).[3] The author's actual identity is unknown and, while certain elements from the canonical Gospels were incorporated into the story, other features were unique. The fourth-century chronicler Eusebius considered the *Gospel* unorthodox, conceivably on the basis of these independent additions.[4]

Although many elements of the *Gospel of Peter*'s Passion narrative are familiar, the most significant difference comes in its unique and mystical resurrection scene. During the night, while the guards were watching Jesus's sealed tomb, they heard a loud voice from above and saw two men come down from heaven to stand on either side of the sepulcher. The stone that had covered the tomb's entrance rolled away on its own and the two men entered. The guards hurried to wake up their centurion as well as the Jewish elders, and as they recounted what they had witnessed, everyone saw three giant men emerge from the cave, two of them assisting the third. The heads of the two assistants reached to the heavens while the head of third was even taller. A giant cross followed this trio out of the tomb, and a voice from heaven spoke to it, asking it if had preached to those who sleep. The cross answered, "Yes."[5]

Although the heavenly question may seem more appropriately directed to the colossal third person who probably was meant to be the resurrected Christ (and who did preach to the dead according to the canonical epistle, 1 Peter 3:19), the narrative emphasizes the agency of the cross as a kind of living being. As such, it might be meant to refer to the Gospel of Matthew's "sign of the Lord" (Matt. 24:29–31), because this agency became a prominent feature in early Christian teachings about the end time. For example, the *Apocalypse of Peter,* another ancient noncanonical book, probably dating from the early to middle second century, incorporates this figure into its description of the Christ's Second Coming and Judgment of the Dead.[6] This document opens with Christ dramatically enumerating the signs of his coming and the end of the world:

> For the coming of the Son of God will not be plain; but as the lightning that shines from the east to the west, so will I come upon the clouds of heaven with a great host in my majesty; with my cross going before my face will I come in my majesty; shining seven times brighter than the sun will I come in my majesty with all my saints, my angels. And my Father shall set a crown upon my head, that I may judge the quick and the dead and recompense every person according to his or her works.[7]

Parallels to this text can be found in other noncanonical documents, including the *Apocalypse of Elijah* and the *Epistle of the Apostles.*[8] Each of these describes the cross as arriving just before Christ at the end of time as his identifying sign.

The *Acts of John,* a second-century collection of fragments or brief narratives regarding the Apostle John's evangelizing mission, relates a series of wonders. Toward the document's midpoint, John recounts to his disciples the circumstances of Christ's death and describes the moment, after the sixth hour, when darkness came over the earth (cf. Matt. 27:45). Suddenly, he says, Jesus communicated directly with him from the midst of a cave, pointing to a cross of light, surrounded by a formless multitude. John describes the cross as containing a single form and likeness, while Lord himself hovered above it, though without any shape but only a voice. In this voice the Lord told John, "This cross of light is sometimes called the Word by me for our sakes, sometimes Mind, sometimes Jesus, sometimes Christ, sometimes Door, sometimes Way, sometimes Bread, sometimes Seed, sometimes Resurrection, sometimes Son, sometimes Father, sometimes Grace."[9] Jesus clarified that this cross of light is not the cross of wood, which John will see when he, Jesus, returns to earth. Nor is he the one on the cross. Rather, this is the cross that "has united all things by the Word, and marked off things transient and inferior, and then compacted all into one."[10] Although clearly having some docetic elements (for example, the Divine Jesus appears to John while the human Jesus is dying on the cross), in this instance the cross itself becomes identified with Christ, having a power of its own, and encompassing a variety of symbols or images.

From Tree of Death to Tree of Life

The followers of Jesus not only viewed the cross as a symbol of triumph but also regarded it as a life-giving tree. This transformation was largely inspired by Paul's typological linking of Adam and Christ (the new Adam) in his first epistle to the Corinthians (cf. 1 Cor. 15). Early Christian writers subsequently elaborated and extended this equation to include the parallel between the cross and the Edenic tree of life (Gen. 2:9). The juxtaposition of the tree of death *(arbor infelix)* with the tree of life *(lignum vitae)* thus became a way of constructing the story of human redemption. While one tree contributed to Adam and Eve's disobedience and downfall, another tree—the cross—ultimately delivered their offspring from the consequences of that disobedience. Thus the cross is a material link between original creation and eventual salvation. It is the counterpart to the Edenic tree of life and the inverse image of the Edenic tree of knowledge.[11]

This linkage is vividly drawn in the apocryphal *Acts of Peter*, which probably was circulating in some form by the middle of the second century. In its concluding account of Peter's martyrdom, the apostle offers his final words to the surrounding witnesses. Just before he was hanged upside down upon his cross and again while he was dying, Peter refers to the cross as the "hidden mystery" and "unspeakable mercy." He urges his followers to recognize the cosmic symbolism of this instrument and the manner of his own execution. He explains that his suspension signifies the position of the first man, who fell downward toward the earth and reversed the natural order of right and left, top and bottom. By contrast, the cross of Christ is an "upright tree" whose image urges those who encounter it to recognize that error and to reverse direction, turn away from sin, and perceive the mystery of their salvation. Peter then identifies the vertical stake with the Divine Word, the crossbeam with human nature, and the nail that affixes them together as acts of contrition and conversion.[12]

A more homely story about the cross as tree occurs in the gnostic *Gospel of Philip*, which describes Jesus's carpenter father, Joseph, building the cross from a paradisiacal tree.[13] More dogmatic equations of the tree of Paradise and Christ's cross turn up in a variety of early Christian documents, including the late second-century work of Irenaeus of Lyons who, referencing the text of Philippians 2, declares that Jesus became obedient unto death on a tree (cross) in order to rectify the disobedience in which another tree had been implicated. In this way, Christ becomes the new Adam, whose suffering on a tree became the remedy for Adam's sin through a tree.[14]

Tertullian of Carthage similarly juxtaposed the tree of Eden with the cross in his working out of God's economy of salvation, while deploying it in a polemical context. In his treatise *Against the Jews,* Tertullian attempts to overcome Jewish refusal to accept a messiah who suffered the cursed death upon a tree (cf. Deut. 21:23). Regarding the "mystery of the tree," he explains the crucifixion's providential symmetry: that what perished through one tree should be reestablished by another tree.[15]

The existence of two trees in Eden sometimes creates a bit of confusion. Eden's tree of Life is the cross's counterpart, just as the tree of knowledge is the cross's antithesis. In one of his catechetical lectures to those about to be baptized at Easter, Cyril, a fourth-century bishop of Jerusalem, offered his version of these juxtapositions of both trees with the cross:

> I am truly amazed at the verisimilitude of the types. In Paradise [the Garden of Eden] was the fall, and in a garden our salvation. From the tree came sin, and until the Tree sin lasted. When the Lord was walking in

Paradise in the afternoon, Adam and Eve hid themselves; and in the afternoon the robber is brought into Paradise by the Lord. . . . The Tree of Life, then, was planted in the earth to bring blessings to the earth, which had been cursed, and to bring release for the dead."[16]

Cyril's contemporary, the illustrious Syrian theologian and poet, Ephrem, wrote several meditations on the Edenic trees and their relationship to the cross. In one hymn on the theme of virginity, he attributed emotions to the tree of life. It first suffers desolation at Adam's expulsion and then joy as it experiences his restoration:

Blessed are you whom they told among the trees,
"We have found Him who finds all,
Who came to find Adam who was lost
and in the garment of light to return him to Eden."
The world in the symbol of the shade of the fig tree
is belabored as if in heavy shadow.
From beneath the fig tree as a symbol of the world, you emerged to meet our Savior.
Very sad was the Tree of Life
that saw Adam hidden from him.
Into the virgin earth he sank and was buried,
but he arose and shone forth from Golgotha.
Humankind, like a bird pursued,
took refuge on it so it would arrive at its home.
The persecutor is persecuted,
and the persecuted doves rejoice in paradise.[17]

The typology continued through the next century with Leo the Great, who adapted the motif of the trees for a Holy Week sermon, extending the symbolism to include a connection between the gall and vinegar offered to Christ upon the cross and the forbidden fruit eaten by Adam and Eve. One kind of food expunged the guilt caused by consuming the other.[18]

These connections were also perpetuated in the ancient belief that Golgotha derived its name (the place of the skull) from the fact that it was the site of Adam's grave.[19] This explains the appearance of a skull (or a skull and crossbones) at the base of the cross in Christian iconography (cf. Figs. 6.1, 7.2, 8.2). Sometimes depictions of the crucifixion alternatively show Adam arising from his coffin at the foot of the cross. The earliest documentary reference to this tradition comes from Origen's *Commentary on the Gospel of Matthew*, although it also turns up in the writings of Epiphanius, John Chrysostom, and Jerome.[20] That Christ's cross should be planted directly over Adam's tomb perfectly symbolized the Pauline assertion that in Adam all die, while in Christ all are raised (1 Cor. 15:22).

The Mystical Symbol of the Cross in the World

Early Christian writers, such as Justin Martyr and Tertullian, saw figures of the cross in just about every aspect of daily life—in masons' tools, ships' masts, farmers' ploughs, trophies set up by victorious troops, or legionary banners carried by cohorts of soldiers. They also perceived the cross reflected in the human form, standing erect with arms extended in prayer, and even in the type of trophy set up by victorious armies, consisting of the helmet, breastplate, and shields of the defeated enemy set upon a crosslike armature.[21] Many of these figures appeared regularly in early Christian iconography and were especially popular as decorations on grave markers. Pointing out the ubiquity of this symbol bolstered the Christian apologists' response to opponents who mocked it as a figure of shame and failure. Hippolytus of Rome (170–236) rebuked those who persecuted Christians by claiming the cross as more than simple proof of the truth of Christian teaching; he also believed it to be a bulwark against attacks of the evil one. He declares that Christians find security and refuge in the safety of the church, which he compares to a strong vessel with the cross for its mast:

> We who hope in the Son of God are persecuted and trampled upon by the nonbelievers. The wings of the ships are churches in the sea of the world; and the Church is like a ship tossed in the waves. Yet, she is not destroyed, for she has Christ for her skilled pilot. Moreover, she carries the trophy over death, the cross of the Lord, in her midsection. . . . The ladder in her leading up to the sailyard is a symbol of Christ's Passion, which allows the faithful to ascend to heaven.[22]

Some writers proclaimed that this ubiquitous cross symbol stretched across the whole universe in its very shape. This idea was rooted in the text of a prayer from the Epistle to the Ephesians, that, being grounded in faith, the followers of Jesus could discern the breadth, and length, and height, and depth of Christ's love (Eph. 3:18–19). Gregory of Nyssa (335–395) referred to this text in his *Address on Religious Instruction* and interpreted it as Paul's attempt to convey the significance and extent of the figure of the cross to the Ephesian Christians. Thus, he equated each directional arm of the cross with one of these dimensions. The top is "height," the bottom is "depth," and the horizontal arms are "breadth and length."[23] Gregory reprised this interpretation in other writings in which he claimed that Christ chose this very shape of the instrument of his death because it revealed his true relationship to the cosmos. In it he is present in all the dimensions of space, holding them together and harmonizing them in himself, even though the cross symbolized the very object through which he was killed.[24]

Augustine of Hippo also frequently cited this Ephesians text as a reference to the cross and interpreted its symbolism.[25] Throughout, he explained that the "width" of the cross is the place where Christ's hands were fixed, and so symbolizes all his works of love. This encourages believers to follow the model of the saints and live virtuously. The cross's "length" refers to the vertical stake and thus not only Christ's perseverance but also the perseverance of the righteous, even through suffering. The "height" is the extension above Christ's head, which points to the ultimate goal and prompts spectators to lift up their hearts and draw strength from on high. Finally, the "depth" is that part that is buried in the ground and cannot be seen, and represents God's inscrutable mysteries. Augustine asked his audience to attend to this particular detail, as it represents the way Christians should be rooted—in their conscious awareness of Christ's self-emptying love, allowing them to understand all the other dimensions and extensions of the cosmic cross.

John Chrysostom (349–407) eloquently lauded the cross in a treatise against unbelievers. Noting the irony of transforming an instrument of torture into a sign of victory, he counters with the standard litany of the cross's ubiquity. His list not only includes the ways the cross appears in the the shapes of various worldly objects, he includes the sign of the cross made on bodies:

> No imperial crown could adorn like the cross, prized by the whole world. That which all once abhorred is now a figure zealously sought out by everyone, found everywhere, among rulers and commoners, among men and women, among virgins and matrons, among slaves and freeborn. For all impress the sign regularly on the noblest part of their bodies and daily carry the figure about on their foreheads. Here on the sacred altar and here in the ordination of priests, here again revealed with the body of Christ in the mystical meal. The cross is everywhere to be seen celebrated, in the home, in the forum, in deserts, in streets, in mountains, in valleys, at sea, on boats, in ships, on islands, on beds, on clothing, on weapons, in bedrooms, at banquets, in silver and gold vessels, in pearls, in wall paintings, on the bodies of beasts of burden, on bodies possessed by demons, in war, in peace, in the day, at night, among those who dance ecstatically, and among groups of somber ascetics. So are all truly eager for this miraculous gift, this indescribable grace.[26]

The Sign of the Cross in Early Christian Ritual

John Chrysostom's reference to the sign of the cross made upon bodies was far from the earliest mention of this practice. In fact, Paul's letter to the Galatians refers to his "carrying the marks of Jesus branded on [his] body" (Gal. 6:17). The apostle implies that these marks should deflect trouble. In the Book of Revelation, an angel who possesses the "seal of the living God" forestalls the destruction of earth and sea until the servants of God are marked with a similar seal on their foreheads (Rev. 7:2–4, cf. also 14.1). These seals clearly identify those who belong to God and thus offer security in times of tribulation.

This sign or seal most likely was derived from the protective mark described by the prophet Ezekiel during his vision of the destruction of the idolaters. In order to separate the righteous from the damned, the Lord sends a scribe through the city of Jerusalem to put a mark on the foreheads of those who sigh and groan over the abominations committed by the guilty (Ezek. 9:3–5). Historians propose that this mark had the appearance of an X or +, a version of the Hebrew letter *taw*, made by the intersection of two straight lines, either horizontal and vertical or two diagonals, that signified some protective purpose or meaning.[27]

2.2 *Ezekiel's Vision of the Sign "Tau."* Enamel plaque, mid-twelfth century, Flemish.

Tertullian associated the mark in Ezekiel with the seal of the saints in the Book of Revelation. According to him, the Hebrew letter *taw* was the same as the Greek letter *tau* and the Latin letter *T;* all of these letters looked (to Tertullian) like a cross. Thus he links the mark of the righteous in Ezekiel with the seal of the servants of God in Revelation.[28] Tertullian's younger contemporary, Origen of Alexandria, claimed to have inquired about the meaning of the *taw* to Jews. He reported that his sources responded that because it is the last of the twenty-two consonants in the Hebrew alphabet, it signifies the perfection of those who despair over sinners. Others, however, said that the *taw* identifies those who faithfully observe Torah, because the title of that sacred book begins with the letter. Finally, he adds, a Jewish convert to Christ explained that as the *taw* resembles the cross, the passage in Ezekiel had already predicted the sacred mark that identified followers of Jesus.[29]

Christian theologians continued to associate the mark of the righteous in Ezekiel with a Christian cross, although they additionally identified it with the mark that the Hebrews applied in blood to their doorposts at the Passover (Exod. 12:7).[30] By linking both Ezekiel's mark and the Passover sign with the Christian cross, Augustine expanded its prophetic significance. To him Christ had become the sacrificial lamb, whose blood marked the lintels of the Hebrews in Egypt and whose sacrifice was symbolized in the cross marks given to Christians on their foreheads at their baptism.[31]

The importance of this cross mark to Christians is evident in descriptions of everyday ritual practices.[32] For example, Tertullian insisted that Christians sign themselves "at every forward step and rising, at every entrance and exit, when we dress, when we put on shoes, when we bathe, when we dine, when we light the lamps, on our couches, on our seats, in everything we do, we trace this sign upon our foreheads."[33] Non-Christians took notice. According to one detractor, Christians not only misguidedly adored the wood of the cross, they drew it on their foreheads and—perhaps with the Passover story in mind—engraved it on their doorposts.[34]

Fourth-century theologians also emphasized the protective value of the cross sign, even believing that it had a powerful exorcistic function. According to his biographer, the great Egyptian ascetic Anthony of Egypt (251–356) urged his disciples to make the sign of the cross on both their bodies and their dwellings in order to repel demons who, he explained, feared the cross and would simply vanish as soon as they see it.[35] The North African teacher Lactantius (250–325) also believed that the sign, if traced on the forehead, would ward off demons.[36] In a late-fourth century letter to Emperor Theodosius I, Bishop Epiphanius of Salamis (310–403) objects to painted images of Christ, preferring the fact that early Christians made nothing apart from "that salutary sign of Christ" (the cross), placing it on their doors and everywhere else.[37]

In his lectures to those preparing for baptism, Cyril of Jerusalem refers to the cross of Christ as a royal sign, urging that it should be worn openly rather than kept hidden. He assures his catechumens that whenever demons see it on a believer's brow, they tremble and flee.[38] Like Tertullian, he urges them to make the sign while eating, sleeping, rising, speaking, entering or leaving, walking—on any and every possible occasion. He tells them that by making the sign of the cross they could silence the objections of unbelievers. Cyril further emphasizes that the sign, while providing powerful protection against demons and dangers, costs nothing. It requires no expenditure of money or labor; it is a free gift from God.[39]

As previously noted, John Chrysostom's praise of the cross urges his followers not merely to trace the "sign of our victory" upon their foreheads but also to inscribe it on the walls and windows of their houses, and to implant it invisibly on their hearts and minds. He declares that it would open closed doors, be an antidote for poison, deflect the imprecations of the devil, and unlock the gates of heaven. In regard to its properties as an antidote, he may have been thinking of the story of Moses and the brazen serpent. John also commends the use of the cross as a protective device for children in place of the magical amulets or other traditional practices he abhorred.[40] In another place, John explains that, though invisible, Christ would clearly recognize it on believers' foreheads. In the final judgment, the sign will "speak" as a pleading on their behalf.[41]

In one of his sermons on the Psalms, Augustine comparably notes that people cross themselves when they are frightened, even though they have already received it on their foreheads at baptism.[42] Elsewhere he recalls an instance when a dying priest signed himself on the forehead and mouth.[43] He also insists that the sacramental gifts of bread and wine are not validly consecrated unless the priest makes the sign of the cross during the prayer of consecration, a rare, early reference to this sign made during the eucharistic liturgy. Augustine sums up his exhortation with a rhetorical question: "What else is the sign of the Christ by the cross of Christ?"[44]

The Cross at Christian Baptism

Augustine's comment about necessity of the sign of the cross in the eucharistic liturgy was preceded by a statement insisting that unless the sign be applied to the foreheads of the newly baptized, to the water in which they are immersed, and to the oil with which they are anointed, they are not truly sanctified.[45] Although making a sign of the cross was widely practiced in a variety of contexts, the cross mark was especially important as the identifying mark given in the Christian ritual of baptism.

Cyprian of Carthage compared the mark of the righteous in Ezekiel and the seal of God's servants in Revelation with this ritual signing of the neophytes.[46] Following the lines in Colossians that linked baptism with Jewish circumcision (Col. 2:11–12), early Christians compared the baptismal mark of the cross with this bodily and indelible sign of membership.[47] In one of his catechetical lectures, Cyril of Jerusalem emphasizes the link between baptism and circumcision: "We receive the spiritual seal, being circumcised by the Holy Spirit through the washing of baptism, not in the foreskin of the body but in the heart."[48] Augustine made the same connection, saying that the cross sign is to the new covenant as circumcision was to the first covenant. He urged his flock to be circumcised in their hearts on the eighth day after their baptism (which often took place at Easter), noting that the eighth day is also the day of circumcision for Jewish male babies.[49]

Cyril, like many of his contemporaries, compared the baptismal signing with the cross to the branding of sheep. He explained that the sacramental seal would permit the Lord to recognize one of his flock.[50] Gregory of Nyssa made a similar comparison, adding that thieves can more easily snatch a sheep that is unmarked than one that has been sealed.[51] Other early writers compare this sign to the soldier's tattoo or the insignia worn by athletes to identify them with their teams.[52]

Resonant with his belief that the cross sign was, in general, an effective device for warding off evil, John Chrysostom believed that the mark given at baptism was an especially powerful shield against spiritual enemies. He says

2.3 Baptismal font from early Christian basilica, Bulla Regia, Tunisia, sixth century.

that once the priest gives the newly baptized the sign on their foreheads, it flashes light and blinds any demon who even tries to look at them. They turn away, frustrated, gnashing their teeth in fury about the loss of a soul they had hoped to ensnare.[53]

Theodore of Mopsuestia similarly declared that once the baptized were signed with the cross, demons see it (even from a long way off) and are deterred from their pursuit. Theodore also explains why the sign is placed on the neophyte's forehead. This, he says, is the highest and noblest part of the body and the place we direct our eyes when we speak to someone. In the future, he adds, if we display this sign before God, we will be granted the privilege of beholding him face-to-face (citing 1 Cor. 13:12). The cross is our proof that we are members of God's flock and soldiers in his army.[54]

Ultimately, the cross sign at baptism incorporates the wearer into Christ's crucifixion and resurrection. By receiving the sign of the cross, the newly baptized bore the mark of having undergone death to an old life, being reborn into a new life, and able to anticipate eternal life.[55] This ritual symbolism was concretely alluded to in the cruciform shape of many early Christian baptismal fonts. The candidate imitated Christ's death as she descended into the cross and then his resurrection as she emerged and stepped out.

Martyrs as Imitators of the Cross

The Gospel of Matthew records Jesus as lambasting his audience of scribes, Pharisees, and hypocrites for killing and crucifying the prophets and wise men he sends them (Matt. 23:34). This prophecy, paired with Jesus's admonition that those who wish to follow him need to take up their cross (Matt. 16:24 and parallels), undergirds the idea that those who died as martyrs imitated Christ, if not in the manner of his death, at least in their suffering and witness.

At least two apostles are reported to have died by crucifixion. According to tradition, the Apostle Peter was crucified in Rome, swept up in a persecution ordered by the Emperor Nero (54–68 CE) in order to deflect blame for a fire that destroyed a large portion of the city. The Roman historian Tacitus reports that a multitude of Rome's Christians lost their lives at this time, accused not of arson but of hatred of humanity. Condemned to die as part of an entertainment in the arena, they were attacked by wild beasts, crucified, or burned alive.[56] Tertullian, writing at the beginning of the third century, also records the belief that Peter was crucified in Rome, although he does not give a specific date.[57] The details of Peter's martyrdom turn up first in the late second-century *Apocryphal Acts of Peter,* which relates that Peter specifically requested to be crucified upside down in order to suffer in a different manner from Christ. The account of Peter's passion includes his explanation for this request: the manner of his suspension was to symbolize the downward spiral of humankind since Adam first sinned and to serve as an admonition to those who witnessed his death to repent and renounce that first error in order to turn upright again, following the true cross of Christ, the upright tree.[58]

According to the *Apocryphal Acts of St. Andrew,* a controversial second- or third-century work denounced by certain church authorities as spurious or heretical, that saint also was scourged and crucified.[59] After one attempt at rescue by the proconsul's brother who had been converted, he finally was led to the site of his execution, where he loudly addressed the cross:

> Greetings, O cross! Greetings indeed! I know well that, though you have been weary for a long time, planted and awaiting me, now at last you can rest. I come to you, whom I have known. I recognize your mystery, why you were planted. So then, cross that is pure, radiant, full of life and light, receive me, I who have been weary for so long.[60]

The text continues, relating that, by order of the proconsul, in order to prolong his death, the executioners tied him to the cross rather than nailing him his hands or feet or breaking his legs. An epitome of the *Acts,* written by Gregory of Tours, states that he continued to preach for three days before expiring.[61] A later tradition elaborates that Andrew specifically requested to be crucified on an X-shaped cross, as he believed himself unworthy to share exactly the same death as Christ.[62]

Few other early Christian martyrs' records reveal that they underwent crucifixion, even though their ordeals were understood as imitating Christ's suffering. Nevertheless, two cases stand out. Pionius, martyred in the Decian persecution, voluntarily stretched himself out, naked, on a stake or cross and allowed the soldier to nail his hands to the beam and raise him aloft. He died, however, from being burned to death in that position.[63] The account of the martyrs of Lyons and Viennes (ca. 177) reports that St. Blandina (d. ca. 177), bound to a stake, appeared to onlookers as if she were actually suspended on a cross. This caused those who watched to perceive Christ crucified in her form and thus to comprehend that the martyr's suffering was a sign of her eternal fellowship with Christ.[64]

Cross Marks on Christian Artifacts

Found in almost every imaginable context, a cross mark is no more than a basic character of two intersecting lines, not necessarily a Christian symbol. Consequently it is difficult to know how to interpret many ancient crosslike images. Crosses found on loaves of bread, as part of game boards, or in masons' alignment marks probably have no religious significance. Yet, when they are found on first-century Jewish burial boxes or tomb markers, they might be versions of the *taw* sign from Ezekiel or—conceivably—specifically Christian symbols.[65] They also may be some kind of magical inscription or simply indications of which side should be placed toward the back of the tomb. In any case, barring other indicators, determining that a simple X-shaped mark has some intentional Christian meaning—much more that it directly alludes to Christ's crucifixion—is often unjustified. Such ambiguous marks are frequently the subject of speculation, even though they only may be crosses in the eyes of an optimistic beholder.

One rather famous and controversial artifact is the so-called Herculaneum cross. Found on the wall of an upper room in that ancient Roman city, it is dated no later than the year the city was destroyed in the Vesuvius eruption (79 CE). If it was undoubtedly shown to be an actual Christian cross, it would be the oldest in existence. Yet, rather than an applied mark, it is a fairly modest depression in the wall plaster, indicating that something of the same shape was attached by nails and then removed at some point. Some scholars suggest that object must have been a wooden cross, hung on a wall of a small Christian chapel and then removed to evade discovery and persecution. Against this explanation, others have simply identified this as a bracket to support a shelf or small cabinet—basically anything that could have been supported on the wall by two pieces of crossed wood.[66] Given the very early date and the lack of any other clearly defined Christian artifacts from Herculaneum or anywhere else in the ancient world for that matter, the case for a cross is difficult to sustain.[67]

In contrast to this ambiguous object, early Christians may have used a kind of cross- or crucifixion-pictogram in certain documents. This device was the combination of the Greek letters *tau* and *rho,* often occurring within forms of the Greek word *stauros,* in order to represent the visual image of a crucified man, as the loop at the top of the *rho* suggests a head, set on the upright of the cross.[68] The earliest example of this character occurs in an early Christian manuscript, the *Papyrus Bodmer* II, which preserves a portion of the Gospel of John and has been dated to around 200 CE, and includes at least ten examples of the so-called staurogram. Each instance occurs within a context that refers to the crucifixion of Christ. The combination of the Greek letters *tau* and *rho* became a widespread device, in mosaics and on tombstones, metal liturgical objects, signet rings, and terra cotta lamps.[69]

The Greek letter *tau* by itself might also serve as a cross. An instance of this, dated to the third century, was found in Rome's catacomb of San Sebastiano,

2.4 *Tau rho* on African red slipware oil lamp, fourth century.

where the capital *tau* was inserted between the *iota* and *chi* in the Greek word *ichthys,* which was itself a well-known acrostic for the title "Jesus Christ, Son of God, Savior."[70] The *tau-rho* cross also may be related to the ankh-cross (often called the *crux ansata,* or handled cross). A sign of life (or eternal life) in Egyptian religious iconography, the ankh became adapted to some Christian images or simply identified as a Christian symbol in retrospect. This is evident in the ancient records of the destruction of the Temple of Serapis in Alexandria, instigated by the bishop Theophilus (392 CE). According to the fifth-century historians Socrates and Sozomen, crosses were found in the ruins. According to Socrates, the Christians interpreted the figures as prophetic and prompted pagan conversions:

> When the Temple of Serapis was torn down and laid bare, there were found in it, engraved on stones, certain characters which they call hieroglyphics, having the forms of crosses. Both the Christians and pagans on seeing them, appropriated and applied them to their respective religions: for the Christians who affirm that the cross is the sign of Christ's saving Passion, claimed this character as peculiarly theirs; but the pagans alleged that it might appertain to Christ and Serapis in common; "for," said they, "it symbolizes one thing to Christians and another to pagans." While this point was controverted among them, some of the pagan converts to Christianity who were conversant with these hieroglyphic characters, interpreted the form of a cross and said that it signifies "life to come." This Christians exultingly laid hold of, as decidedly favorable to their religion. But after other hieroglyphics had been deciphered containing a prediction that "When the cross should appear,"—for this was "life to come,"—"the Temple of Serapis would be destroyed," a very great number of the pagans embraced Christians, and confessing their sins were baptized.[71]

Thus, despite the importance of making the sign of the cross in everyday religious practice or in tracing it on the foreheads of the newly baptized, early Christians did not—to any significant degree—incorporate plain crosses in their homes, tomb epitaphs, or even on small personal objects (rings, dishware, clothing). It would be the middle of the fourth century before crosses began to show up to any extent on such objects. Rather, these early believers favored devices like doves, anchors, or fish, which presumably alluded to the cross without actually depicting it. For example, in an introduction to living as a Christian, Clement of Alexandria enumerated the figures that believers might appropriately inscribe on their signet rings. While he approved of doves, fish, ships, lyres, and anchors, his instructions specifically omitted a cross.[72]

Based on the surviving evidence, the anchor was among the most popular of these figures. It has been found inscribed on gems, on glassware, pottery,

2.5 Fish and anchor gem from the Christian Schmidt collection, Munich.

and on early Christian tomb epitaphs. Although the anchor bears a similarity to the cross, its meaning may also be drawn from a passage in the Epistle to the Hebrews: "We have this hope, a sure and steadfast anchor of the soul" (Heb. 6:19). The anchor is frequently accompanied by fish, which simultaneously symbolizes the faithful (caught in the nets of the church and anchored by their faith) and Christ himself, based on an acrostic made from the letters of the Greek word for fish *(ichthys)*. Each letter begins one of the words of the title, "Jesus Christ, Son of God, Savior."

Some historians have proposed that another word puzzle, in this case a rather mysterious device—or anagram—known as the Rotas-Sator square may also have been an esoteric allusion to the Christian cross. In discussions since the end of the nineteenth century, scholars have taken widely different views on whether this is even a Christian object. It has been found in a variety of places, including a Coptic papyrus, a temple in the Syrian city of Dura Europos, a wall

2.6 Acrostic Rotas-Sator Square from Dura-Europos, ca. 165–256 CE.

from British Circencester, a first-century house underneath Rome's Basilica of Santa Maria Maggiore, and a Carolingian Bible.[73]

Although its meaning is disputed and scholars have offered diverse interpretations, it generally appears in the form of a square of five words arranged in an acrostic: ROTAS OPERA TENET AREPO SATOR. One of the most vexing problems is the translation of the word *arepo,* which could mean "plough," according to some scholars. *Rotas* probably means "wheels," *sator* means "sower," *tenet* is a verb meaning "holds," while *opera* is taken as a form of the adverb *operosus,* so "carefully." Put together, the five words arguably construct the sentence,

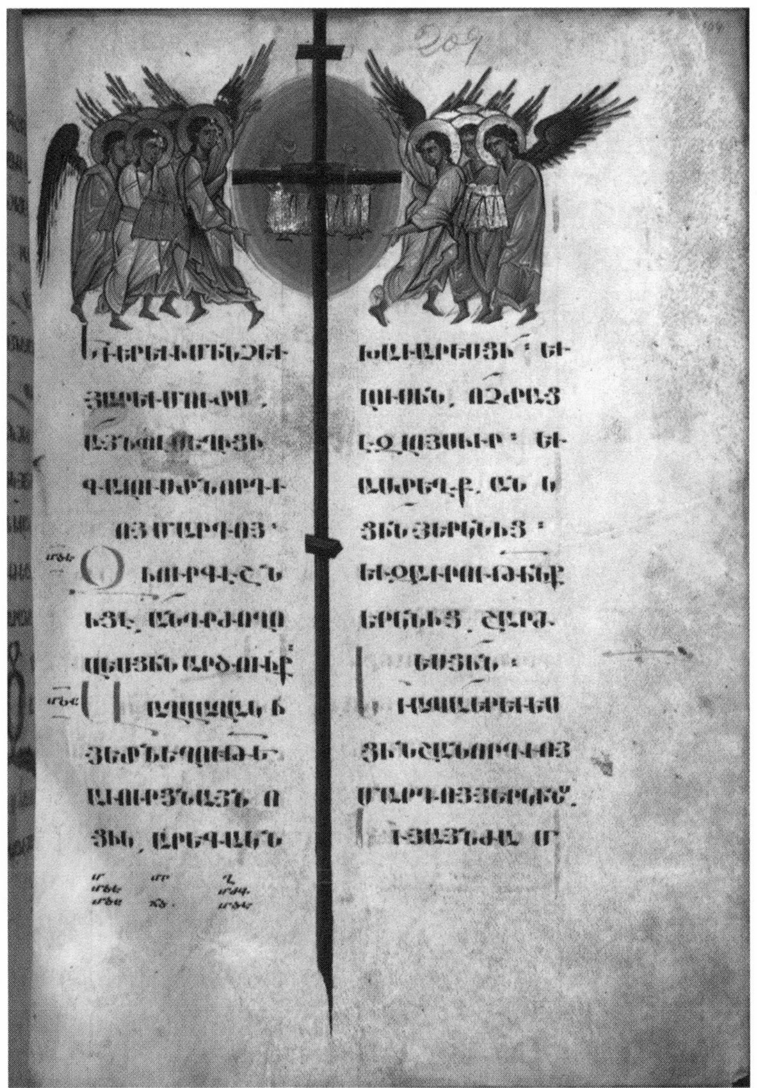

2.7 Sign of the Son of Man in Heaven, T'oros Roslin, Armenian (scribe), ca. 1262.

"The sower with his eyes on the plough holds the wheels with care." Of course, this legend contains nothing specifically Christian or even religiously significant; quite possibly it was a simple word puzzle or game. However, if one rearranges the letters, they can be plotted on the form of a Greek (equal-armed) cross to form the words *Pater Noster* twice, intersecting at the central *N*.

The remaining four letters, two alphas and two omegas (note the inclusion of Greek letters), are then set into the four corners and thus make a Christian symbol.

Rather than allow the cross to be a figure of scandal or shame, Christians regarded it as a triumphant and potent cosmic symbol. It summed up the story of their salvation insofar as it overrode the sin of the first humans in the Garden of Eden and heralded the return of the savior, the last judgment, the resurrection of the righteous, and the New Creation. Its very shape, pointing in all four cardinal directions, had a mystical significance. As an emblem of their hope, Christians received it on their foreheads at baptism and made it daily on their bodies. Invisible to ordinary eyes, the sign of the cross was vividly apparent to those with supernatural vision. It offered protection from demons and identified the members of the flock to their Good Shepherd, at once their holy talisman and a reminder of their own potential for glory. Martyrs accepted death, believing their imitation of Christ's crucifixion assured them of a triumphant (and immediate) admission to heaven.

Depiction of the cross as the cosmic sign of the Son of Man is evident in Christian art through the centuries. It appears, for example, on a thirteenth-century Armenian book illumination that depicts the eschatological cross as a slender black trophy with a gilded banner, set against an oval opening of blue sky, and accompanied by angels. The surrounding text comes from Matthew 24:30. Here we see something quite distinct from the instrument of Christ's execution; it portends the world's final reckoning and the safe deliverance of the faithful from eternal damnation. However, centuries before this illumination was created, artisans will already have rendered the cross as dazzling, gilded, and covered with jewels, emerging from a star-studded sky.

Given its centrality in ritual and its attributed power and cosmic significance, the cross's appearance in the Christian material culture seems surprisingly late. However, when it does eventually appear, it continues to refer more to Christ's conquest of death than to his mode of death. The cross will remain empty, devoid of the body of the Savior, for many more years. The cross as a reference to Jesus's victimization, physical suffering, or humiliation will not emerge until much later.

3

Inventio Crucis

Discovery, Dispersion, and Commemoration of the Cross

> Indeed, this cross of inanimate wood has living power, and ever since its discovery it has lent its wood to the countless, almost daily prayers of men. Yet it suffers no diminution; though daily divided, it seems to remain whole to those who lift it, and always entire to those who consecrate it. Assuredly it draws this power of incorruptibility, this undiminishing integrity, from the Blood of that Flesh which endured death yet did not see corruption.
>
> —Paulinus of Nola

DESPITE THE CENTRALITY of Christ's cross in scripture and early Christian texts, it rarely occurred in visual form before the fourth century. Symbolic allusions to the cross that showed up on small personal objects or grave markers—anchors, ships' masts, or other implements—were not graphic references to Jesus's crucifixion. Some early Christian epitaphs with crosses have been dated to the third century, but it was the middle of the fourth century before the cross emerged as a regular feature in Christian iconography. Two precipitating events may be most responsible for this development: the Emperor Constantine I's vision of the cross (or christogram) before his decisive battle against his enemy Maxentius, and the discovery and subsequent distribution of the relics of the actual cross in Jerusalem.

Both of these events were popular subjects for Christian legend and art through the ages and were told and represented according to different accounts.

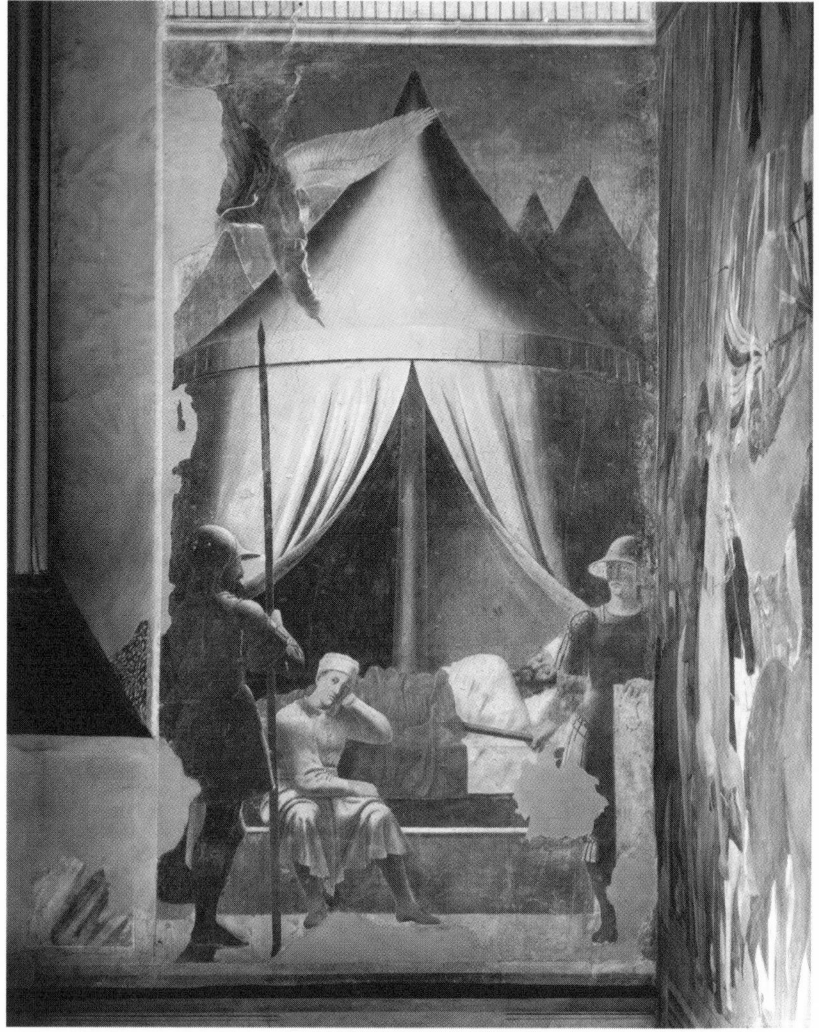

3.1 Piero della Francesca (ca. 1420–1492), "The Dream of Constantine," from the *Legend of the True Cross* fresco, Arezzo, Church of San Francesco.

For example, depictions of Constantine's supernatural vision depended on the version that guided the artist's composition. The story was an especially popular subject in the Renaissance. A painting by Piero della Francesca, for example, presents the prodigy as being delivered by an angel who comes to Constantine while he sleeps, a supernatural light bathing the scene and alerting the emper-

3.2 Raphael (school of), *Apparition of the Cross to Constantine the Great,* Stanze di Raffaello, Vatican Palace.

or's bodyguards to its arrival. This contrasts dramatically with the slightly later composition attributed to the School of Raphael, in which the event takes place on the battlefield in the clear light of the day. Deciding which work is more historically accurate is impossible, as both paintings bear some correspondence with the details found in historical documents.

Similarly, the tale of Constantine's mother's discovery of the cross—also a popular subject for Renaissance artists—exists in divergent narratives, even with different actors. This, however, did not dampen the enthusiasm that accompanied the dispersion and reception of fragments of the Holy Cross or inhibit the development of ceremonies that commemorated its invention. From the fourth century until the present, the cross is exalted with its own special feast, and its place in the narrative of Christ's Passion is understood as a reason to venerate it on Good Friday.

The actual events surrounding the emperor's visions and his mother's discovery of the cross may be uncertain, but perhaps that is not so important as the fact of these stories' impact on the story of the cross and its emergence as a distinctly holy object in the next centuries. Without doubt, the emergence of these legends in the fourth century was rooted in the earlier construction of the cross as a cosmic sign rather than an instrument of death; but in these narratives, that cosmic sign came to acquire more earthly and tangible significance, at once an imperial symbol of God's patronage of a particular ruling dynasty or nation as well as a portent of Christ's Second Coming and the establishment of the Kingdom of God.

Yet, the imperial symbol—the christogram—although initially mounted atop a military standard—soon transcended its particular and exclusive connection with the ruling imperial dynasty. By the mid to late fourth century, a cross surmounted by a christogram began to signify Christ's conquest of death, a triumph that would be ultimately shared by his faithful followers. Before long, the christogram was a popular decoration for a Christian tomb, supplanting the praying figure and the dove as a symbol of hope.[1] In time, the christogram itself was displaced as the cross emerged to become the primary symbol of the Christian faith.

Constantine's Vision of the Cross

According to two more or less contemporary sources, the then-pagan Emperor Constantine I had a vision of the cross just before his famous battle for dominance of the Western Roman Empire against his rival, Maxentius. His army had proclaimed Constantine, the son and heir of the Caesar Constantius I, to be the western Augustus (senior emperor) upon his father's death in 306. However, Maxentius, the son of Augustus Maximian, had already seized the title and was ensconced in Rome, where he successfully fended off attempts to remove him. In 312, Constantine organized an army and began a march on Rome after successful victories over Maxentius's supporters at Turin and Verona. Just before his final battle against his imperial rival, Constantine reportedly received a heavenly vision of the cross, which he interpreted as a sign of the Christian God's will that he would conquer his rival and enter Rome as its new ruler.

The two versions of Constantine's heavenly cross vision differ in certain significant respects, even though they are not so very far apart in date. The earlier of the two accounts comes from the North African historian, Lactantius (250–325), and was probably written only a year or two after Constantine's victory.[2] The other is generally ascribed to Eusebius of Caesarea (263–339) and dates to the late 330s.[3] Both men were Christians and intimates of the emperor; Lactantius was the emperor's religious advisor and his son's tutor; Eusebius was his biographer and political theologian. According to Lactantius, on the evening before the decisive battle, Constantine was directed in a dream to place a certain symbol on the shields of his soldiers before battle. Lactantius described the sign as having the form of the letter *X* bisected by a perpendicular line that was looped at the top. This, he adds, was a symbol for Christ. Constantine did as he was commanded and advanced toward Rome, routing Maxentius's forces at the Milvian Bridge over the Tiber River.

Eusebius's version, written shortly after the emperor's death and incomplete at the time of his own (ca. 339), relates that Constantine, believing that he needed some divine intervention in order to be successful in battle, turned to his father's god for assistance instead of the many other gods of the Roman pantheon. Imprecating this god with earnest prayers, he received a noonday vision of a cross of light in the sky, rather than a dream with the sign of the *chi-rho*. The cross was accompanied by the Greek words, *"En touto nika"* ("by this you will conquer"). Pondering the meaning of this vision, Eusebius continues, Constantine also had a dream in which Christ appeared to him with the same sign and commanded him to make its likeness into a military standard (*vexillum* or *labarum*).[4]

What Constantine ordered, however, was not a cross-shaped object but rather a long, gilded spear, bisected by a horizontal bar, topped with a golden and gemmed wreath that surrounded two letters, *chi* and *rho:* the first two letters of *Christos*. Like Lactantius, Eusebius explains that this looked like the intersection of the Latin letters *X* and *P*. In addition, a banner hung from the bar, embroidered with portraits of the emperor with his two sons.[5] Eusebius insists that this christogram was not simply Constantine's military emblem and explains the emperor learned (through some Christians in his entourage) that it was the sign of Christ's triumph over death. Seeking instruction in Christianity, Constantine came to be persuaded that he should honor the Christian God above all others, since he was the one who must have appeared to him in his waking and sleeping visions.[6] Yet, he adds, the emperor habitually wore the *chi-rho* device on his helmet, a fact borne out by rare images found on coins from his reign.

According to Eusebius, whenever this standard accompanied the emperor's armies into battle, the enemy fled. As a kind of lucky charm, it was credited with granting Constantine's troops speedy and unconditional victories.[7] Constantine's sons' coinage also depicts this sign attached to soldiers' standards, shields, and helmets, although it was not a common feature of imperial iconography—military or otherwise—before the 320s. His subsequent victory resulted in his adoption of the Christian god and his patronage of the church. However one evaluates the character of Constantine's conversion, he clearly believed that the Christian God was his ally. Thus the cross, or its counterpart, the christogram, became a trophy of victory, not only over demonic foes but also over ordinary human ones.

Apart from its origins in a purported miraculous vision, the source of Constantine's famous christogram remains rather mysterious. It bears some simi-

3.3 *The Legend of the Cross,* attributed to Antoniazzo Romano or Melozzo da Forli, late fifteenth century. Apse fresco from the Basilica of Santa Croce in Gerusalemme, Rome.

larities to the symbol of the sun god found in the area around the Danube (home of Constantine's ancestors) and, again, the Egyptian ankh—a symbol of life.[8] Rare instances of this symbol in Christian contexts are thought to predate Constantine, mostly on small, personal objects (such as signet rings and tomb inscriptions).[9] Moreover, the sign must have been incomprehensible to most western observers, especially to those who knew no Greek or were unaware of this title for the Christian savior god.

Eusebius's account of Constantine's visions explains the centrality of this symbol for Constantinian coinage and how he understood his special relationship to Christ. Nevertheless, the narrative is problematic, not only because it is different from Lactantius's earlier version but because Eusebius did not refer to it again in his other major work, *The History of the Church,* probably written a year or two earlier than his *Life of Constantine*. Arguably, Eusebius's elaborations on Lactantius's version reflect the desire of the emperor to be remembered as a God-chosen, pious, and heaven-protected ruler. Eusebius also suggests that Constantine's father had been devoted to the Christian God for his whole life. Nevertheless, some surviving evidence indicates that Constantine himself was originally devoted to Apollo, supported by the fact that the god Sol Invictus continued to show up on the reverse types of Constantinian coinage until the mid-320s, while the christogram remained relatively rare during his reign (appearing mainly on the coinage of his sons and their rivals).[10]

Nevertheless, a kind of cross-shaped labarum shows up on one Constantinian coin dated to the mid-320s. The reverse of this coin shows a military standard that more or less corresponds to the one Eusebius described, as it includes the wreath with the *chi-rho* and a banner apparently bearing three royal portraits. The standard pierces a serpent, perhaps indicating Satan, or one of Constantine's human enemies, most likely his rival Licinius, whom he defeated at the Battle of Adrianople in 324. The legend reads *SPES PUBLICA* (the "public hope"). This iconography may have been replicated in part of a figured panel that stood over the entrance to the imperial palace in Constantinople, built in the 330s, shortly after Constantine gained control of the eastern part of the empire. According to Eusebius, the composition included a portrait of the emperor and his children. The christogram stood over their heads, while below their feet was a depiction of a serpent being speared and falling headlong into the abyss.[11]

The christogram was not the only Constantinian talisman, however. According to Eusebius, Constantine affixed a large, gilded, gem-studded cross on the ceiling of one of the rooms of the imperial palace, which he deemed as the protective insignia for his empire.[12] Eusebius also described a portrait statue of Constantine, set up in Rome, in which he brandishes a cross in place of (or as) a scepter or spear.[13] Yet while Constantine's vision equated the *chi-rho* emblem with the cross, the former was—at least initially—a specific imperial symbol of the Constantinian dynasty, particularly its military conquests. According to historians, Constantine also took the step of prohibiting crucifixion as a form of capital punishment, an indication that he may have regarded it, now, as a sacred death rather than a dishonorable one.[14]

Constantine's vision of the cross (or christogram) was not the last. Later fourth-century documents report at least two other staurophanies. One took place in Jerusalem on the Feast of Pentecost (May 7) in 351, according to a letter of Bishop Cyril to the then-emperor Constantius II.[15] This portent lasted for many hours and was observed by all of the city's inhabitants (not only by the emperor). Nevertheless, Cyril interpreted this omen to be analogous to the one Constantius's father (Constantine) had seen decades earlier. Just as the earlier omen was a prophecy of the emperor's victory over his human enemy Maxentius, this one predicted the victory of Constantius II over the usurper Magnentius.

The second vision, recorded by the Cappadocian father, Gregory of Nazianzus, took place in 363. Gregory describes it as a cross of light visible in the sky above Jerusalem, and he interpreted it as portending divine repudiation of the pagan apostate Emperor Julian's efforts to rebuild the Jerusalem Temple. The prodigy followed a great blast of wind, an earthquake, a fire that consumed the building project, and finally, standing in the midst of the heavens, a great luminous cross. Gregory continues with noting that cross marks miraculously appeared on the clothing and bodies of participants and spectators alike.[16] According to the slightly later report of Rufinus (ca. 402), these marks could not be washed away or otherwise removed, no matter how hard one tried.[17]

Finding the True Cross

Arguably, no relic has been more celebrated or worthy of veneration in the history of Christianity than the purported remains of Jesus's cross. According to tradition, the True Cross was discovered in Jerusalem, around the year 324 or 325, and most ancient historians attribute its finding to the Emperor Constantine's mother, Helena. Constantine's patronage of the church included his taking a particular interest in discovering and developing the actual site of Christ's crucifixion and burial. Thus—according to some traditions—his mother, Helena, traveled to Jerusalem where she unearthed the remains of the actual cross. Despite the wide acceptance of this story, the literary record is complicated, showing multiple variants dating from the fourth century through the Middle Ages. These myriad versions thus make this *inventio crucis* (discovery of the cross) tradition an extremely unstable one, offering endlessly divergent plot details and characters.

The earliest mention of the existence of a relic of the True Cross comes from Cyril of Jerusalem's catechetical lectures, dated to the early 350s. In one, Cyril tells those preparing for baptism that Christ's Passion was real and Christians are not ashamed of that fact; they even boast of it. He adds that he could not deny it even if he wished because he speaks from a church directly across the city from the site of Golgotha and which possesses precious fragments of the very wood on which Jesus died. He adds that those fragments have also been distributed throughout the world.[18]

Curiously, however, Eusebius describes Constantine's establishment of the Jerusalem shrine on the site of Christ's crucifixion and burial in his laudatory *Life of Constantine* (probably written shortly after Constantine's death in 337), but omits any mention of the cross relic or Helena's involvement in its discovery. Eusebius reports Helena's journey to the Holy Land around 324 and mentions her involvement in the establishment of churches on the sites of the nativity in Bethlehem and the Ascension on the Mount of Olives, but says nothing about the cross.[19]

In his biography, Eusebius includes a letter from Constantine to Macarius, bishop of Jerusalem, with the emperor's instructions for the church's construction. Here the emperor also mentions the monument of Christ's Passion, which may refer either to the cross or simply to Golgotha—or even to the empty tomb.[20] As detailed as this narrative is regarding the site's discovery and the buildings' construction, Eusebius never comments on finding the relics of the cross or mentions Helena's role in determining the actual locations of Jesus's death and burial. Rather, Eusebius credits Constantine himself with the discovery of the "holy cave" (the site of Christ's tomb) under a temple to Venus built by the Emperor Hadrian when he transformed and renamed Jerusalem as Aelia Capitolina.[21]

Some scholars have argued that if Eusebius knew about the finding of the wood of the cross, he would have highlighted it in his narrative.[22] Yet, there are reasons to suspect that Eusebius might have known of, but downplayed, the discovery in his *Life of Constantine*. Some scholars believe that, as bishop of a neighboring see (Caesarea), he may have been jealous of the importance of Jerusalem and its drawing power for pilgrims. Others think Eusebius may have had a theological purpose in his omission in that he may have been concerned about attaching too much importance to Christ's death or to the power of relics.[23] In any event, the relics of the True Cross were an important possession of the see of Jerusalem no later than the time of Cyril's lectures to his catechumens in 351.

Another witness, the so-called Bordeaux Pilgrim, writing a few years earlier (ca. 333), similarly makes no mention of the cross relics, although he describes visiting the rock of Calvary.[24] Thus, unless there were reasons for Eusebius to repress the discovery or the Pilgrim of Bordeaux to omit it, it is most likely that the relics were found sometime after construction of the basilica on the site of Christ's death and burial had begun under the supervision of Bishop Macarius (312–335) or even after its official dedication on September 14, 335.

The fact that Helena died in 328 or 329, well before any documentary mention of her discovery, makes it additionally problematic to credit her with the deed. A likely scenario is that the Helena story originated in Jerusalem, either as a way to enhance the importance of the bishop (and his church) or a response to the growing number of pilgrims seeking the very place of the crucifixion and desiring something tangible to authenticate it. Although the circumstances can never be established with certainty, the fact that the earliest surviving attribution of the cross's discovery to the empress actually comes from Ambrose of Milan's funeral oration for the Emperor Theodosius, delivered in 395, is significant.

In his sermon, Ambrose expresses his grief over the death of the emperor and consoles his listeners with the image of the emperor being reunited with members of his family and even Emperor Constantine I in heaven. He uses this opportunity to introduce a topic that seems somewhat extraneous: the story of how Constantine's mother found the cross as well as the nails of the crucifixion. According to Ambrose, the Holy Spirit prompted her to find the place where the three crosses had been buried. She was able to distinguish Christ's from the two thieves' because the title—the charge against Jesus ("King of the Jews") that Pilate had inscribed on a plaque—had remained attached to his. Thus, in Ambrose's version, Helena not only found the cross and the title, she also recovered the nails. These, he says, she sent to her son in Constantinople, one to be incorporated into the emperor's bridle, another into his crown.[25]

Slightly earlier (ca. 390), John Chrysostom mentioned the title's discovery in a sermon on the Passion in John's Gospel. Although he seems unaware of any association with Helena, he explains that the wood of the cross had lain hidden for centuries because Jesus's followers were too afraid and distracted to have saved it. When it came time for it to be found, he explains, it would need to be distinguished from the other two buried with it, first by the fact that it would be lying between them, and second because it would be the only one with the title.[26] In any case, at least by the mid-fourth century, Christians in Jerusalem knew and venerated what was proclaimed to be the wood of the actual cross. It may have been unearthed during the construction of the basilica by an ordinary workman, and, after the fact, its discovery attributed to the emperor's mother.

Around this same time, another detail emerged in the story of Helena's discovery: a miraculous cure as additional proof of the identity of the True Cross. This element in the story turns up in a continuation of Eusebius's church history written by Rufinus of Aquileia and dated to the turn of the fifth century (ca. 402). According to this version, when the workmen unearthed the crosses, Helena and her assistants could not verify which of the three was Christ's by the titulus alone, so the bishop of Jerusalem, Macarius, resolved the matter by bringing forward a woman suffering from an illness and had each of the crosses brought forward to see which would effect a miraculous healing. Accordingly, the moment the True Cross was brought near the woman, it instantly removed the disease from her body.[27]

Rufinus's addition may have been based on a previously lost account, included in a church history attributed to Gelasius of Caesarea, dated sometime in the mid 390s and reconstructed on the basis of a late fifth-century work by a certain Gelasius of Cyzicus.[28] Gelasius may have written his version at the behest of Cyril of Jerusalem, which would make it significant insofar as it would then recount the story of Helena's discovery as it was recalled in late fourth-century Jerusalem.

The story of the miraculous healing, in addition to Helena's finding of the title and the nails, is recounted in subsequent and slightly differing versions of the story of the True Cross's discovery. In a letter dated to his friend, Sulpicius Severus (ca. 403), Paulinus of Nola recounts an alternative tale of the relics' discovery. He reports that when Helena arrived in Jerusalem, she was eager to find the cross, but after searching in vain, she sought out locals, both learned Jews and Christians, to give her some assistance. With their help, along with a divine revelation, she knew just where to dig and soon unearthed three crosses. Fearing that they might mistake the cross of one of the thieves for that of Christ, Helena (following divine inspiration) sent for a newly dead corpse and ordered that each cross touch it in turn. The first two had no effect, but at the touch of the third the corpse immediately came to life, like Lazarus emerging from the tomb. Thus authenticated, the True Cross was placed with great reverence in the basilica built on the very site of Christ's Passion.[29]

Sulpicius included this story in his own history, presumably drawing upon his correspondence with Paulinus.[30] Subsequent historians, Sozomen, Socrates, and Theodoret, writing in the 430s and 440s, retain the story of the cure of the woman at the behest of Bishop Macarius, although Sozomen also includes the resuscitation of the dead man.[31] This part of the story became especially popular

3.4 Follis of Constantius II, ca. 350, minted in Siscia.

in the Middle Ages and appears prominently in works of art well into the Renaissance. The one major discrepancy between these accounts occurs in Sozomen's version, which alludes to the rumor that a certain Jew had inherited some documents that identified the site and so led Helena to the spot. Sozomen immediately dismisses the idea, as he says it would be more accordant with truth to assume that God would reveal the place by means of visions or signs.[32]

Other Versions of the Inventio Crucis *Legend*

Sozomen's references to a Jewish guide to the site of the cross have some resonance with a slightly different and possibly earlier version of the Helena story, in which this Jew is named Judas. In this legend, Helena gathers all of Jerusalem's Jews and interrogates them about where the True Cross might be found. Judas remembers something that his father told him, that he should reveal the place should he ever be asked. Nevertheless, Judas at first refuses his assistance and Helena throws him into a well. After a week's imprisonment, he finally agrees to show her the spot, prays at Golgotha that it be disclosed to him, and then helps to dig up the three crosses as well as the nails. He witnesses the resuscitation miracle and is so moved that he converts to Christianity and is baptized on the spot. He changes his name to Kyriakos ("Belonging to the Lord"), eventually becomes the bishop of Jerusalem, and dies as a martyr during the reign of Julian the Apostate.[33] This character occurs in the writings of Gregory of Tours, although his name is Latinized as Quiriacus.[34]

Other versions of the story also exist, including one from the apocryphal book *The Doctrine of Addai*, which attributes the discovery to the fictional, Christian wife of the Emperor Claudius, Protonice, said to have been converted by the Apostle Peter. Dated to around 400 and originally written in Syriac, the text relates the tale of the queen visiting Jerusalem with her children and asking James, the brother of Jesus, to take her to visit the place where Christ had been crucified. James tells her that the place is under the control of Jews who will persecute them if they venture to do so. Protonice then commands the leaders of the Jews to give the site of Golgotha and the relics of the cross to James, and then she goes there herself and finds the three crosses. At the moment she enters, her daughter falls down dead and is then miraculously revived.[35]

The Protonice story has many common elements with the Helena narrative, which makes the untangling of their various sources and folkloric traditions difficult. Like the different versions of Constantine's vision, the retelling is amplified and elaborated, in particular the miraculous details. The legend of the discovery of the True Cross appears in subsequent histories of the church and continues on through the Middle Ages, when it perhaps found its ultimate expression in the *Golden Legend*, a collection of saints' stories compiled by Jacobus de Voragine.[36] Its popularity was such that it became the subject of countless works of art, from Byzantine icons to Renaissance fresco cycles, and one can still find representations of Helena presenting her cross in everything from mass-produced holy cards to monumental statuary.[37]

Early Feasts of the Cross

That workmen found the fragments during the building process may also explain why the feast of the dedication of the basilica includes a commemoration of their discovery. One of the most famous witnesses to this annual liturgy is the pilgrim Egeria, who visited Jerusalem in the 380s. She reports on the commemorative Feast of the Dedication of the Basilica and the Invention of the Cross (September 14) and testifies to the centrality of the relics in the service (although she does not mention Helena's role in finding them). She specifies that the liturgy is especially magnificent and joyful because the cross was supposed to have been discovered on the same day as the original dedication of the basilica. It was also the very day that Solomon dedicated his temple, according to (she says) the Book of Chronicles (2 Chron. 6:12).[38]

Egeria was also present in Jerusalem for the liturgies of Holy Week and describes the ritual veneration of the cross relics on Good Friday. She and her fellow pilgrims followed the narrative of Christ's last week, tracing the path of his entry to Jerusalem on Palm Sunday through the various episodes of his arrest, flagellation, and trial. On Good Friday afternoon, they all gathered within the shrine at Golgotha and beheld a relic of the cross that had been stored in a precious, gilded silver reliquary casket. One by one, the pilgrims come forward to kiss and otherwise venerate the relic along with the title that had been found with it. Egeria adds that, as long as the wood is exposed, the bishop rests his hands upon either end and the deacons keep careful watch over it. This is to prevent a repeat of an earlier occasion when someone bit off a piece of the holy wood and stole it away.[39]

Although it may seem odd, the place of Golgotha was never incorporated into the large basilica (the Martyrium) but rather was marked by a small, open-air shrine within the courtyard that connected the Martyrium with the domed shrine that Constantine had constructed over the site of Christ's tomb (the Anastasis rotunda). Thus, some—if not all—of the ceremonies described by Egeria that took place "before the cross," or simply "at the cross," must have been staged in that courtyard.[40] Her explanation, although a bit confusing, suggests the likely existence of a monumental, freestanding cross, which formed the backdrop of many of the Good Friday rites. Yet, because her descriptions often indicate that the rituals sometimes took place indoors, it is conceivable that a movable object or even a two-dimensional image constituted part of the basilica's furnishings or decorative program.[41]

Paulinus of Nola later described the Good Friday liturgy at Jerusalem in the letter to his friend and fellow bishop Sulpicius Severus. In his letter, Paulinus recounts how the bishop of the city conceals the cross in a hidden sanctuary, brings it out to be venerated on that day, and leads the people in their veneration. But, he adds, due to the desire of some especially devout pilgrims who beg for the honor, the relics are sometimes shown apart from this holy day. This request, granted only occasionally by the bishop, might even be accompanied by tiny fragments of the sacred wood, given as gifts to be taken away by the most privileged of pilgrims.[42]

The Relics' Dispersion

As Paulinus's letter indicates, the presence of an actual cross relic at the shrine of the Holy Sepulcher in Jerusalem made the site a major pilgrimage destination. Egeria's description of its display and veneration on Good Friday provides a vivid example of its drawing power. Jerome reports that when his protégé, the matron Paula, arrived in Jerusalem from Rome, around the year 385, she came directly to the place where the cross was preserved and prostrated herself in adoration, almost as if she saw Christ himself still suspended from it.[43]

Guides led subsequent pilgrims to the very spot, under the basilica's altar, where the cross had been unearthed. A short fifty paces then led them to the site of Golgotha and from there they could enter a small room where the actual wood was kept for veneration. The Piacenza Pilgrim, arriving in the 570s, reported that at the moment the cross was displayed, a star appeared in the sky and stopped over the place, hovering while worshippers offered their reverence and presented small flasks of oil to be blessed. He noted that as the open mouth of each flask touched the wood, its contents immediately bubbled over, and so the flask had to be quickly recorked so that the oil would not all spill out.[44]

Egeria recounted the concern that clergy had about visitors kissing the cross and trying to take away a sliver in their mouths.[45] Privileged dignitaries, however, did not need to be so devious. They received them as gifts. In addition, according to Ambrose and several fifth-century historians, after the Empress Helena encased a large portion of the wood and left it in Jerusalem, she sent some to her son in Constantinople, to be deposited within his statue atop the porphyry column in that emperor's new, circular forum.[46] These same ancient sources also share Ambrose's claim that Helena sent the nails of the crucifixion back to Constantinople to be incorporated into her imperial son's bridle bits and his helmet.[47] The inclusion of the nails into the emperor's bridle supposedly fulfilled a prophecy from Zechariah: "What is placed in the mouth of the horse will be holy" (Zech. 14:20). Helena and Constantine both clearly believed that the relics would protect the city and the emperor himself from harm.

A late sixth-century story about the nails comes from Gregory of Tours (538–594), who affirmed that Helena found them after the discovery of the Holy Cross. He, like others, reports that according to his sources, she inserted two of them into the emperor's bridle so that it would repel enemies. Gregory adds the colorful detail that she threw one of them into the sea to protect herself from shipwreck on the way home. He states the fourth went into the diadem of the emperor's statue in Constantinople, adding that it was instrumental in exposing the demonic curse of a magician against the Emperor Justin.[48]

Cyril of Jerusalem acknowledged the transmission of cross relics throughout the world, as noted previously.[49] This distribution apparently did not reduce the volume of fragments that were preserved in Jerusalem, nor did it cause any attenuation of their potency or value. Paulinus of Nola similarly reported an instance of this multiplication and translation of relics when the elder Melania, aristocrat, ascetic, and spiritual companion of Rufinus, returned to Italy around 403 carrying some fragments of the cross as a gift for him and his wife, Therasia, from Bishop John. Paulinus in turn sent a small portion to his friend, Sulpicius Severus, and his mother-in-law, Bassula, in Aquitania. Paulinus excitedly explains that, although tiny, the sliver of wood has great power. Not only is it a protective talisman but, as a portion of the whole cross of Christ, also a guarantor of eternal salvation. He adds that if Severus can behold in the particle the actual wood on which the Lord of Majesty was hung, he should both tremble and rejoice.[50] He further insists that although inanimate, the cross has the living power to multiply, and that, though constantly divided, it suffers no diminution.[51]

The distribution (without decrease) of fragments of the cross is evident in many subsequent stories about gifts of the holy wood. Some of them may have been diplomatic gifts as much as purely spiritual ones. For example, the Emperor Justin II (565–574) gave one such precious gift to Queen Radegund of the Franks around 569. Seeking the protection of the church after the murder of her husband, Radegund founded a monastery in Poitiers to house the relic and named it for the Holy Cross.[52] The solemn dedication of the relic was embellished by a hymn written by Venantius Fortunatus, then bishop of Poitiers. Congregations and choirs still sing his hymn "Vexilla Regis" at the annual Feast of the Holy Cross in the Latin Catholic rite.[53]

Justin and his consort, the Empress Sophia, also presented a fragment encased in a gilded and gemmed cross to Pope John III in Rome. A few years later, Pope Gregory I sent a portion of the cross to Reccared I, the Visigoth King of Spain, and to Theodelinda, Queen of the Lombards.[54] Gregory of Tours recounted a series of miracles related to a different fragment of the cross, one originally belonging to the Empress Sophia, which she had entrusted to a certain Abbot Futes in Jerusalem. According to Gregory, the abbot passed along the fragment to one of his acquaintances, who then wrapped it in a silk cloth and brought it with him on a visit to Tours. Gregory, initially skeptical, audaciously washed the cloth in which the relic had been wrapped and used the water to cure fevers. He then gave small bits of the silk to others to be used for other healing miracles.[55]

Procopius of Caesarea (500–565) described a different type of miracle. According to Procopius, the city of Apamea had received a large portion of the wood of the cross, secretly conveyed there from Jerusalem by a local pilgrim upon his return. Believing it would be a significant protection for the city, the pilgrim turned it over to some of the town fathers, who placed the relic in a wooden casket and entrusted it to the care of the local clergy who unveiled it once a year for the citizens to worship. The relic was later credited with saving the populace from death or enslavement when the Persian army invaded, its saving power demonstrated by a miraculous flame hovered over it as the people prepared themselves to face the enemy. Even though the city surrendered to King Chosroes and his army, the citizens were spared the likely destruction they would have experienced without the divine protection afforded by the holy wood.[56]

Some evidence from the fourth century indicates that those lucky enough to receive slivers of the cross encased them in tiny reliquaries and wore them on their bodies. Gregory of Nyssa reports that his sister Macrina wore an iron cross, suspended around her neck by a thin chain. In addition, she had a ring engraved with a cross and a cavity that held a sliver of the relic.[57] John Chrysostom referred to crosses worn as protective amulets.[58]

Ironically, the one place that apparently lacked a cross relic was the Roman shrine purportedly built to honor the True Cross and the woman who supposedly discovered it, the Basilica of Santa Croce in Gerusalemme. According to some historians, following a notice in the *Liber Pontificalis,* a few years after her death, Constantine converted Empress Helena's palace (the Palatium Sessorianum) into a basilica dedicated to the True Cross. The entry adds that Constantine placed some of the Holy Wood there and sealed it with gold and jewels. He also apparently chose its name, simply "Jerusalem," at the church's dedication.[59] Other scholars have argued that the association of this building with Helena is actually somewhat tenuous, and that the transformation of palace to church should be dated to the mid-fifth century and the donation of the imperial family of Valentinian III, Galla Placidia, and Honoria.[60]

At this time, a mosaic was installed that recognized these donors and named the church as Sancta Ecclesia Hierusalem. A unique building, as it evidently was founded to be neither an episcopal church nor a place for regular liturgical services, its title of Santa Croce appears to date no earlier than the time of Gregory I. Thus, even though the *Liber Pontificalis* asserts that the church was founded by Constantine I and that the emperor himself installed a cross relic there, the earliest clear evidence for such a relic dates only to the late fifth century, and the tradition that Helena herself installed it cannot be dated

3.5 Statue of St. Helena by Andrea Bolgi, 1639. St. Peter's Basilica, Rome.

before the fifteenth.[61] It is possible that a relic was there in the fourth century and then lost during the sack of Rome by the Visigoths (ca. 410) or Vandals (ca. 455).

Pope Leo I (440–461) may have received a relic of the wood from Bishop Juvenal of Jerusalem along with a letter confirming his (Juvenal's) return after having taken the opposition's side in the Christological debates and, according to the *Liber Pontificalis*, both Popes Hilarius (461–468) and Symmachus (498–514) installed relics in the basilica at the Lateran and at St. Peter's.[62] As late as the seventeenth century, Pope Urban VIII donated some portion to St. Peter's Basilica, placing it in a gold casket at the base of Andrea Bolgi's monumental statue of St. Helena in one of the four niches that support the church's dome.

In any case, based on the records of Pope Gregory's donation of some of the wood to King Reccared and Queen Theodelinda, the holy wood seems to have been in Rome no later than the sixth century, and it seems reasonable to assume that at some point a portion was kept at Santa Croce and that it was alternatively removed and returned over time. While Santa Croce was the primary destination of the medieval Good Friday liturgy, it seems the pope walked barefoot from the Lateran Basilica bearing a casket with the relic stored in the papal chapel (the Sancta Sanctorum), where it was venerated with a kiss and then returned to the treasury of relics at the Lateran.[63] Despite the confusion about whether the relic was ever at Santa Croce, today one can still visit a small chapel there that contains a display of relics that are identified as portions of the wood of the cross, Pilate's title (probably a medieval artifact), a nail, and two thorns from the crown of thorns.[64]

The Empty Cross on Fourth-Century Sarcophagi

Constantine's labarum, which appeared mainly on coin reverses and primarily in a military context, shows up in a new form on later fourth-century sarcophagi.[65] From the 340s to the 370s, it became the central motif on a series of so-called Passion sarcophagi, the majority of them found in the ancient Christian cemeteries of Rome. Some of these sarcophagi include abbreviated references to episodes in Christ's arrest and trial, along with other scenes, including the arrests of Peter and Paul, and Old Testament figures. Others show a queue of apostles, in two groups of six, processing toward the central motif, a large empty cross, surmounted by a christogram within a wreath, conceivably a replacement for the figure of Christ who would normally be positioned among his disciples. This motif is the unifying element of the group and often is referred to as the *crux invicta* (the unconquered cross). Ordinarily, doves perch on the horizontal arms of the cross, and ribbons flow from the wreath. An eagle often holds the wreath in his beak, and the busts of the personified sun and moon, Sol and Luna, appear beneath his spread wings.

In several instances, two helmeted Roman soldiers sit beneath the cross's arms, one on each side; the one on the viewer's right normally leans on his shield as if sleeping. These may be depictions of the guards posted to keep watch (cf. Matt. 27:36). Yet they are iconographically parallel to the soldiers on the coinage, as well as the figures of captives, often shown seated and bound beneath a military standard. This transformation of a symbol initially linked with military victories validates the parallels drawn by Justin Martyr, Tertullian, and Minucius Felix, who, long before Constantine had his vision, saw the actual standards or banners of Roman armies as displaying the sign of the cross, and—to their eyes—a representation of Christ's crucifixion.[66]

One of these sarcophagi, now in the Vatican Museum, is divided into several architecturally distinct niches, separated by spiraling columns. Each niche contains an episode from scripture. On the far left, Simon carries Christ's cross; in the center left, a Roman soldier crowns Jesus with a jeweled laurel wreath instead of one made of thorns. To the right of the central motif (the *crux invicta*), a soldier presents Jesus to Pilate, who turns away while attendants pour water into a basin so that he may wash his hands. These are among the earliest depictions of episodes from the trial and death of Jesus and, undoubtedly, they deemphasize his suffering and clearly avoid showing his actual death on the cross. Rather, the empty cross—a perch for doves and a framework for a victory wreath—anticipates the image of a crucifix.

Another fourth-century sarcophagus employs the trunks of olive trees rather than spiraling columns and niches to separate its scenes. In the center is the cross with christogram. On the far left, Cain and Abel present their gifts to God. Just to the right is the arrest of Peter. On the other side, a soldier draws his sword to execute Paul; beyond this a somewhat enigmatic scene has usually been identified as Job and his wife but could be Pilate with his wife. Here, the Passion

3.6 Fourth-century sarcophagus with scenes of the Passion and empty cross. Museo Pio Cristiano, Vatican.

scenes are those that pertain to Rome's two founding apostles rather than Christ. Crowns suspended above their heads signify their saintly status.

While the *crux invicta* on these sarcophagi parallels aspects of the imperial labarum, it emerges in a new context, one that is clearly different from the reverse of a coin or the face of a public monument. While the sign alludes to victory, its funerary context suggests that the victory is Christ's conquest of death and not of some earthly, human enemy. The figure occurs elsewhere in grave décor, from elaborate mosaic tomb covers to simple epitaphs, often accompanied by a dove holding an olive branch or the inscription *in pace* (in peace). Clearly, the image suggests that the deceased within the sarcophagus or tomb hopes to be resurrected like Christ, thus experiencing his own triumph over the final foe. The conquest here is one that Paul refers to in 1 Corinthians: "Death has been swallowed up in victory. Where, O death, is your victory? Where, O, death is your sting?" (1 Cor. 15:54–56).

The Passion sarcophagi clearly substituted the figure of the *crux invicta* for an actual depiction of the crucifixion. They never show Christ affixed to the cross, even as part of an ensemble of scenes that represent episodes from the story of his arrest, trial, and execution. Depictions of crucifixion do not occur with any regularity until the following century.[67] In a variation on the theme, some sarcophagi present scenes from the Christ's Passion on either side of the figure of Jesus ascended (standing on the rock of Eden, from which four rivers flow). In one of its earliest appearances in visual art, he holds a gemmed cross in his right hand. Even apart from the fact that it is studded with oval jewels, it is far too slender and short to be an instrument of torture. Rather, here it has become his personal standard of victory.

The cross began to turn up regularly on Christian monuments as well as small personal items fairly soon after Constantine's prophetic heavenly vision and the momentous discovery of the relic of wood of the True Cross in Jerusalem. Because both of these events were associated with the imperial house, the emergence of the cross often has been seen at least initially as a symbol, employed by the emperor or his agents to be a sign of divine protection and patronage. Yet, almost immediately following its discovery, the cross

3.7 Fourth-century sarcophagus with Traditio Legis and Arrest of Peter. Museo Pio Cristiano, Vatican.

began to distinguish itself from those imperial associations to become a devotional object in itself, without bearing any necessary or direct political or military meaning. The fragments of the wood of the True Cross or even oil poured over them were the centerpieces of ceremonies and rituals of veneration that had more to do with the role the cross played in human salvation than its use as an imperial emblem. These relics were recognized as repositories of sacred power, able to heal physical infirmities and to repel all kinds of human and supernatural enemies. They were valued above the gold and bejeweled reliquaries that typically housed them. Bishops treasured them and occasionally presented them as gifts to secular princes or queens. Commoners merely glimpsed them, but even so felt themselves to be in the presence of the holy.

4

Crux Abscondita

The Late-Emerging Crucifix

> The death on the Cross, then, for us has proved seemly and fitting, and its cause has been shewn to be reasonable in every respect; and it may justly be argued that in no other way than by the Cross was it right for the salvation of all to take place. For not even thus—not even on the Cross—did He leave Himself concealed; but far otherwise, while He made creation witness to the presence of its Maker, he suffered not the temple of His body to remain long, but having merely shown it to be dead, by the contact of death with it, He straightway raised it up on the third day, bearing away, as the mark of victory and the triumph over death, the incorruptibility and impassibility which resulted to His body.
>
> —Athanasius

The image of Christ crucified is so ubiquitous in Christian art that it seems impossible that it was not there from the first. Yet, art historians have been unable to identify an unambiguously Christian crucifix before the fourth or early fifth century, and only a few examples before the sixth century. Though crosses and episodes from the events of Christ's Passion began to appear on Christian artifacts by the mid-fourth century, none ever depicted Christ on the cross. Rather, as on the fourth-century Passion sarcophagi, they usually showed only an empty cross surmounted by a wreathed christogram (cf. Fig. 3.6). Even when they show Jesus being judged by Pilate or accompanied by Simon of Cyrene carrying the cross (cf. Fig. 3.7), they omit any actual depiction of crucifixion.

The exclusion of crucifixion scenes from Passion iconography is similarly evident on a late fourth-century ivory casket now in the Museo di Santa Guilia

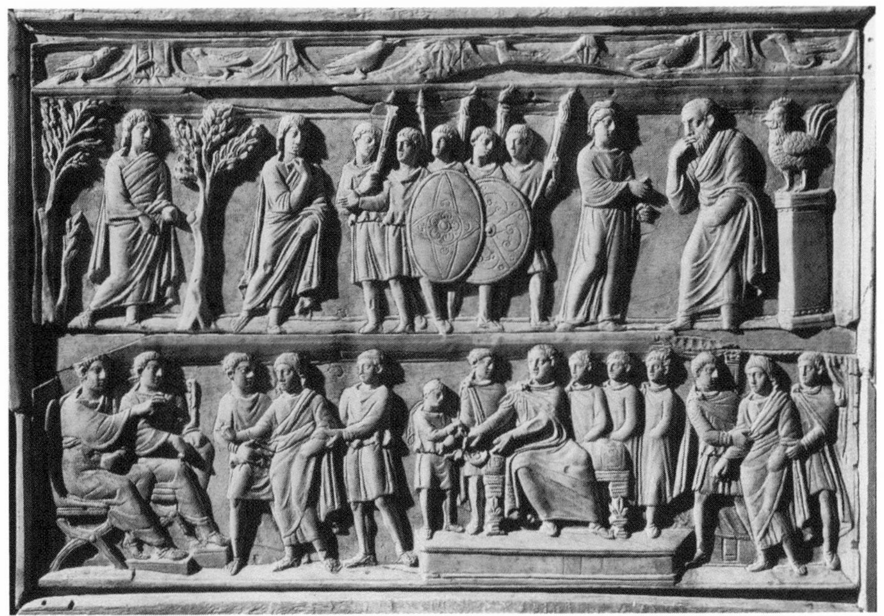

4.1 Scenes of Christ's Passion, relief from the Brescia Lipsanoteca (ivory casket), fourth century.

in Brescia (Italy). This casket's lid displays what may be the oldest pictorial narrative of Christ's arrest and trial in several sequential scenes. The upper of two registers shows Jesus in the Garden of Gethsemane, Judas's betrayal, and Peter's denial. The lower register shows Jesus before Herod and then before Pilate, who washes his hands. The conclusion to the narrative—the death of Jesus on the cross—is absent, even though one must assume that viewers knew how the story ends. Similarly, a late fifth-century cycle of Passion episodes in Ravenna's Basilica of Sant'Apollinare Nuovo includes depictions of Jesus in the Garden, his arrest, his trials before Herod and Pilate, and his carrying the cross to Golgotha. In this case, however, the latter image is immediately followed by a depiction of the women arriving at the empty tomb, which makes the exclusion of a crucifixion scene even more conspicuous.

Given the theological significance of Christ's crucifixion and death accorded by early Christian writers from Paul onward, the relatively late appearance of both cross and crucifix in visual art is perplexing—particularly in light of these images' dominance in later Christian iconography. Allegorical figures like the Lamb of God, or typologies such as the sacrifice of Isaac, may have been deemed acceptable visual substitutes. Yet, early Christian art tends to represent Jesus in episodes from his earthly ministry—as healer, teacher, lawgiver, and wonderworker—as more than images from his last days on earth. Evidently, depictions of his crucifixion were regarded as distinct or problematic in a way that representations of other episodes from the Gospel narratives were not. Yet, for reasons that may have more to do with the emergence of pilgrimage to the Holy Land and the dissemination of the cross relics than an evolution in Christian teaching, the visual image of the crucifixion eventually made its formal appearance.

Crucifixion Scenes on Gems

Possibly the oldest surviving visual depictions of crucifixion images are found on small gems most likely fabricated by workshops in the eastern part of the Roman Empire.[1] Although their dates (and sometimes even their origins) are disputed, scholars believe they date to the mid-fourth century, and some would place them even earlier. Their depictions of crucifixion are the most striking aspect of their unusual iconography.

One of these, an inscribed carnelian now in the British Museum, depicts a crucified man, apparently standing on the ground, and affixed to a *tau*-shaped cross. He is nude and bearded, which is unusual for depictions of Jesus in this era. His face is in partial profile and he gazes off to his right. His arms, bent at the elbows, appear to be tied to the crossbar of the cross at the wrists; his feet are free of either bonds or nails. Identifying this depiction of Christ's crucifixion depends primarily on two details: first, the Greek word *IXΘYC* (an acrostic for the title *Jesus Christ, Son of God, Savior*) is inscribed over the scene; second, two groups of six faceless figures stand to each side. Identical, bareheaded, and beardless, these characters in their identical, tightly wrapped mantles are about half of Christ's size. Based on their number, they could be meant to represent the twelve apostles. Even though the canonical Gospels did not place the twelve at the crucifixion, the scene does not have to be a simple illustration.[2]

A second gem that bore distinct similarities to this carnelian was at one time in the private collection of a nineteenth-century British cleric, Rev. George Frederick Nott. Now lost, it is known only from a plaster cast currently owned

4.2 Crucifixion on third- or fourth-century carnelian, the "Constanza Carnelian."

by the German Archeological Institute in Rome. Its composition has many of the same features, except here Christ (or his cross) seems to be raised above the ground by a column. Additionally, his arms are straight, he faces forward rather than to the side, and a halo circles his head. Each of the twelve apostles on either side of him wears some kind of hat or helmet and garments that look vaguely military. The lead apostle in each group reaches out to touch the top of the column. Rather than the word *IXΘYC*, the legend that runs across the gem and beneath Christ's arms reads *EHCO XPECT*, which may be completed in the lower part of the gem with the letters *O* and *C* on either side of a lamb (likely an unusual form of the name Jesus Christ).

The similarities between the British Museum carnelian and the Nott cast suggest that they were not unique.[3] Yet, a third gem—an engraved jasper also in the British Museum—is significantly different. It portrays a crucified figure in two-thirds profile, his hands are outstretched, and it appears that he has a halo.

No cross is visible, and two devotees seem to adore the crucified one. Because halos are rare in depictions of Christ before the late fourth century, their inclusion argues against an earlier date for these gems.

Added to the problem of establishing their dates, it is difficult to know if workshops fabricated these gems exclusively for Christian patrons or whether they could have been owned or used by anyone—Christian or otherwise—as magical amulets. The existence of two other crucifixion gems, one of them a possible forgery, supports the latter possibility. The first, a fairly well-authenticated example, is an inscribed bloodstone also in the British Museum. Dated to the late second or early third century, it portrays a man crucified on a *tau*-shaped cross. According to a leading scholar of ancient gems, its style, material, legend, and iconography are typical of Greco-Roman magical amulets fabricated in Egypt and Syria and exported to all parts of the Roman Empire around that time.[4]

The figure is quite unusual for Jesus, especially if this gem was manufactured in the third century. Like the British Museum carnelian, he is both bearded and nude, but here the image lacks the twelve apostle figures. His arms appear to be tied to the horizontal crossbar by the wrists, while his legs and feet dangle free on either side of the cross. The words inscribed above and around him are difficult to interpret; they seem to be a collection of magical names, including some strange combinations that approximate the words on similar amulets (such as *Badetophoth* and *Satraperkmephthe*). The back of the gem contains similar phrases in a nine-line legend that has been interpreted as a reference to the titles "Son, Father, Jesus Christ."[5] The use of Jesus's name or title for incantations was mentioned in the New Testament Book of Acts, which recounts the case of traveling Jewish exorcists invoking the name of Jesus to cast out evil spirits (Acts 19:13–15).

Another frequently discussed amulet is a small, engraved hematite stone that appears to show a crucified figure beneath the name "Orpheus Bakkikos." Dated to the second or third century and at one time in the Kaiser-Friedrich-Museum (now the Berlin Bode Museum), it was lost during the Second World War and is now known only from old black-and-white photos. This is unfortunate because many modern scholars believe that it may have been a forgery and the object's loss leaves that question unresolved.[6] Even if authentic, this gem may have had a non-Christian origin and use.

The cone-shaped gem had a hole drilled through it, suggesting that it was worn as a pendant. Its face depicts a naked figure attached to a cross. He was slightly turned, his knees together and bent, his ankles attached to the base of the cross. Two large objects, perhaps nails, appeared at the bottom of the figure. A crescent moon was attached to the top of the cross, under an arc of seven stars, or possibly planets.

The identifying inscription, "Orpheus Bakkikos," suggests that this may not be an image of Christ but of the hero-god Orpheus, who is himself aligned with Bacchus. Although Orpheus' myth includes his violent death, it does not mention his being crucified. Nevertheless, Christian sources, both literary and iconographic, do in fact draw parallels between Orpheus and Christ, just as Jewish art draws them between Orpheus and David. These, however, normally refer to the story of Orpheus as a musician whose playing could tame wild animals. Early Christian texts and images then adapted this theme to describe Christ as a "new Orpheus" who could tame human souls.[7] In any case, this artifact is at least syncretistic, if not entirely pagan.[8]

The two angled wedges or nail-like objects that meet at the base of the cross may hint at the gem's purpose. Like the name of Jesus, nails from crucified victims may have been supposed to possess some healing or magical powers. Rabbinic texts mention this, as do certain second-century Latin documents that recommend nails from crucifixions for use in healing rituals or concocting magical spells. According to Pliny the Elder, a fragment of a nail used in crucifixion could be wrapped in wool and attached to a patient suffering from fever. Once the patient was cured, the fragment should be buried in a hole to keep it out of the light.[9] Both Lucan and Apuleius include nails from crucifixions among the contents of a sorceress's laboratory.[10]

Fifth-Century Depictions of the Crucifixion

The earliest surviving and undisputed depiction of Jesus's crucifixion occurs on one of four surviving ivory panels of a small casket in the British Museum.[11] Known as the Maskell Ivories after its nineteenth-century owner, the box was probably fabricated in Rome around 420 CE and likely designed either as a reliquary or a container for consecrated eucharistic bread. As a group, the four panels of equal size (7.5 × 9.8 cm) display scenes from Christ's Passion,

4.3 Panel from an ivory reliquary box, the "Maskell Casket," ca. 420–430.

resurrection, and postresurrection appearances. A skilled artisan crafted the panels in a polished, classicizing style.[12] The iconography of all four scenes is nearly unprecedented; each being one of the earliest, if not the earliest, of its type.

The first panel conflates several episodes from Jesus's Passion narrative. On the left, Pilate sits on an elevated throne. A servant holds a jug and a basin and Pilate turns to wash his hands. In the center, Jesus carries his cross and a soldier gestures as if to direct him forward. The soldier's gesture draws the viewer's eye to the figure of Peter at the lower right. Peter sits before a small brazier and holds his arms out as if indicating incomprehension. Above Peter, a female figure points directly at him, and a rooster perches above his head, ready to fulfill Jesus's prediction that Peter would deny him three times before the cock's crow.

The second panel juxtaposes Christ crucified with Judas's suicide (cf. Matt. 27:5). On the left, Judas hangs from a tree; his moneybag lies open on the ground, spilling its contents (Matt. 27:3–5), its drawstring evoking a slithering serpent. Judas's lifeless body provides a dramatic counterpoint to Christ's living body on the cross. The tree on which he hangs arches gracefully to draw the viewer's eye to the crucified Christ to the right. Rather than suffering or dead, Jesus is portrayed as vigorously alive, arms outstretched, and eyes wide open. He wears only a loincloth *(subligaculum)*, and his body shows no evidence of physical agony. In fact, his facial expression makes him seem stoically detached. The nails through his palms are the only indication of his suspension; his feet are neither bound nor nailed and, although the image implies the possibility of a footrest *(suppedaneum)*, he evidently supports his body on the cross; there is no indication of slumping. Pilate's title rests just above his head and displays the abbreviated title, *REX IUD* (*Rex Iudaeorum* = "King of the Jews"). Mary and John stand together as witnesses between the figures of Judas and Jesus (cf. John 19:26). On the right, a Roman soldier drives his lance into Christ's side. The weapon is lost but its end is still visible in the soldier's right hand, and the wound is apparent. Unlike the gems discussed earlier, this crucifixion scene fairly closely follows the biblical narrative in its details.

The third panel depicts two women arriving at the empty tomb of the resurrection (Matt. 28:1). Contrary to the biblical description, Jesus's tomb is shown as a small, elaborate monument. Corinthian columns rise on either side of a decoratively carved double door. A brick cupola pierced with windows and covered by a peaked tiled roof tops this small, cubical structure. The structure may have been a visual reference to the actual shrine at the Holy Sepulcher in Jerusalem. The relief carvings on the doors depict Christ's raising of Lazarus. The doors themselves are slightly ajar so that viewers may see the empty slab inside. The two women stand on either side of the tomb, behind the pair of Roman guards who have evidently fallen asleep leaning on their shields.

The final panel shows one of the postresurrection appearances of Jesus to four of his apostles. One of them—undoubtedly Thomas—inserts his index finger into Christ's side wound (John 20:19–29). Jesus stands on a small platform and his raised left hand makes the gesture of an orator, indicating that he is delivering his final teachings to his disciples. Here, as in the crucifixion panel, Jesus has a halo.

Perhaps a decade or less after the Maskell Ivories were made, someone carved a very different depiction of the crucifixion on a small wooden panel decorating the doors of Rome's Basilica of Santa Sabina. Among the smaller of an ensemble

4.4 Crucifixion on wooden panel from the door of Rome's Basilica of Santa Sabina, ca. 432.

of twenty-eight carved scenes that included episodes from both the Old and New Testaments, the crucifixion scene is rather unremarkable and was possibly placed (as it is today) in the upper left corner—almost out of the viewer's range of vision.

This composition shows Christ for the first time between the two thieves. The thieves are about half of Jesus's height, and all three are naked except for simple loincloths. Here Christ is bearded and has long flowing hair. All three figures face forward, their arms outstretched while still bent at the elbows, as if they are in the posture of prayer rather than suspended on crosses.[13] In fact, no crosses are visible, nor are there indications of nails or bindings. The three figures seem to stand on the ground rather than hang. Their eyes are open, and they show no evidence of suffering. Behind the trio is a three-gabled brick structure that could be meant to represent Jerusalem's city walls, or possibly the walls of the Jerusalem basilica founded by Constantine on the site of the crucifixion.[14] No other figures appear.

Sixth- to Eighth-Century Depictions of the Crucifixion

No other artifacts survive from the fifth century, though there must have been others. Gregory of Tours (d. 594) mentions a crucifix, probably made in the 440s for the Cathedral of Saint-Just in Narbonne. According to Gregory, this crucifix depicted Jesus girded with only a simple loincloth. This description matches the representation of Christ on the Maskell Ivories and the Santa Sabina door. Nevertheless, Jesus's seminudity apparently caused something of a scandal at that time and place; it even prompted a prodigy, involving a priest named Basileus who experienced a vision in which a stranger appeared to him, saying, "All of you are clothed in various garments, but you see me always naked. Come now as quickly as possible, cover me with a curtain!" According to Gregory, the priest did not understand the import of the vision, and so the stranger returned and repeated his demand. When he came a third time, he even hit the priest and threatened death if he did not obey. When Basileus finally went to his bishop to ask what to do, his superior ordered him to cover the image with a curtain.[15]

The story of the Narbonne crucifix gives some context to the shift in Jesus's garments in subsequent images of the crucifixion. By the sixth century, images of Christ's crucifixion were becoming more widespread, and most show him covered from shoulders to toes by a purple robe. That said, they also come from a different part of the Roman Empire, originating in Syria-Palestine.

One of these, a full-page illumination from the Syrian Gospel of Rabbula, dates to the 580s and comes from the Monastery of St. John of Zagba. It resides now in the Biblioteca Medicea Laurenziana in Florence. The page is divided into two parts. The upper section (about two-thirds of the space) depicts Christ's crucifixion. The lower panel connects two different scenes associated with his resurrection: two women meet the angel at the empty tomb and then, as they run to bring the angel's message to his disciples, encounter Jesus, take hold of his feet, and worship him (Matt. 28:1–10).

The crucifixion is depicted in a style that is often described as the "eastern" or "Syrian" type. Here, Christ is fastened to the cross with nails in his palms and both ankles. His hair and beard are long and dark, his gold halo is banded with blue, and he wears a sleeveless purple robe with two vertical gold stripes, commonly depicted in crucifixion images and often referred to by its Latin name

4.5 Crucifixion from the Rabbula Gospels, fol. 13a, ca. 586.

(colobium). His eyes are open but his head tilts slightly down toward his right shoulder; his face expresses sorrow and pain. The two crucified thieves are shown slightly lower and shorter than (or perhaps slightly behind) Christ. They are naked except for knotted skirt-like garments *(perizomata)* that cover them from their hips to their upper thighs. Ropes across their bare chests bind them to their crosses. Like Christ, the two thieves have nails through their palms and ankles.

The crucifixion scene is set outdoors against the backdrop of Jerusalem's two hills, Agra and Gareb. Small images of the sun and the moon appear on either side of Christ. The entire scene is populated with a number of other characters as well. On the far left stand Jesus's mother and the Beloved Disciple. On either side of Christ are two figures, one holding up a lance to his right side and identified by name as Longinus. The other, unidentified (though tradition later names him Stephaton), lifts up a sponge with his right hand and holds a bucket, presumably containing vinegar or sour wine, with his left (cf. Matt. 27:48). At the foot of the cross are three men, apparently casting lots for Christ's garments (Matt. 27:35). A group of women witnesses appears at the far right (Matt. 27:55).

Jesus's purple vestment may refer to the robe that soldiers gave him in mockery (Luke 23:11; John 19:2). It shows up on the inside lid of a seventh-century Palestinian reliquary (the Sancta Sanctorum reliquary) now in the Vatican Museum, an eighth- or ninth-century enameled reliquary box probably from Constantinople and now in the Metropolitan Museum in New York, and an icon at the Monastery of St. Catherine on Mount Sinai usually dated to the eighth century. The *colobium* begins to disappear by the ninth or early tenth century, however; and from this time, Jesus is more commonly shown, like the thieves, wearing a knotted *perizoma*, which some medieval interpreters understood to be Mary's veil, given to him in order to cover his nudity.[16]

The Crucifix on Ampullae, Reliquaries, Processional and Pectoral Crosses

The seemingly late emergence of crucifixion iconography begs some explanation. Given the timing, it is conceivable that historical events, including the identification of the site of Golgotha, the discovery of the True Cross relics, and the increase in pilgrimage to the Holy Land partially account for this development. Once the cult of the cross was inaugurated, depictions of crucifixion may have emerged naturally. Although no written or archeological evidence exists to confirm this supposition, conceivably a very early (if not the earliest) depiction of Jesus's crucifixion was created for the basilica built on that Jerusalem site.

Depictions of Jesus's crucifixion were often directly connected to objects made in the Holy Land and intended to be containers for relics, including fragments of the True Cross. These objects—some of them humble bits of the sacred landscape (e.g., rocks or earth), others made from precious materials or of fine workmanship—served as souvenirs of a pilgrim's visit to the places of Jesus's life, death, burial, and ascension. Many of these objects include pictorial images that depict the events at the sites the pilgrims visited, including some of the earliest depictions of Christ's crucifixion, insofar as these travelers' most prized destination was the site of Golgotha. This connection between site, object, and iconography was reinforced by the incorporation of some kind of material remains from the holy place that could be transported home, not only as a reminder of the journey and a focus for prayer but also as a powerful medium of blessing, healing, or protection.

Pilgrimage Ampullae

Small metal, clay, or glass flasks *(ampullae)* associated with pilgrimage sites in the Holy Land were fabricated to hold oil that had been poured over a fragment of the True Cross (or otherwise had some contact with sacred sites or relics in the Holy Land).[17] These were inexpensive objects, locally manufactured in molds and sold by vendors. Pilgrims would have brought them home as souvenirs, their contents both blessed and capable of transmitting blessings. Some have inscriptions that refer to the contents of the ampulla, typically reading as follows: "Oil of the wood (or Tree) of life from the holy places of Christ."[18]

The best known and most elaborately decorated of these objects are a group of thirty-eight sixth- or seventh-century pewter vials preserved in the treasuries of the Italian cathedrals of Monza and Bobbio. Some show a variety of scenes from the life of Christ, including the adoration of the magi, the baptism in the Jordan, the story of doubting Thomas, and the ascension. The majority (twenty-nine) display crucifixion scenes, many of which occur above an image of the women arriving at the empty tomb.[19] Arguably, the juxtaposition of crucifixion and empty tomb has as much to do with the spatial connection between Golgotha and the Anastasis rotunda at the Holy Sepulcher as it has to do with the narrative of the events of Good Friday and Easter.

These objects' depictions of the crucifixion vary. In a small number of instances, Christ wears the *colobium;* he has a cruciform halo; his arms are bent at the elbows with hands outstretched; and his feet are together. The two thieves who flank him are nude from the waist up. Sometimes their hands seem to be bound behind their backs; in other instances, they also have arms bent at the elbows and hands outstretched. Normally their knees are bent with legs apart. Often only the top of an upright stake, visible above their heads, indicates the cross. Far more commonly, the central cross has no corpus. Rather, Christ is shown only in an encircled bust portrait *(imago clipeata)* that appears to hover over it. Yet, even in these examples, the two thieves are on their crosses and, as in the other instances, nude from the waist up. On many of these ampullae, the central cross has arms of equal length and rests on a tall column; in rare examples, the cross is fashioned from palm branches, perhaps an allusion to the tree of life mentioned in the surrounding inscription.[20] Normally, the cross

4.6 Pilgrimage ampulla with crucifixion. © Dumbarton Oaks Research Library and Collection (BZ.1948.18).

rises from a small outcropping of rock out of which flow four rivers, representing a conflation of Golgotha with Eden. The sun and moon appear to either side of Christ's head, providing a cosmic witness to the event.

In nearly every example, two smaller figures kneel at the base of the cross in veneration, reaching out to touch it. Their presence in the image elides the historical image of the crucifixion with the contemporary practice of pilgrims at the site of Golgotha, allowing them to become witnesses or even participants in the events they have come to experience firsthand. By fusing past and present in one image, the souvenir synthesizes the story of Christ's death with a contemporary traveler's experience of commemorating that event at its actual site and venerating the relics (or monuments) displayed there.[21] If, in addition, the vial on which the image was impressed held oil poured over the Holy Wood, the pilgrim could return home with a material as well as iconographic testimony to her experience.

Reliquaries

In addition to the modest ampullae just described, more elaborate reliquaries were made to contain actual fragments of the True Cross, and some of these included depictions of the crucifixion. One of these, mentioned earlier, is a small wooden box discovered in the Sancta Sanctorum of the Papal Palace at the Lateran Basilica and now residing in the Vatican Museum. Probably made around the turn of the seventh century, it contained small stones or bits of wood, some of which bear labels identifying the sites from which they were taken. The box's inside lid displays a series of five small paintings in tempera and gold leaf, showing scenes from Christ's life: the nativity, the baptism, the empty tomb, the ascension, and the crucifixion. The crucifixion scene, the largest of the five, takes up the central section and shows a scene that parallels the Rabbula manuscript crucifixion (cf. Fig. 4.5). Christ wears the *colobium;* the bare-chested thieves (in *perizomata*), the spear- and sponge-bearers, Mary, and the Beloved Disciple all flank him. Agra and Gareb again stand in the background.

Other early reliquaries with crucifixion images include two enameled, precious metal boxes. One, a cruciform casket, was commissioned by Pope Paschal I (817–824) for the relics preserved in the Lateran Palace's Sancta Sanctorum. A second is the ninth-century Fieschi Morgan Staurotheke in

New York's Metropolitan Museum. The Vatican reliquary opens to reveal five small compartments for relics. Its front (top) surface shows a series of episodes from Christ's nativity and early life: the annunciation, Mary and Joseph traveling to Bethlehem, the nativity, the adoration of the magi, the presentation in the temple, and Jesus's baptism by John. Inside is a dedicatory inscription addressed to the Virgin Mary from the Pope: "Please accept, my sovereign, queen of the world, this *vexillum* of a Cross, which Bishop Paschal offers you."[22]

The Metropolitan's Fieschi Morgan Staurotheke was constructed from gilded silver and decorated with enamel work and likely was fabricated in the early ninth century, probably in Syria, Palestine, or Constantinople. Its sliding lid opens to reveal a series of compartments. The central one is cross-shaped to indicate the place where the True Cross fragment would have been inserted. A series of four episodes from Christ's life (annunciation, nativity, crucifixion, and resurrection) appear on the underside of the lid, rather than on the top, which shows only the crucifixion. Here Christ wears the *colobium* and stands upon the *suppedaneum*. Mary and the Beloved Disciple stand to either side, hands lifted to their faces in grief. The Greek inscription reads, "Behold your son; behold your mother," a reference to the scene at the foot of the cross in John 19:26. Twenty-seven busts of saints and apostles, with their names, surround the central crucifixion scene on the lid's edges and sides.

Pectoral and Processional Crosses

Around the beginning of the seventh century, small crosses made of silver or other precious metals were fabricated to be worn around the neck *(encolpia)*. Unlike earlier cross amulets, they depicted the image Christ on the cross, alive and wearing the *colobium*. Often they were made to house a small relic, either a sliver of the True Cross or a scrap of material that had come into contact with it.[23] An especially fine example, dated to the seventh century and now in the British Museum, has medallions at the terminations of the four arms of the cross. The top medallion depicts the sun and the moon, those at the ends of the horizontal arms contain portraits of the Virgin and the Beloved Disciple (in lieu of displaying them standing to Christ's right and left), while the bottom medallion contains the scene of the two soldiers casting dice for Jesus's garments.

4.7 Byzantine gold pectoral cross, sixth to seventh century.

The ninth-century Beresford Hope Cross, in the Victoria and Albert Museum, was hinged so that it could be opened for the relic's insertion. Decorated on both sides, this cloisonné-enameled object shows the crucified Christ on the front and the Virgin Mary on the back. The image of Christ has been partially destroyed; at the center of his body is a hole, probably directly over the place where a relic would have been placed. The sun and moon appear above him, and Adam's skull lies beneath his feet. Bust portraits of the Virgin and the Beloved Disciple are at his right and left. Portraits of John the Baptist, Peter, Paul, and Andrew surround the Virgin on the cross's back.

The fact that these objects were pendants implies a special connection between the wearer and the article (or its contents). Although the inclusion of relics might have led their owners to regard them as protective devices, the fact that they also depicted the crucifixion suggests that they were also the focus of private devotions.[24] This is the point at which public display and personal piety meet—where the image is worn on an individual's body and visible to all, but is not large enough to be an object of veneration by anyone other than its owner. Their intimate size makes them more like the ampullae than crosses made to be carried in liturgical processions, especially because they are often containers for relics. Yet, their visibility and often-exquisite fabrication from precious metal put them in a different category from more simple pilgrimage souvenirs.

Processional crosses, by contrast, were designed for public, liturgical ceremonies rather than private devotion. Large gemmed and reliquary crosses may have been in use by the late fourth century, particularly for the annual commemorative feasts of the cross, but they may have been used on almost any other significant occasion, including rituals of coronation, dedications of churches, civic processions, or the formal visits of important persons (bishops, imperial representatives, and so on).[25] According to Bede, St. Augustine of Canterbury carried a silver cross before him as he embarked on his evangelizing mission to England.[26] Eventually, a processional cross would be prescribed for the entrance rites of both eastern and western liturgies. The earliest examples of these crosses were aniconic; by the sixth or seventh century, they began to display images of Christ giving his blessing or the Virgin in a position of prayer. Only in the tenth century did they more commonly depict Christ crucified.[27] The relatively late appearance of images of the crucifixion on Byzantine processional crosses might be tied to the aftermath of the eastern iconoclastic controversy, when inclusion of Christ's Passion could be understood as support of the reaffirmed Orthodox position confirming the place of icons in the liturgy.

Aniconic Crosses and Iconoclasm

Reticence about making or viewing images of the crucifixion was not eclipsed by their gradual appearance from the fifth through the ninth century. A seventh-century debate over whether Christ's human and divine natures shared a common will (monothelitism) or activity (monoergism) had a direct impact on Christian iconography. The long-standing question of how Christ's two natures were joined in the one person of Jesus was theoretically resolved by the Council of Chalcedon in 451, which recognized the presence of two distinct but inseparable natures in Christ, a position that preserved the impassible divine nature from suffering and death. The Second Council of Constantinople reaffirmed this position in 553. However, many Christians resisted Chalcedon's declarations, including those who claimed that both Christ's divine and human natures suffered the agony of crucifixion and that in so doing divinity overcame death and conferred immortality upon humanity.

A famous chapter of this controversy is recounted in the work of the monk Anastasius, who lived at Sinai in the 640s. Encountering a version of the teaching that God suffered on the cross (associated with the non-Chalcedonian, so-called miaphysite, or one-nature Christology), he not only tried to refute it verbally in the twelfth chapter of his handbook on orthodoxy *(Hodegos)* but also reportedly illustrated his text with an image (or perhaps a diagram) of the crucifix.[28] Unfortunately, the surviving manuscripts of the text differ in their presentation of this visual aid. One of these merely shows a cross inscribed within a circle. However, the other three show Christ dead on the cross, eyes closed, and partially nude—a type that corresponds to later Byzantine crucifixion scenes.[29] As Anastasius quoted chapter 53 of Isaiah to emphasize the physical agony of the crucifixion, his illustration may have emphasized the human and excruciating death of Christ in his bodily nature. The Sinai icon's depiction of Christ with closed eyes and streaming wound arguably suits this purpose: to emphasize Christ's corporeal, human nature as he is shown suffering on the cross.

By the early eighth century, however, inhibitions about representations of Christ's crucifixion started to reemerge, as the Church in the East experienced a long-running debate over the validity of holy images. These so-called iconoclastic controversies moved from the realm of theological debate to official action during the reign of Constantine V (741–775), son of Emperor Leo III (717–741), whom tradition has often credited with the first imperially mandated removal of Christian holy images or icons.

The extent of Leo III's negative attitude toward and action regarding holy images is not altogether clear, nor is it certain that he ordered the removal of an image of Christ from the imperial residence, despite the assertions of Theophanes, a pro-image chronicler, writing some decades after the supposed events.[30] Yet, however Leo regarded religious iconography, he clearly perceived the cross as acceptable; he included it on his coinage, sometimes set upon a stepped base, sometimes mounted on an orb.

During the reign of his son, Constantine V, the anti-image faction gained official imperial support. Constantine convened a synod in 754 that condemned iconic depictions of Christ and the saints. Under the direction of the patriarch Niketas (741–775), iconoclasts removed figurative portraits (probably saints' busts) from the council hall of the church of Hagia Sophia and replaced them with plain crosses.[31] Already, by 743, Constantine V had rebuilt the earthquake-damaged church of Hagia Eirene and ordered its apse decorated with a simple, unadorned cross. Somewhat surprisingly, this cross has remained its sole decoration to this day. Plain crosses replaced images of Christ and the saints in other parts of the empire, as in the apse of the Church of the Koimesis of the Virgin at Nicaea, where a cross supplanted a mosaic image of the Virgin.[32] After the reaffirmation of the orthodoxy of icons in the ninth century, iconophiles removed the cross and reinstalled an image of the Theotokos holding the Christ child.

Meanwhile, theological debate raged over the legitimacy of the cross versus the crucifix. Iconoclasts viewed the cross as an adequate memorial of the crucifixion. As it was the instrument of salvation and the long-established and venerable emblem of Christ, they deemed it appropriate for liturgical use and acceptable for church décor. As it was an abstract symbol, they did not classify it among potentially idolatrous images. Although not equal to the consecrated elements of the eucharist, it could be reverenced. Moreover, its associations with imperial iconography made it valuable to retain for purely secular and political contexts. It had, after all, once assured the emperor of God's divine protection.[33]

The iconophiles, however, would not concede this distinction between cross and crucifix and argued that the representative depiction of the crucifix was necessary to affirm the true humanity of Christ. For this reason, they regarded the removal of crucifixes as both heretical and sacrilegious. Illuminations in the ninth-century Chludov Psalter went so far as to equate the whitewashing of an icon of Christ with the act of crucifixion itself. The iconophiles further argued that by allowing plain crosses, the iconoclasts were, themselves, actually permitting the veneration of images made by human hands.[34]

John of Damascus (676–749) particularly poses the question of why it would be acceptable to venerate the wood of the cross—and the *form* of the cross—but not to venerate the image of the crucified Christ on the cross. For, he says, it is not the material that we adore but what the image typifies and calls to our memory.[35] John's three treatises justifying the use of holy images, written during the first half of the eighth century, essentially summarize the iconophile argument. John, a Syrian monk active at the beginning of the first iconoclastic controversy, defends the image of Christ largely on the basis that it affirms the doctrine of the incarnation.

Ninth-century defenders of images, namely Theodore the Studite and the patriarch Nicephoros, were even more assertive in defending the crucifix, arguing that whatever value there might be in adoring the plain cross as a symbol, so much more would be gained by venerating the figure of the crucified Christ.[36] Nicephoros judged a plain cross to be frankly insufficient as a memorial of Christ's Passion. The crucifix, he argued, was far better, as it presented corporeal reality, showing both Christ's likeness and human suffering. Unlike the cross, the crucifix had a recognizable, physical similarity to the appearance of the Incarnate Savior.[37]

The eighth-century icon now at St. Catherine's Monastery in Sinai was one of the earliest to show Christ upon the cross with his eyes closed. It also features a dual stream of blood and water spurting from his side wound (cf. John 19:34). As in other depictions of this type, he wears the *colobium* but also—possibly for the first time—a crown of thorns. His closed eyes indicate that he has died, but the blood and water suggest that his death has only just occurred.

4.8 Crucifixion on panel, eighth century. Monastery of St. Catherine, Sinai, Egypt.

Thus, while this depiction has some elements in common with an image like the Rabbula illumination (cf. Fig. 4.5), it illustrates a new type of crucifixion image by showing Jesus bleeding and dying. Within a short time, in addition to showing Christ's death, these crucifixion images also begin to show Jesus wearing only a loincloth *(perizoma)* rather than the purple *colobium*.

This transition in iconography may reflect certain aspects of renewed theological discussion about the meaning of Christ's death in the century before the creation of the Sinai panel.[38] Arguably, such depictions emphasize Christ's physical vulnerability and mortality—and therefore his complete human nature—rather than his heroic victory over death and the devil. They even direct the viewer's attention to his death as such.[39] This raises the long-debated question of whether in his divine nature Christ could suffer and die, which may be why such images took centuries to emerge. Theologians had long condemned the teaching that Christ could be subject to pain and death in his divine nature, as that necessarily was impassible and immortal.

This theological formulation, however, did not deal with the problem of how to visualize Christ's Passion. Did those who actually saw Jesus's agony on the cross see only his human suffering, or did they, by implication, perceive him suffering as God? The fourth-century bishop Athanasius of Alexandria had stressed the significance not only of Christ's bodily death but specifically the fact that eyewitnesses had seen it taking place, which he insisted was so that they could testify to the truth of his resurrection. Christ's death could not have been a private or secret act, nor in any way staged or false. He contended that by this especially humiliating form of execution, Christ could all the more victoriously overcome death, conquer the devil, and open the way to the salvation of humanity. He also explained that the visual image of his crucifixion had two important purposes. First, it was the only manner of death in which Christ could stretch out his arms to embrace both Jews and Gentiles and draw them to himself. Second, as Christ was suspended on the cross, his upright body pointed the way to heaven.[40]

5

Adoratio Crucis

Monumental Gemmed Crosses and Feasts of the Cross

The Cross purifies the man that
pursues the energies cast forth from it.
The Cross is the holy mystery.
The Cross is the consolation of those who are
in distress because of their sins.
The Cross is the straight way, not leading astray
those who walk on it when they are estranged.
The Cross is the high tower which
receives those who are running to it.
The Cross is the ladder which raises
the man to the sky.
The Cross is the garment which the
Christians are wearing.
The Cross is the helper
of the poor and the help for those who are distressed.

—Ps. Theophilus

Eusebius's *Life of Constantine* describes the emperor commissioning a replica of his celestial vision to be his imperial military standard. According to Eusebius, this object consisted of a long spear, covered with gold and enhanced with a transverse bar to give it the shape of a cross. A wreath of precious stones surrounded the christogram that crowned it, an embroidered banner hung from its crossbar, and portraits of the emperor and his sons decorated its shaft.[1] In a later chapter, Eusebius asserts that Constantine, out of his deep devotion for the Christian God, also affixed an enormous, golden, and bejeweled cross to the center of an imperial palace ceiling. This object—the labarum—was to serve as a protective amulet for the whole Roman Empire.[2]

Although none of these artifacts have survived, from the mid-fourth century onward, visual depictions of both the cross and the christogram show it as fashioned from precious metal and adorned with gems. Although the widely distributed relics of the True Cross attested to its having been made of ordinary wood, its depictions show it more as a scepterlike object than a rough-hewn pair of timbers (cf. Fig. 3.7). Even the cross's relics were enclosed in caskets of silver or gold and studded with jewels. Mosaics, relief sculptures, wall paintings, and textiles alike reproduced the image of the gem-encrusted cross. Depictions of gilded and gemmed crosses also appeared on imperial coinage and were carried in processions. A fifth- or sixth-century Coptic sanctuary curtain was woven with an image of a jeweled cross set into a stepped base. The pomegranate wreath that encircles it bears a resemblance to the *crux invicta* on fourth-century Roman sarcophagi (cf. Fig. 3.6).

Because they lacked any reference to Christ's dying body, viewers would not be prompted to associate these objects with Christ's suffering; rather they were an extravagant testimony to his divine glory. In many instances, they were augmented with the Greek letters *alpha* and *omega*—a reference from the Book of Revelation (Rev. 21:6, 22:13), and an allusion to his Second Coming. They could be depicted as enthroned, emblazoned upon starry skies, or surmounting the rock of Eden with its four primordial rivers. Their brilliant gems and gleaming gold connected them more closely to the Book of Revelation's New Jerusalem than to Golgotha.

Although the figure of the cross evolved into a gem-encrusted scepter, the relics of the True Cross became the focus of liturgical ceremonies and an annual feast. Yearly commemorations of its discovery and exaltation included elaborate processions and were enriched by special hymns and prayers. On Good Friday, the church's memorial of Christ's Passion, the cross was held up and incensed while the people venerated it with prostrations and kisses. Through these actions, the cross was transformed into an object of devotion—a commemoration of Jesus's sacrifice to be sure but also a sign of an anxiously

5.1 Coptic tapestry (curtain), fifth to sixth century, Egypt. Minneapolis Institute of Art (83.126). The Centennial Fund: Aimee Mott Butler Charitable Trust, Mr. and Mrs. John F. Donovan, Estate of Margaret B. Hawks, Eleanor Weld Reid.

anticipated future, when Christ would return in glory, sit in judgment, and establish his kingdom.

The Cross at Golgotha

Some decades after Constantine commissioned the bejeweled cross for his palace, a similar kind of cross might have appeared at the site where the actual cross had been unearthed. Although Eusebius never mentions it, nor does it appear in the travelogue of the fourth-century Bordeaux Pilgrim or the writings of fourth-century bishops of Jerusalem, it is implied in the diary of the pilgrim Egeria, who mentions some kind of cross around which the Jerusalem congregation assembled on Sundays and especially on Good Friday. For example, according to Egeria, on Sunday mornings the faithful gather in the main basilica, a space that she designates as "behind the cross." The community returns in the afternoon to accompany the bishop from the Anastasis rotunda to "behind the cross," and then, she says, repeat the rituals that they had enacted "before the cross" (that is, in the Anastasis). On Holy Thursday, they gather "before the cross" to hear the story of Jesus's trial, and before daybreak on Good Friday they are dismissed "at the cross" to go home and rest. Before long they return and gather around the bishop's chair that is placed on Golgotha "behind the cross" to venerate the actual relic, which she describes as being kept in a silver casket.[3]

Egeria could have meant the relic when she described people gathering behind, before, or at the cross, but her words seem to denote a monumental and possibly moveable object that would have been erected within a chapel or small shrine, either within or attached to the basilica and as something distinct from the relic, which she refers to in different terms. Such an object also fits a mention in a letter from Jerome to Eustochium, describing a visit by her mother, Paula, to Jerusalem. Apparently, when Paula entered the basilica, she threw herself down in adoration before the cross and imagined that she could see Christ hanging upon it.[4] Paula's need to imagine Christ on the cross not only implies that this was not a portable reliquary box but also that Paula knelt before a cross rather than a crucifix.

Another early reference to a jeweled cross comes from the anonymously authored *Brevarius de Hierosolyma,* a pilgrim's guide book to Jerusalem's sacred places, dated anywhere from 400 to 530. The guide alerts visitors to a cross made from the lance that pierced the Lord and another cross displayed at Golgotha, adorned with gold and gems and placed beneath a dome. It is unclear whether the author indicates the existence of a monumental cross or refers to the jeweled reliquary box containing the remnants of the holy wood.[5]

Other evidence for a monumental cross at Golgotha include images on sixth-century pilgrimage ampullae that depict devotees kneeling on either side of a cross as if to venerate it.[6] A sixth-century gem, possibly originating in Palestine and now in the Kunsthistorischen Museum in Vienna, has a similar composition, although here Peter and Paul stand on either side of a cross that, like the images on most of the ampullae, is surmounted by the bust of Christ. Both apostles raise their right hands in a gesture of acclamation. Although none of these crosses is gemmed, they do seem to illustrate some kind of object enshrined in Jerusalem's basilica complex as well as the ritual of reverencing it.

Added to these small objects is a monumental mosaic that may have adorned the Chapel of Adam in the Basilica of the Holy Sepulcher (located just below Golgotha). Based on a seventeenth-century eyewitness description, art historian Christa Ihm hypothetically reconstructed the mosaic as it supposedly looked in the seventh century. It depicts a gemmed cross guarded by two angels. A medallion portrait of Christ appears at the center of the cross with the inscription NIC / KA to either side.[7] This mosaic conceivably depicted a splendid golden cross donated by the Emperor Theodosius II (401–450) to the Great Church to replace an earlier, simpler model, at least according to the ninth-century *Chronicle* of Theophanes that reports Theodosius's receiving some of St. Stephen's relics in exchange.[8] Jeweled crosses that occur for the first time on Theodosius's coinage could refer to this imperial gift. Even more evocative is a sixth-century silver paten, probably made in Constantinople and now in the Hermitage Museum in St. Petersburg. Here, in a composition closely paralleling the Adam chapel mosaic reconstruction, a gemmed cross is inserted into a starry orb and guarded by the archangels Gabriel and Michael. Beneath the cross are the four streams of Paradise.

Thus, the existence of a monumental cross at Golgotha in the fourth to sixth centuries is uncertain but not inconceivable. Arguably, the only reliable witness to a large memorial cross at the Great Church comes from the Frankish bishop Arculf, who visited Jerusalem around the year 680 and reports seeing a large silver cross mounted on the rock of Calvary. By this date, however, the actual relic of the True Cross had disappeared, first acquired by the Persians in 614, then supposedly returned to Jerusalem by the Emperor Heraclius around 630, and finally translated for safekeeping to Constantinople by that same emperor around 640. According to one scholar, Arculf's silver cross initially may have been a substitute for the absent relic, not for a looted gold and gemmed monument.[9]

Gemmed Crosses

Whether or not a gemmed cross *(crux gemmata)* adorned Jerusalem's Great Church, images of jeweled crosses had emerged elsewhere in the Christian world by the mid to late fourth century. These early examples include pottery lamps (cf. Fig. 2.4), a recently discovered glass paten from southern Spain, and a late fourth-century sarcophagus currently in the Vatican Museum (cf. Fig. 3.7).[10] More monumental examples begin to appear in the fifth- and sixth-century churches, especially in Rome and Ravenna. Gemmed crosses almost suddenly seem to appear everywhere, from mosaic apses to covers of Gospel books, and from sixth-century Coptic tapestries to Byzantine silver patens. Whether these crosses were iconic references to a prototypical object or image in Jerusalem is unclear, yet the coincidence and consistency of their design makes this an appealing theory.

Rome: Santa Pudenziana and San Stefano Rotondo

The apse of Rome's Basilica of Santa Pudenziana contains the oldest surviving example of a golden, gemmed cross in mosaic. This church, known up to the sixth century as the Titulus Pudentis, was reconstructed at the end of the fourth century. Its apse mosaic—the earliest extant in any Roman church—was installed during the papacy of Innocent I (402–417). The mosaic's composition, although much restored, especially in the nineteenth century, shows the enthroned and golden-robed Christ amidst his apostles in front of a backdrop that appears to depict the cityscape of the New Jerusalem (Rev. 21). Christ's throne is gold and richly adorned with colored stones; his book declares that he is the "protector of the Church of Santa Pudenziana." Rising from behind the city walls is a huge rocky hill, no doubt intended to represent Golgotha, and an enormous, golden, jewel-studded cross rises from it. In the sky above are the four living creatures (Rev. 4:7–8): the winged man, the lion, the ox, and the eagle, figures that by this time had come also to represent the four evangelists (Matthew, Mark, Luke, and John). Two female figures hold crowns over the heads of Rome's founding apostles, Peter and Paul. The gemmed cross here need not allude to an actual monument, or even primarily to the cross of crucifixion, but instead to the cross of Christ's Second Coming—which would announce the arrival of the New Jerusalem (Rev. 21). This identification is supported by the presence of the Lamb of God, also a figure from the Book of Revelation, positioned just below Christ's feet in the original composition, but lost in later baroque-era reconstruction.[11]

The apse at Santa Pudenziana had contemporary—if not earlier—parallels that have not survived. One adorned a basilica at Nola (Italy), built by Bishop Paulinus sometime around the turn of the fifth century. While the basilica's apse is long lost, Paulinus described it in a letter to his friend, Sulpicius Severus, as a depiction of the Holy Trinity: Christ was represented as both a lamb and a wreathed cross, the Holy Spirit by a dove, and the Father by a voice from the sky (perhaps depicted as a hand). The twelve apostles were represented as doves, circling this cross. Because Paulinus specifies that the cross was wreathed, it is conceivable that it was a modified *crux invicta* type, as opposed to a *crux gemmata*.[12]

A similar type of Trinity image can be seen on a sixth-century silver paten, found as part of a hoard near Canoscio, Italy. In its center the paten displays the image of a gemmed cross, flanked by two lambs. The cross stands on a small hill from which the four Edenic rivers flow. An *alpha* and an *omega* hang from the cross's arms. Above, the hand of God reaches from the sky and to the right is a descending dove with an olive branch in its beak.

Built shortly after the Vandal sack of Rome in 455 and consecrated by Pope Simplicius, the circular basilica of San Stefano Rotondo was dedicated to St. Stephen the Protomartyr, whose relics had only recently been translated to the West. Architectural historians have suggested that the building's unusual shape was intended to evoke the Anastasis rotunda in Jerusalem. It also has a

5.2 Mosaic apse, Basilica of Santa Pudenziana, Rome, early fifth century.

5.3 Mosaic from seventh-century chapel of Primus and Felicianus, San Stefano Rotondo, Rome.

cruciform character, insofar as it originally incorporated four equilateral transept arms extending from an interior circular nave; today only one of these transepts survives.[13]

Sometime in the seventh century, Pope Theodorus I (642–649) renovated this surviving transept arm to accommodate an apsed chapel for the relics of the martyrs Primus and Felicianus, brought there from the catacomb of St. Alessandro. The apse was then decorated with a mosaic showing the two martyrs flanking a gem-studded cross. Above the cross is a bust portrait of Christ within a medallion, a composition noticeably similar to the iconography on pilgrimage ampullae from the Holy Land (cf. Fig. 4.6).[14] As on those objects, the image avoids depicting Christ as crucified, perhaps in an effort to indicate his triumph over death and allude to his glorious return at the end of time.

Three other gemmed crosses occur as paintings in a less frequented space—the catacomb of Pontianus, in the Monteverde neighborhood of Rome. Probably dating to the late sixth or early seventh century, one of these crosses appears between the figures of Saints Milix and Pumenius, the other at the back of what has been identified as an underground baptismal pool. The image, now completely submerged in water, just beneath a painting of John baptizing Jesus, includes lit tapers above and the *alpha* and *omega* below the cross's arms. The third gemmed cross is only partial, seen on a wall adjacent to the image of the baptism that includes a depiction of Christ crowning four saints.

Ravenna: Galla Placidia Mausoleum and Sant'Apollinare in Classe

One of the oldest surviving Christian buildings in Ravenna, the so-called Mausoleum of the Empress Galla Placidia, was built sometime in the early fifth century. This small, cross-shaped structure was originally attached to the south end of the narthex of the mostly destroyed Church of Santa Croce. In light of the fact that she was actually buried in Rome, Galla Placidia may have commissioned the small oratory to house a relic of the True Cross (as its shape and the church's name suggest), rather than as an imperial mausoleum.[15]

The lavishly decorated interior of the mausoleum displays glorious mosaic panels and lunettes, set off by decorative geometric and floral bands. In the center of its dome, an enormous golden cross floats on a dark blue, star-spangled ground. Surrounding the cross are more than 550 eight-pointed golden stars, laid out in concentric circles. The cross is oriented toward the east, rather than aligned with the north-south axis of the building—possibly an indication that it was intended to point toward Jerusalem. The four living creatures of Revelation (symbols of the four evangelists), also depicted in gold, appear in the pendentives.

Scholars have ventured different interpretations of this golden cross. Some believe it depicts Christ's Second Coming (Matt. 24:30) and/or his reigning presence as ruler of the cosmos. Others say it refers to Constantine's vision of the cross in 312, or connect it with the heavenly prodigy observed in Jerusalem's skies in 351.[16] Similar golden crosses show up in the so-called mausoleum's lunette mosaics, including the one held by the regally garbed Good Shepherd, and another carried by a martyr usually identified as St. Lawrence.[17]

Another such cross appears a few miles from Ravenna, in the sixth-century basilica dedicated to St. Apollinaris in the neighboring port city of Classe. The apse mosaic in this basilica, one of the most beautiful in the world, is divided

5.4 Apse mosaic, Basilica of Sant'Apollinare in Classe, ca. 540.

into two zones. The upper shows an unusual version of the Transfiguration, in which Christ is portrayed as a large gemmed cross instead of a human figure. Half-length figures of Moses and Elijah float in a golden sky and gesture toward a large, dominating medallion surrounded by a jeweled band. This medallion encloses the gemmed cross, emblazoned on a starry ground; a small bust portrait of Christ lies at the intersection of the cross's arms. The Greek letters *alpha* and *omega* float among the stars to the cross's left and right. Above the cross, the Greek word *IXΘYC* (fish) refers to the ancient acrostic "Jesus Christ, Son of God, Savior"; below are the Latin words, *SALUS MUNDI* (salvation of the world). At the vault's apex, the right hand of God reaches down from the sky. In the lower zone, St. Apollinaris stands in the prayer posture within a lush, flower-dotted green meadow. Two rows of processing lambs flank him, while three other lambs, symbolically representing Peter, James, and John at the Transfiguration, are above, looking toward this unique allusion to Christ's Transfiguration combined with the sign of his Second Coming: a gemmed cross set against a star-studded night sky.

Gemmed crosses also occur elsewhere in Ravenna. The upper, domed chamber of the mausoleum of the Ostrogothic King Theodoric, who ruled from 475 until his death in 526, contains the remnants of an enormous mosaic cross dominating the center of its ceiling vault. More than five meters across, this equal-armed cross was originally completely gold and decorated with gems. Other examples include the mosaic depicting Justinian and his retinue in San Vitale, which shows the bishop carrying a gemmed processional cross or a gemmed cross in Christ's halo from the mosaic program of Sant'Apollinare Nuovo.

Enthroned Crosses

A different type of gemmed cross appears in both of Ravenna's famed baptisteries: the older completed in the latter half of the fifth century for the Orthodox cathedral under Bishop Neon (451–475), and the newer constructed several decades later for the Arian community. Both baptisteries are renowned for their mosaics, including depictions of Christ's baptism located at the apex of each of their vaulted ceilings.

The incredibly rich mosaic program of the Orthodox baptistery includes a series of jewel-covered thrones surmounted with fairly simple, empty crosses. The slightly later Arian baptistery similarly displays a jeweled, enthroned cross at the terminus of the band of processing apostles that surrounds the baptism scene. The apostles, in two groups of six, led by Peter and Paul, respectively, move in opposing directions and meet at this throne. The throne, standing on a stepped pedestal, contains a purple, gold-striped cushion and is draped on the sides and back. The gemmed cross is itself draped with a purple cloth.

This cross-on-throne motif is often known by its Greek title, *hetoimasia*, which means "preparation." Often described as an "empty throne," it has parallels in the iconography of earlier Greco-Roman emperors and gods, as well in as other ancient religions, including Buddhism. It became a popular means of depicting the throne prepared for Christ at his Second Coming—and yet, as it frequently holds a cross or a Gospel book or even the Lamb of God, this throne is not actually "empty." The motif resonates with the text of Revelation 4–5, which describes a figure who looks like jasper and carnelian, seated on a heavenly throne, surrounded by twenty-four elders wearing white robes and golden crowns, seven flaming torches, and the four winged creatures.

5.5 Empty throne with gemmed cross, Arian Baptistery, Ravenna, late fifth century.

One of the earliest examples of this image can be seen in mosaic at the apex of the triumphal arch in Rome's Basilica of Santa Maria Maggiore (ca. 435). Here, within a blue-banded medallion, a jeweled cross sits on a throne that also holds a jeweled diadem. A seven-sealed scroll lies on the throne's footstool—a reference to the scroll in the hand of the enthroned figure of Revelation 5.1. As in the Arian baptistery, Peter and Paul stand on opposite sides of the enthroned cross. Above them hover the four winged creatures (ox, angel, lion, and eagle).

Jeweled Cross Reliquaries

The fourth-century pilgrim Egeria describes a gold and silver box that housed the relic of the True Cross in Jerusalem.[18] She does not mention that it was gem-encrusted, although it might have been. However, the anonymous author of the *Brevarius de Hierosolyma* refers to a golden, gemmed reliquary, which suggests the original container might have been replaced with something more opulent.[19] Other containers for relics were likely adorned in similar fashion. Many of them were designed in a cruciform shape, or were themselves monumental crosses. Many also appear to have been aniconic—that is, they did not include a figure of Christ. As such, they were direct allusions to the cross as a relic in itself, and perhaps also to the cross as a sign of Christ's Second Coming.

5.6 Reliquary cross of Justin II (the Crux Vaticana), Constantinople, 568–574.

The *Liber Pontificalis* records that Pope Symmachus (498–514) installed a gold, jeweled cross for the Basilica of Santa Croce in Rome and placed a fragment of the relic within it.[20] According to the ninth-century historian Agnellus, Ravenna's bishop, Maximian (546–556), commissioned a large golden cross for that city's cathedral. He describes this cross as adorned with pearls and precious gems (aquamarines, amethysts, carnelians, and emeralds). After its completion, the bishop inserted a relic of the True Cross into its center.[21] The cross that Maximian carries in the famous mosaic of Justinian and his retinue in Ravenna's Basilica of San Vitale might refer to this, despite its relatively small size.

Although Maximian's gem-encrusted reliquary cross has not survived, it might have been much like the celebrated reliquary cross of Justin II, also known as the Crux Vaticana. Little documentary evidence testifies to the actual origins, ownership, or fabrication of this object, but its inscription declares that it was a gift from Emperor Justin II (565–574) and his wife, Sophia, to the city of Rome or more likely to the city's bishop, John III (561–574). Today the cross resides in the treasury of St. Peter's Basilica in Rome.

This impressive (though much-restored) object was constructed from bronze sheets, overlaid with gilded silver. Its front side was inlaid with gems; four gems also hung from its arms; a capsule at its center contained a fragment of the True Cross. The inscription on the horizontal arms and vertical shaft reads, *JUSTINUS OPEM ET SOCIA DECOREM/LIGNO QUO CHRISTUS HUMANUM SUBDIDIT HOSTEM DAT ROMAE* (Justin and his consort give to Rome a glorious gift, the wood by which Christ subdued the enemy of humanity). Five medallions on the reverse side show Christ twice (at the bottom and top), a Lamb of God in the center, and what likely are portraits of Justin II and Sophia at the ends of the horizontal arms.[22]

Feasts of the Holy Cross

The Christian church calendar has historically celebrated the cross on two different dates. The one most modern Christians observe falls on September 14, but an alternative date of May 3 has a long tradition. A number of other holy days commemorate the cross as well. These include Good Friday, the Orthodox Veneration of the Holy Cross on the third Sunday of Lent, and an originally

Constantinopolitan liturgical procession of the cross on August 1, in which the relic was carried through the streets to sanctify the city and ward off sickness. These various feasts commemorate distinct yet intersecting events and serve different purposes. They not only commemorate the cross's fourth-century rediscovery but also its return from Persian captivity in the mid-seventh century. In addition, the feast honors the cross itself as an instrument of Christ's Passion, an object worthy of veneration in its own right, and a relic through which miracles are accomplished. As such, the feasts' ceremonial includes displaying a cross or an actual relic of the True Cross before worshippers for their veneration. The September and May feasts typically go by the name the Invention of the Holy Cross *(Inventio Sanctae Crucis)* or the Exaltation of the Holy Cross *(Exaltatio Sanctae Crucis)*.

Invention and Exaltation of the Cross

The *Inventio* and *Exaltatio* feasts undoubtedly originated in Jerusalem. According to Egeria, writing some time in the 380s, the feast of the Holy Cross was initially celebrated in conjunction with the anniversary of the dedication *(encaenia)* of the two churches built at the site of Jesus's crucifixion and burial: the Anastasis and the Martyrium (now the Church of the Holy Sepulcher). The shared feast, she explains, reflects the fact that the buildings' consecration in the year 335 exactly coincided with the discovery *(inventio)* of the holy wood and, moreover, on the very day of the year that Solomon consecrated his temple (in the autumn month of Tishri, according to 1 Kings 8:2). She asserts that the festival, which lasts for eight days and draws huge crowds, ranks with Easter and Epiphany in importance.[23]

The oldest version of the Armenian lectionary, which preserves ancient practices of the Jerusalem church, basically accords with these details, noting that the Feast of the Dedication began on September 13 and lasted for eight days, on the second of which (September 14) the Holy Cross was displayed *(exaltatio)*.[24] Another witness, the early sixth-century pilgrim Theodosius the Cenobiarch, records that the feast was held on September 14, and that the relic was displayed for seven days.[25] Thus the feast was a double—or even triple—commemoration: first for the founding of the basilica; then for the discovery of the relics of the True Cross, which validated the site on which the basilica stands; and finally as a symbolic link between the Holy Sepulcher and Solomon's Temple, insofar as they were supposedly dedicated on the same day of the year.

The Feast of the Cross soon spread to other parts of the Christian world. The seventh-century Greek *Chronicon Paschale* mentions an exposition of the Holy Cross *(staurophaneia)* on September 14 as well as an exaltation *(hyposis)* of the cross in Hagia Sophia on that same day. On the basis of entries in a ninth-century sacramentary, some scholars have dated the first indications of its observance in Rome also to the first half of the seventh century and the reign of Pope Honorius I (625–628).[26] In addition, a Roman celebration of the feast is found in the *Liber Pontificalis,* which recounts the story of Pope Sergius's (687–701) discovery of a gemmed cross lying neglected in a dark corner of St. Peter's.[27] According to the anonymous (perhaps ninth-century) author of this portion of the papal history, the object's existence was divinely revealed to Sergius, who found it in a tarnished casket, hidden under a feather-and-silk pillow. Sergius removed the cross and took off its four jeweled plates to discover a large relic of the holy wood hidden inside. From that day onward, the story continues, this was the very relic that was kissed and venerated on the Feast of the Exaltation of the Holy Cross, held in the Basilica of the Savior (the Lateran Basilica).

The text does not report the date on which Sergius celebrated this discovery. However, lectionaries dating from the mid-seventh century note that the Feast of the Cross supplanted—or possibly supplemented—the celebration of the martyrs Cyprian and Cornelius, originally held on September 14 (now September 16). In the meantime, the feast spread further west and became part of the liturgical calendar of the Frankish churches, which adopted Roman liturgical books and rituals.

Yet the *Gelasian Sacramentary,* which reflects a mix of Roman and Gallican practices, specifies the liturgy for the Feast of the Invention of the Holy Cross for May 3 (the fifth day before the *nones*—or 7th—of May). This alternative date had already been observed in other parts of the world and may be connected to the fifth-century *Legend of Judas Kyriakos.*[28] At the conclusion of this elaborated account of Helena's discovery of the cross with the help of a local Jew, the empress herself decrees that the discovery should be commemorated annually, on the third day of the third month. This, the *Legend of Judas Kyriakos,* evidently reached the West fairly rapidly, where the date of this discovery was taken to be May 3, the alternative date of the feast.[29] Another reference turns up in the *Liber Pontificalis,* under the entry for Pope Eusebius (308–310), which claims that it was in Eusebius's time and on May 3 that Jesus's cross was found and Judas known as Cyriacus was baptized.[30] This tradition was eventually condemned in the West, although the date of May 3 continued to be honored until the suppression of this complementary feast in 1961.

Good Friday Veneration of the Cross

According to Egeria, Good Friday in Jerusalem was celebrated with a series of processions and liturgies, including a veneration of the True Cross relic between the second and sixth hours of the day.[31] Paulinus of Nola added his witness to this practice, stating that the bishop of Jerusalem marked every annual commemoration of Christ's death by bringing out the cross to be venerated by his congregation.[32]

The Jerusalem practice was initially unique. Public veneration of the cross then spread to other eastern churches around the sixth century. At some point the churches of Constantinople and Antioch included a veneration of the cross on Good Friday, as Rome did around the late seventh or early eighth century.[33] Yet, Gregory of Tours (538–594) mentions a veneration of the cross on Wednesday and Friday, presumably of Holy Week.[34] Nevertheless, the most fully developed rituals are found in later documents, including the eighth-century *Ordo of Einsiedeln,* the roughly contemporaneous *Gelasian Sacramentary,* and the tenth-century *Concordia Regularis of St. Athelwold.*[35]

According to the *Ordo of Einsiedeln,* which describes a papal liturgy, the Roman Good Friday veneration began with a mid-afternoon procession from St. John Lateran to Santa Croce in Gerusalemme. The city's clergy walked barefoot behind a deacon carrying the relic in a gemmed casket, which apparently had been taken from the Lateran treasury, as it appears that the Basilica of Santa Croce was without an actual relic of its own at this point. The company likely chanted Psalm 118 with the antiphon "Behold the wood of the cross on which hung the salvation of the world."[36] Upon arrival at Santa Croce, the box with the relic was placed upon the main altar and opened. The liturgy continued with the pope prostrating himself before the relic and offering it a kiss, followed by veneration by the clergy, and finally the laity. The *Concordia Regularis of St. Athelwold* adds details that describe the pope entering the Sancta Sanctorum adjoining the Lateran palace and removing the relic from under the altar before setting out for Santa Croce. At the conclusion of the vigil (with the singing of vespers), the pope bore the cross back to the Lateran and replaced it under the altar in the Sancta Sanctorum, an action that suggests Christ's burial in the Holy Sepulcher.[37]

The *Gelasian Sacramentary* details the ritual of a Good Friday nonpapal mass. The account omits any procession but describes the veneration of the cross and reception of communion after the reading of the Passion and the invocation of solemn prayers. According to the eighth-century *Ordo XXIV,* the antiphon *Ecce lignum crucis* ("Behold the wood of the cross") would have been chanted during the veneration rather than the procession. The ninth-century *Ordo XXXI* elaborates further, describing acolytes entering the church with a veiled cross, stopping three times to allow cantors to intone the Greek *trisagion* ("Holy God, Holy Mighty One, Holy Immortal One, have mercy upon us"), which concludes with the bishop unveiling the cross and proclaiming, "Behold the wood of the cross."[38]

The intonation of these words emphasizes the significance of the cross itself, even within a liturgy primarily commemorating Christ's crucifixion. The papal procession from the Basilica of St. John Lateran to Santa Croce also suggests a replication of the spatial locus of the original Jerusalem liturgy and the necessity of an actual relic for veneration. However, over time it is evident that other objects were substituted for shards of the True Cross—a simple wooden cross could even have been used for Good Friday veneration. Bishop Amalarius of Metz (780–850) acknowledges that churches without a relic of the holy wood were not disadvantaged because the power of Christ's cross would equally reside in a manufactured image thereof.[39] The tenth-century work of Pseudo-Alcuin confirms that an empty wooden cross could be used for veneration; he explains that while offering such veneration, one should *mentally* discern Christ hanging upon it.[40]

Although these liturgical celebrations of the cross were inextricably linked with the story of Christ's Passion, they did not emphasize his suffering and dying. Rather they concentrated on the cross as the instrument of his victory over death and Satan. The story of the crucifixion was not the central element.

It would be only later that these liturgical rites centered on the cross as a memorial of Christ's sacrificial death and encouraged participants to mourn rather than rejoice.

The Captivity and Return of the Cross

The spread of the Feast of the Cross from Jerusalem to other centers, especially to Constantinople and notably in the mid-seventh century, is partially explained by a new chapter in the holy wood's story. According to various accounts, the relic was captured in 614 and taken out of Jerusalem by the Persian ruler Chosroes II (588–628). An archenemy of the Byzantine Emperor Heraclius (610–641), Chosroes pillaged Jerusalem, set the city on fire, destroyed the Church of the Holy Sepulcher, captured the patriarch Zacharius, and seized the relic of the cross and brought it to Persia, where, according to some sources, he installed it next to his throne as a kind of magical talisman.[41] Some accounts report that one of Chosroes's wives, a Nestorian Christian, secreted the relic in the women's quarters; others say that the bishop of the local Nestorian church took possession of it, at least briefly.[42]

Heraclius retaliated. He organized a successful counterattack against the Persians and destroyed the temple of Zarathustra in Ganzak in revenge. The Byzantines eventually defeated the Persian army at Nineveh (627), overthrew and executed Chosroes II, and made peace with his successor, Kavadh II. Heraclius returned to Constantinople as a victorious hero—a reputation that soon suffered, as he was almost immediately faced with Arab invasions. He lost the decisive Battle of Yarmouk to the Rashidun Caliphate in 636.

Although tradition claims that Kavadh II returned the True Cross to Heraclius in his suit for peace, Heraclius fails to mention this in a letter written back to Constantinople at the time. However, a year later, in 630, the story of the holy wood is picked up again when Heraclius is said to have undertaken a pilgrimage to Jerusalem to restore the relic to its rightful place. This episode, the emperor's triumphant restoration of the cross to the Holy Sepulcher, became the second basis for the Feast of the Holy Cross. The story of Heraclius's capture and return of the cross became linked with Helena's discovery and was even celebrated within the same feast.

The tale of Heraclius's return of the cross circulated widely in the early Middle Ages, especially in the West. A homily delivered by Hrabanus Maurus (780–856), abbot of Fulda and archbishop of Mainz, provides the earliest evidence of the western reception of the legend. The homily opens with a reference to Constantine's vision of the cross before his battle with Maxentius, and then moves forward in time to recount Heraclius's military victories up to and including his defeat of Chosroes II and his reclaiming of the holy wood.[43]

Hrabanus's account includes some details that became part of the standard retelling of the story: When Heraclius returned to Jerusalem ceremoniously bearing the relic, he descended the Mount of Olives to the city gate. However, the gate had been miraculously bricked up so that he could not enter. Soon he received the vision of a flaming cross and an angelic message that commanded him to set aside his imperial array and to enter the city humbly, on a donkey, as Christ had at the beginning of his Passion. Once Heraclius removed his diadem and shoes and replaced his imperial robes with a linen tunic, the gate opened to admit him. The relic performed many miracles as it passed through the city, healing the crippled and sick.

Heraclius's recovery and return of the cross also appears in the popular thirteenth-century *Golden Legend (Legenda Aurea)*, compiled by Jacobus de Voragine. Its popularity led to the story's becoming the subject of a number of early Renaissance painting cycles, including a series of frescoes by Agnolo Gaddi in the Chancel Chapel of Santa Croce in Florence (1385–1387), and by Piero della Francesca in the Church of San Francesco in Arezzo (1452–1466). Usually, depictions of Helena discovering and miraculously confirming the wood of the True Cross are combined with these representations of Heraclius bringing the cross back to Jerusalem, sometimes even showing the pair together as if they were contemporaries. Thus their stories as well as their feasts are linked in visual representations, despite the chronological separation of these events by almost three hundred years.

August 1 inaugurated a week of veneration and procession of the relic through the streets of Constantinople, leading up to the Feast of the Dormition of the Virgin on August 15.[44] By the seventh century, perhaps soon after the event itself, Heraclius's return of the cross to Jerusalem came to be commemorated on the third Lenten Sunday in addition to September 14. The establishment of the

5.7 *Saint Helena and Heraclius Taking the Holy Cross to Jerusalem*, Miguel Jiménez and Martin Bernat, Retable of the Holy Cross of Blosa, Museo de Zaragosa, Spain, 1481.

Lenten celebration was based on the tradition that Heraclius's restoration historically took place on the third Sunday of Lent (March 6) in 630. Based on this dating, some eastern churches chose to commemorate the event annually on March 6 rather than the third Sunday of Lent. However, in addition to the Lenten observation, most Orthodox communions also continue to celebrate the Elevation of the Cross on September 14 and hold it as a joint feast commemorating Helena's discovery, Heraclius's restoration, and the dedication of the basilica at the Holy Sepulcher in Jerusalem.[45]

The Relic's Final Disappearance

Ultimately, the eastern parts of the empire were unable to withstand Persian invasions and the rapid Arab expansion that followed the death of Mohammed in 632. Because the Arab conquest of Jerusalem in 637–38 endangered the recently rescued and restored relic of the True Cross, Heraclius once again instigated its rescue and safe removal, this time to Constantinople.[46]

The relic was most likely installed in the basilica of Hagia Sophia, which shared with the Holy Sepulcher some comparison to the ancient temple of Solomon.[47] As mentioned earlier in this chapter, the main source for this location is the account of a bishop from Gaul, Arculf, who happened to visit Constantinople around the year 680, on his way home from Jerusalem, where he had seen a monumental silver cross mounted on the rock of Golgotha.[48] In his diary, Arculf records attending a liturgy in the Great Church (Hagia Sophia) and seeing a large and beautiful cabinet *(armorium)* containing the cross fragments. Three pieces of the holy wood were elevated in their casket above a golden altar on the three holy days of the Easter Triduum (Thursday, Friday, and Sunday). On these days, he says, the casket was opened to display the relics and to allow clergy and members of the imperial family to venerate them with a kiss. Whatever Arculf saw in the seventh century, by the tenth century the holy wood had been removed to the Lighthouse Church, built by Constantine V within the Sacred Palace. On certain feast days, the wood could be removed to other churches or processed around the city and then returned to safekeeping with the rest of the relics in the imperial treasury.

A fragment of the cross must have remained in Jerusalem, because it was supposed to have been again a spoil of war—captured by Saladin at the Battle of Hattin in 1187 and brought to Damascus, where it was paraded in triumph and subsequently disappeared from the record.[49] The last witnesses to the True Cross in Constantinople include King Louis VII of France, who was given permission to see and venerate the relics in 1147, and the crusader Robert de Clari, who reports seeing them just before the sack of Constantinople by western troops in 1204.[50] Interestingly, Robert is also one of the last to report seeing the Holy Shroud before it turns up later in Turin. The crown of thorns was purchased in 1239 by Louis IX from Baldwin II—who had been proclaimed the Latin Emperor of Constantinople—along with the Edessan image (the *Mandylion*). The crown was brought to Paris and installed at the Sainte-Chapelle. Fragments of the cross and the lance came to Paris in 1246. Presumably, western troops seized the relics of the True Cross (along with the nails) at Constantinople and carried them home to be distributed, perhaps in fragments, either for profit or spiritual gain.[51] Byzantine power was restored in 1261, but by then the cross fragments apparently had been dispersed throughout Europe.

Shortly after its discovery in the fourth century, the True Cross became an object of veneration for its own sake. Its role as the instrument of Christ's Passion gave it a place in the salvation story, and it became the sign or symbol of the Lord's triumphant return at the end of the age. For this reason, the cross could be depicted without the corpus of Christ upon it and fashioned from precious metals and adorned with gems. Arguably, the foremost example of a gem-studded cross appeared first at Jerusalem's shrine of the Holy Sepulcher and became the inspiration for almost endless copies. Large versions of such crosses were carried in processions, while smaller ones might be worn as pectoral crosses by bishops or other important clergy. Visual representations turn up in apse and dome mosaics, on sanctuary curtains, liturgical vessels, Gospel book covers, wall paintings, and even on ordinary domestic objects. Despite some inhibitions about stepping on the image of the cross, some of these even found their way onto pavements. The mosaic floor of a baptistery from La Skhira in southern Tunisia displays a series of gemmed crosses within a colonnade framed by a guilloche border. The spiral-fluted columns have basket-style capitals and support elaborately decorated arches in which birds perch. Lit lamps (or

5.8 Baptistery pavement, Benefensis (La Skhira, Tunisia), fifth century.

chalices) hang from the crosses' arms. The purpose of decoration may be to link the idea of Christ's return with the salvation offered in baptism.

Thus, over the centuries, the cross changed from being a mere prop in the Passion story to a symbolic manifestation of Christ's power and glory. Its relics were objects of veneration and the focus of solemn liturgies and ceremonial processions. However, even though fragments of the actual holy wood were distributed throughout Christendom, in practice, any likeness of the cross, however ordinary or grand, could contain and convey the spiritual power of the original object. Its simple iconic image was—like the wood itself—infinitely reproducible. The image itself became a relic, a transformation that grew even more important in the centuries after the original relic had been captured and desecrated by its enemies.

Eventually the cross would even become the subject of its own story, and the ancient link between it and the Tree of Paradise was elaborated by a legend that reframed it as the Tree of Life. This development, moreover, emphasized the unbreakable relationship between the instrument of death and the divine body that died upon it, and a different kind of attention to the events of the Passion emerged.

6

Carmina Crucis

The Cross in Poetry, Legend, and Liturgical Drama

> Owing to our first-formed parent's
>   injury, the maker grieved;
> when he bit the baleful apple
>   and thereby collapsed in death,
> he himself the wood then marked out
>   that wood's damage to repair.
>
> —Venantius Fortunatus

THE GEMMED CROSSES that became so widespread from the fourth to the sixth century demonstrate the degree to which the cross had become an object worthy of veneration for itself, that is, even without a corpus. By the early Middle Ages no other Christian symbol or artifact was—or would ever be—so revered in its own right. Gold sheathing and jewels were merely a means of further glorifying something intrinsically glorious. Although its holiness was rooted in the narrative of Christ's Passion, it transcended the historical episode and acquired a distinct sanctity that bridged the gap between event and meaning or between symbol and reality. It was the single holy image that iconophobes never regarded as potentially idolatrous. Even to them it was a valid recipient of pious devotion.

Such reverence is depicted in a fifteenth-century altarpiece showing John the Baptist and St. Francis of Assisi presenting a plain cross to two devotees. The cross appears to be planted in a green landscape that recedes into the

6.1 The Pérussis Altarpiece, circle of Nicolas Froment, ca. 1480.

distance toward an idealized city of Jerusalem. A golden panel divides the upper and lower sections of the painting, creating a division, like a curtain, between the natural and the supernatural world. Apart from Adam's skull and bones at the foot of the cross, narrative details that one would expect in a crucifixion scene are lacking (for example, the mourning Virgin and the Beloved Disciple). Instead we see the donors on their knees, attentively gazing at the cross under the tutelage of the two saints, their family coat of arms prominently displayed as if to assert their social importance as well as their piety.

During the centuries that followed the relics' discovery and in which the cross itself became a holy image, theologians continued to elucidate the link between the two trees of Eden and the cross. Artists envisioned the cross as a fertile plant that sprouts leafy branches, blooming flowers, or fruit-bearing vines. Storytellers elaborated legends in which the tree of life lived on outside the Garden, eventually growing up to fulfill its divine destiny at Golgotha.

Poets even described the splinters and gore left on its wooden beams to be sweet and life-giving. Thus the cross continued to be reimagined as something beautiful. But rather than the gems and pearls of an imperial New Jerusalem, these crosses allude to the Garden of Eden: an original pristine paradise.

In this time, the cross also moved beyond its status as holy artifact and began to be lauded as an autonomous character in the story of Christ's Passion. In some cases, it was given a voice and a personality, to the extent of becoming both a hero and a martyr, even a partner to Jesus in his Passion. Like a much-expanded version of the *Gospel of Peter*'s walking and talking cross, it moves beyond simple animation and monosyllables to possess memories, emotions, and even physical sensations. The kind of imaginative minds that produced such stories and images also turned to the creation of dramatic liturgical ceremonies and eventually to the staging of religious and secular theater in which the cross became an actor as much as a prop.

Hymns to the Holy Cross

The various feasts of the cross discussed in Chapter 5 would have featured hymns along with solemn processions and acts of veneration. Early poetic and theological literature that praised or addressed the cross shaped the language and imagery of these texts.[1] Some of the most vivid were written in Latin and date from the fourth through the seventh centuries. Among them is one by Paulinus of Nola, which concludes by addressing the cross directly with words of gratitude, calling it "God's mighty love, glory of heaven, perennial salvation of humanity, dread of the wicked, strength of the righteous, light of the faithful." He continues,

> Through you truth's light is revealed and evil's darkness has fled.
> You have destroyed the pagan shrines, cast down by believers.
> You are the brooch of peace joining people together,
> Reconciling humanity through the covenant of the mediator, Christ.
> You have become a ladder for humanity to climb to heaven.
> Be a pillar for the faithful and our anchor,
> So that our house may safely stand and our ship be safely steered
> Relying on the cross, receiving from the cross both faith and a crown.[2]

Another example comes from the Spanish poet Prudentius (d. ca. 413). His poems, mostly written at the beginning of the fifth century, include a collection dedicated to the saints and martyrs of the church (*Liber Peristephanon* [*Book of Crowns*]) and a group of twelve organized around the hours of the day (*Liber Cathemerinon* [*The Daily Round*]). In the latter, the poem of the sixth hour, written for the time just before sleep, speaks of the cross as the protection from fear, dispelling all darkness and sin.

A particularly vivid work, "A Hymn on the Lord's Pasch," was discovered among the writings of Cyprian of Carthage (d. 258) and erroneously attributed both to Cyprian and his African predecessor Tertullian, and even to a certain (obscure) Victorinus from the fifth century.[3] Sixty-nine lines in length and written in hexameters, the poem incorporates a motif that reprises the ancient theme of the cross as the tree of life *(lignum vitae)*.[4] As in the early tradition, the crucifixion reverses the consequences of Adam's and Eve's eating the fruit of the tree of Eden. The cross as the tree does this by providing a different kind of fruit—one that produces life rather than causes death. Commonly, this motif not only associates the tree of Eden with the cross, but also asserts that they are, in fact, the very same tree. The poem opens with a description of the cross as tree, sprung from a barren stump, planted at the center of the world (the *axis mundi*), yet able to produce life-giving fruit:

> There is a place, we believe, lying at the center of the world,
> which the Jews in their native language call Golgotha.
> I recall that a tree was planted here.
> Cut from a barren stump, it yet produced health-giving fruit.
> Yet, it did not produce for those who lived there;
> rather foreigners picked those lovely fruits.
> The tree looked like this: it rose from a single stem,
> then extended its two branches like arms,
> much like the heavy yardarms that support sails,
> or the yoke that harnesses oxen to the plough.[5]

The poet first describes this tree as having only an upright, bare trunk with two horizontal branches. Yet, he says, in three days it produced a third branch, then in forty days, twelve. The tree then grew so tall that it reached heaven, spread its branches over the whole world, and produced life-giving fruit. It sheltered a spring of pure water and people of all ages and races sought its shade. However tempting, these people could not pick the fruit before they had washed in the sacred spring. Once washed, they ate the fruit and were changed from greedy and selfish beings into shining souls, destined for heaven. Here, the tale of the fruit-producing cross continues past the crucifixion and into the age of the church by providing the elements for the sacraments of baptism and eucharist.

Sixth-century Greek poet Romanos the Melodist, a widely acclaimed father of Byzantine hymnography, wrote a series of hymns (or *kontakia*) on the cross, especially for use in the great church of Hagia Sophia in Constantinople. Romanos was probably born in Syria and perhaps was influenced by the works of writers such as Ephrem. His hymns include themes of Mary at the foot of the cross and the Passion of Christ, among others. One, crafted as a dialogue between Hades and the serpent Belial, mutually lamenting the loss of their human prey, repeatedly juxtaposes with the tree of Eden. Here the cross is characterized as the instrument by which Adam and his progeny will be rescued and returned to Paradise. In the sixteenth stanza, Belial cries out,

> It is so, Hades. Wail! I shall echo your groans. Let us weep as we behold the tree we planted transformed into a sacred trunk. Beneath it some creatures pitch their tents; on its branches others build their nests. Who are these settlers? Thieves, killers, extorters, harlots. They want to taste the now-sweet fruit of a withered tree. They cling to the cross as if it were the Tree of Life. Holding fast to the cross, they ride out the currents, finish their voyages, and come to anchor. They find a peaceful harbor in the return to Paradise.[6]

Although the tree of life motif was widely popular with ancient Christian authors, perhaps the most stirring praise of the cross as deflector of evil, symbol of victory, and antitype of the Edenic tree came from the pen of a sixth-century Gallican poet and bishop named Venantius Fortunatus (d. ca. 600). Fortunatus ended his life as bishop of Poitiers, where he also served the Thuringian princess and Frankish queen, Radegund, widow of King Clothair I. In the 560s, near Poitiers, Radegund had founded the Abbey of the Holy Cross, named for the relic of the True Cross that she had received as a gift from the Emperor Justin II and his consort, Sophia.[7] In honor of this donation—and to celebrate the arrival of the relics in Poitiers—Fortunatus, Radegund's personal friend and admirer, composed six hymns of thanksgiving, of which three are still in use: *Crux benedicta nitet* ("The Blessed Cross Gleams Forth"), *Pange lingua gloriosi* ("Sing My Tongue of the Glorious Battle"), and *Vexilla regis prodeunt* ("The Royal Banners Go Forth"). The *Vexilla regis* and perhaps also the *Pange lingua* were written expressly for the procession of the relics. The *Crux benedicta nitet* was composed for morning prayer, following the closing salutation *(Benedicamus)*.[8] All three incorporate the theme of the cross as a life-giving tree. For example, the *Pange lingua* contains the following stanzas, in which the cross is praised above all other trees and encouraged to become supple in order to tenderly support the body of the dying Christ. It closes by associating the cross with the ark, the vessel that saved the world once before:

> Cross so faithful, tree of all trees
> glorious, having no peer;
> such a tree no forest brought forth
> with such blossom, leaf, and bud;
> sweet the wood, with which sweet nails
> its sweet burden undergoes.
>
> Bend your branches, tree so lofty,
> loose your tight-knit inner core;
> let that stiffness grow more supple
> which your native birth imposed,
> that you may stretch forth the limbs
> of heaven's king from gentle trunk.
>
> You alone were then found worthy
> all the world's ransom to bear,
> yachtsman to prepare the harbor
> for our shipwrecked universe,
> you whom sacred blood anointed,
> pouring from the Lamb's spent frame.[9]

The *Vexilla regis* is specifically addressed to the cross and became a standard hymn for western liturgies celebrating its feasts (especially the Exaltation of the Cross on September 14). It is also sung at vespers from Palm Sunday until Holy Thursday. The opening stanza reprises the imperially inspired image of the cross as a battle standard. Yet, rather than describe an earthly conflict, the hymn tells of the mysterious victory in Christ's conquest of death and identifies the cross as the sign that will precede his Second Coming:

> The standards of the king advance,
> the mystery of the cross shines forth,
> whereby the founder of our flesh
> in flesh upon a gibbet hung.

The hymn continues, however, with a paean to the cross as sweet, blessed, and heroic:

> O beautiful and shining tree,
> adorned with purple of the king,
> selected, as its trunk deserved,
> to touch so close such sacred limbs!
>
> O blessed tree, upon whose arms
> there hung the ransom of the world!
> it weighed his body in its scales,
> and bore away the prey of hell.
>
> From your bark fragrance you diffuse;
> sweeter then nectar is your taste;
> rejoicing in your fecund fruit,
> that splendid triumph you applaud.[10]

Although not explicit in Fortunatus's texts, his and other works continue the link between the Edenic tree, which bore the fruit of death, disgrace, and expulsion and cut off humanity from the tree of life, and the tree of the cross, which redeems all the harm done by its counterpart. In addition to St. Paul's parallel between Old Adam and New Adam, the poet draws on the image of the tree of life that appears again in the Book of Revelation, where it grows alongside the river of life that runs through the Heavenly Jerusalem (Rev. 22:1–2) and yields twelve kinds of fruit, which, along with its leaves, are for the healing of the nations.

Poets and hymn writers subsequently elaborated this motif. A particularly striking instance is St. Bonaventure's allegory, *The Tree of Life*, written in the third quarter of the thirteenth century. In his prologue, Bonaventure adapts the text from Revelation 22, asking his reader to form a mental image of a twelve-branched tree, watered by an ever-flowing spring. The spring becomes a great river, fed by four living streams that water the garden of the Church. The leaves of the tree yield a remedy for every kind of illness; the flowers are a delight to the eye and their scent sweet to the nostrils. The twelve fruits of the tree, formed in the Virgin's womb, come to full ripeness on the cross and endlessly feed God's faithful servants, who never tire of their taste. He addresses the tree with these words:

> O cross, salvation-bearing tree,
> Watered by a living fountain,
> Your flower is spice-scented,
> Your fruit an object of desire.[11]

Bonaventure goes on to describe each of the tree's fruits, outlining the mysteries of Christ's origin, life on earth, Passion, resurrection, and final judgment.

The Tree of Life in Visual Art

In *The Tree of Life*, Bonaventure indicates that his manuscript was illuminated with the image of a twelve-branched tree (based on Rev. 22:21), watered by a living source, and with a single fruit hanging from each branch. Although Bonaventure's original manuscript has not survived, depictions of a twelve-branched tree, each branch bearing a single fruit, were extremely popular in the thirteenth and fourteenth centuries. These served as allegorical guides for meditation on Christ's life and salvific death. Most depict Christ's body suspended upon the great, fruit-bearing tree. Date palms frame the mosaic apses of early Roman basilicas, and one can usually find a phoenix—a symbol of resurrection as the bird that rose alive from its own ashes—perching on a branch to symbolize the victory of Christ (and the saints) and the resurrection to eternal life.

Among the most elaborate are frescoes from two fourteenth-century churches in Florence, one by Taddeo Gaddi in the refectory of Santa Croce (ca. 1340), and an earlier model painted by Pacino di Bonaguida for a convent of Poor Clares and now in the Galleria dell'Accademia (1305–1310). Like the Gaddi, the Bonaguida shows Jesus suspended upon a twelve-branched, tree-like cross. Medallions (fruit) depicting scenes from Christ's life hang from the arms. Episodes from the story of Adam and Eve—their creation, fall, and expulsion from Eden—run along the painting's base. At the top, Mary and Christ preside over the celestial court. A pelican feeding her young with blood she has drawn from her own breast nests at the top of the cross (a common medieval allusion to Christ's redemptive bloodshed). At the bottom, a rocky crag encloses an enigmatic figure, possibly Adam, whose face has been mutilated, nearly scratched away, apparently by some effort to repudiate him (or his sin).

Depictions of the cross as a tree appeared in earlier Christian iconography, just as they had occurred in earlier literature.[12] Some fifth-century sarcophagi show the cross surmounting a rocky ledge. Four streams flowing out of that ledge make the link between the cross and Eden. Peacocks, curling vines, birds, and flowers often surround the cross, adding to the paradisiacal allusions. Occasionally, the sixth-century pilgrims' souvenirs (ampullae) from the Holy Land depicted a cross constructed from leafy branches, a fitting visual reference to the description of their contents inscribed on the edge of these vials: "Oil from the wood of life of the holy places of Christ."[13]

Other cross-tree motifs occur in a variety of contexts from the ninth century onward: in manuscript illuminations, stained glass windows, wall paintings, liturgical vessels, reliquaries, and processional crosses of ivory and precious metals. Among these are illuminations such as the *Te Igitur* page of the *Drogo Sacramentary* (ca. 850), which depicts the cross entwined with vines forming the first letter *(T)* of the word that opens the consecratory prayer of the Mass. More examples include the eleventh-century *Arundel Psalter* (folio 12v), in which the cross is a palm tree with pruned branches; and the renowned twelfth-century ivory Cloisters Cross, which displays almost a hundred different

6.2 *Tree of Life*, Pacino di Bonaguida, 1305–1310.

6.3 *Te Igitur* page (fol. 15v) from the *Drogo Sacramentary*, Metz, ninth century.

figures, including a depiction of Moses raising the brazen serpent, and scenes from Jesus's Passion, resurrection, and ascension attached to a pruned tree-cross. Adam and Eve cling to the cross's base in a posture of supplication.[14]

Similar in some respects to the Ravenna sarcophagi are stone crosses found in Armenia and Georgia. Although the earliest date from the ninth century, such crosses continue to be made into the modern period. These memorial steles, called *khachkars,* typically display crosses enclosed within interlacing

6.4 Armenian *khachkar*, Noraduz Cemetery, probably thirteenth century.

designs of vines, fruit, and flowers. The cross's arms generally flare and are tipped with buds. Only a few of the later examples show a corpus on the cross.

Like the two Florentine frescoes, the tree of life motif became more elaborate in the art of the high and late Middle Ages. One of the most striking of these depictions is the twelfth-century apse mosaic found in Rome's Basilica of San Clemente, attributed to the artist Masolino da Panicale. Filled with vibrant color and set upon a gold ground, the image shows a crucifix rising out of an acanthus plant whose scrolling tendrils enclose birds, animals, and various small human figures harvesting or herding. Flanking the crucifix—and larger—are the Virgin Mary and the Beloved Disciple. The hand of God reaches down from heaven with a crown. Twelve doves sit upon the cross above and beneath Christ's body and to the right and left of his hands. Deer come to drink from the four rivers that emerge from the base of the plant. The Latin inscription running directly beneath the tree reads, "We liken the church of Christ to this vine, which the law makes wither, but the cross makes

6.5 Tree of Life, apse mosaic, Basilica of San Clemente, Rome.

verdant."[15] The inscription also mentions some relics embedded within the body of Christ: wood from the True Cross, a tooth of St. James, and a tooth of St. Ignatius.

The Dream of the Rood and Stone High Crosses

The tree of life motif is especially prominent in the medieval poem "The Dream of the Rood." Probably first written in the late seventh or early eighth century, the extant version of this Anglo-Saxon epic poem was discovered among a collection of other Old English religious literature in the Cathedral library at Vercelli in northern Italy. The text recounts the Passion from the cross's point of view, making it the chronicler of its own story, starting from its youth as a green sapling, and concluding with its being hewn down and fashioned into the instrument of crucifixion.

The poem is divided into three parts. It opens with a narrator recounting a dream in which he speaks to the cross. At first, the speaker describes a wonderful tree, surrounded by light—a golden and bejeweled cross. Soon, however, he notices that the glistening gems are blood-drenched, and he hears the tree begin to speak.[16] In the second part, the cross takes on the role of the narrator. Speaking in the first person, the cross relates the events leading up to and through the crucifixion. The third section tells the rest of the story also from the cross's perspective, vividly elaborating its feelings as it is pierced with nails, spat upon, then cast aside. The poem concludes when the original narrator awakens. The cross charges him to hold it in awe, share the vision with others, and to follow the path to righteousness. The narrator praises God, expresses his anticipation of seeing the cross again after he dies and arrives at the heavenly banquet, and gives thanks for the miraculous dream.

In the central section of the poem, Christ is a young hero, willingly embracing his crucifixion, even running up to and climbing upon the cross. The cross wills itself not to bend or break but to remain steadfast as it is raised from the ground. The cross thus not only witnesses but also shares in Christ's suffering, being pierced with nails and covered with blood. Like Christ, the cross is buried after Jesus's death. And while Christ is resurrected, the cross is itself—in time—exhumed from its pit. Like the victorious Christ, the rediscovered cross receives its own kind of glory and honor, enshrined with gold, silver, and jewels. It is venerated above all other trees as the tree of life. In this sense, the cross replicates Christ's ascension and enthronement.[17] In triumph, the cross declares,

> Now you may hear, beloved hero,
> how I had to abide the deeds of bullies,
> sorrowful cares. The time has now come
> that people on this plain far and wide
> and all this wondrous creation worship me,
> pray to this sign. On me God's Son
> suffered a time; thus glorious I now tower
> under the heavens, and I may heal
> all and some of those in awe of me.[18]

The Ruthwell Cross and Standing Crosses of the British Isles

An excerpt from "The Dream of the Rood" was inscribed in Northumbrian runic script on an eighth-century sandstone monument, the Ruthwell Cross, reconstructed after its destruction by Protestants in the seventeenth century and now housed within a small church in Dumfriesshire, Scotland. While the stone cross (about 5.5 meters tall) is a fascinating monument in itself, the existence of these runes justifies the proposed seventh- or eighth-century dating of the original poem.[19] The inscribed text is roughly half the length of the Vercelli text, presumably shortened in order to fit onto the cross's two narrow sides. Here the runes form a border surrounding a lush vine inhabited by birds and animals. Its four stanzas begin at the point Christ ascends onto the cross and end with the crucifixion. What makes this particularly remarkable is the link between the object and the text. The poem speaks in the first-person voice of the cross and, in this case, the actual stone cross voices its own story (albeit in carved runes).

The Ruthwell Cross is one among many tall, freestanding, elaborately carved stone crosses in the British Isles that were erected between the eighth and thirteenth centuries. The Irish examples are particularly ancient and justifiably famous, as they display some of the most intricate and well-preserved reliefs. Conceivably modeled after smaller objects of wood or metal, their purpose is unclear. Some scholars believe they were intended to identify a particularly holy place, such as a saint's grave. Others argue that they marked monastery foundations, distinguished boundaries, and graves or simply served as devotional monuments or village landmarks (for example, market crosses).

The ringed, Celtic-type crosses resemble the crosses surmounted by wreathed christograms *(crux invicta)* on fourth-century Roman sarcophagi (cf. Figs. 3.6 and 3.7). Yet, because many display small half-spheres that could have originally been colored, art historians also have likened them to early gemmed crosses, including Theodosius II's presumed donation to the Holy Sepulcher, and Coptic crosses (Fig. 5.1, for example), thus making a iconographic link between eastern Mediterranean and insular art.[20] One of the most famous, the Kello "Wheel Cross," dates to about 1200 and is decorated with depictions of Helena discovering the cross, making an explicit connection with the Jerusalem relic.

The crosses are often set upon stepped platforms and topped with gabled or beehive-shaped capstones. Most have multiple panels of relief sculpture on all four sides: the front and back usually depict stories from scripture or groups of saints or apostles, and the sides are typically covered with interlacing designs. A crucifixion scene sometimes appears prominently in the center, but in other instances is found in the margins or omitted altogether. The style of the narrative scenes suggests that they drew upon earlier artworks, perhaps late antique or Carolingian ivories, while the interlacing designs have more in common with local metalwork patterns.

The tenth-century ringed cross known as Muiredach's is connected with Monasterboice (in County Louth), an ancient ecclesial complex and graveyard that features a group of high crosses. The west face features an image of the crucifixion in its center. An image of St. Michael weighing souls at the Last Judgment occurs at the same position on the east face. Other iconography includes images of Cain and Abel, and David and Goliath.

The Ruthwell Cross's iconography is unique in that it features an image of the crucifixion at its base rather than at its center. This may have been intended to accommodate pilgrims who could view it at eye level and so direct their devotions. Rising above the scene is a series of panels showing other biblical episodes interspersed with typical Celtic geometric designs, bosses, and interlacing knot work. The remaining motifs have virtually no direct association with the Passion. Above the crucifixion are, in order, the Annunciation, Christ healing the blind man, Jesus with the woman anointing his feet, and either the Visitation or Mary with Martha. The north side figures include the flight into Egypt, Saints Paul and Anthony breaking bread, Christ trampling on beasts (in the center of the shaft), and an image often identified as John the Baptist holding the Lamb of God (although it might be Christ in Majesty).[21] Latin inscriptions—usually quotations from scripture—identify the scenes. For example, the scene of Saints Paul and Anthony is encircled by the inscription, SCS PAULUS ET ANTONIUS EREMITAE FREGER(UN)T PANEM IN DESERTO (the Eremite Saints Paul and Anthony broke bread in the desert). The cross piece and central designs of a Trinity symbol and rosette are later restorations.[22]

In the mid-seventeenth century, members of the General Assembly of the Church of Scotland judged the Ruthwell Cross to be an idolatrous object and ordered it to be taken down, broken, and defaced. Two hundred years later, a local minister, Henry Duncan, found various pieces around the grounds of his

6.6 Muiredach's Cross, west side, tenth century, Monasterboice.

church, reassembled the cross, and initially installed it as an obelisk in his garden. Duncan, wishing to reconstruct the cross as he imagined it had once looked, designed a hypothetical replacement for the missing cross piece and commissioned a local mason to carve and install it.[23] Today the cross stands in a specially built apse within the Ruthwell church.

The Irish high crosses have undergone a parallel rehabilitation to the Ruthwell Cross. After centuries of neglect, the Celtic Revival of the mid-nineteenth century adapted the iconic figure of these crosses as a symbol for Ireland and Irish culture. During the Irish War of Independence (1919–1921), they also became an emblem associated with the resistance of Catholic Ireland to English occupation. An exhibition of plaster copies of these crosses in the National Museum of Ireland demonstrated the modern interest and demand for everything from full-scale replicas to small reproductions on a variety of items, from gravestones to tattoos.

The Cross in the Apocryphal Lives of Adam and Eve

The link between the tree of Eden and the Cross of Christ was elaborated in a series of apocryphal legends that emerged sometime in the third to sixth centuries. These stories narrate the events of Adam and Eve's life following their expulsion from Eden. They have a complicated literary history, probably relying on one or more now-lost sources, likely including some ancient Jewish narratives to which Christianizing features were subsequently added. The main versions of the tale exist in Latin, Greek, Armenian, Georgian, and Slavonic, each of which has some unique details as well as overlapping elements with one or more of the others.[24] One of the best known is a Latin *Life of Adam and Eve,* which has a Greek parallel also known as the *Apocalypse of Moses.* Distinct—but bearing similarities—are sections of the *Gospel of Nicodemus* (or the *Acts of Pilate*). Significantly, the tree of life shows up in all of these in respect to certain incidents related to Adam's death and burial.[25]

In the Latin *Life of Adam and Eve,* as Adam lies dying, he asks that all his children should gather so that he can speak with them and bless them. Seth asks Adam if he longs for some of the fruit of the tree in the Garden. At this, Adam recounts the story of the fall and expulsion, explaining that his current affliction is a result of that ancient transgression. He then wonders aloud whether God would finally take pity upon him and ask his angel to gather some of the oil of mercy from the tree of life and give it to Seth in order to anoint Adam so that he might have relief from his pain. Thus, Eve and Seth set out for Eden and arrive at the gates of the Garden. After an encounter with the Serpent, Seth and Eve finally arrive and penitently plead with God to give them some of the oil of mercy. The archangel Michael appears and tells them that they may not yet have the oil from the tree, explaining that at the proper time in the future, Christ will come to resurrect Adam's body and, with him, the bodies of all the dead. Michael also tells them that, before any of this happens, Christ also will be baptized in the Jordan and, once he emerges from the water, he will anoint all who believe in him with the oil of mercy. Then, he adds, the Son of God will descend into the earth to lead Adam back into the Garden and to the tree of mercy. In one manuscript, Seth and Eve return home bearing a small branch as well as incense and spices.[26]

A parallel legend is included in the apocryphal *Gospel of Nicodemus*. This story is set in the context of Jesus's harrowing of Hell and the release of the dead from their tombs (Matt. 27:52–53). Here, Adam asks Seth to tell the other prophets and patriarchs in Hades about the events surrounding his (Adam's) death. Accordingly, Seth relates a similar story: that, on his sickbed, Adam asked him to go to the gate of Paradise and petition God to send him an angel who could lead him to the tree of mercy, from which he might gather oil to anoint and thus restore his dying father. Seth did this, but in answer to his prayer, the angel told Seth that the tree could not be found. Instead, the angel tells Seth he should return to his father with the news that in 5,500 years from the creation of the world, the only-begotten Son of God would come to earth, and only then anoint Adam with that oil. At that time, Adam would rise along with all his descendants and be washed with water and the Holy Spirit. Then they could be healed of every disease.[27]

In later renditions of the *Life of Adam and Eve,* the archangel Michael gives Seth a twig from the tree as a consolation prize, which he carries back to place on Adam's grave. The twig grows up to be a lofty tree and, in time, is hewn down and becomes Christ's cross. This legendary detail occurs in other early medieval stories. The long-standing tradition that the site of Jesus's crucifixion, Golgotha, was so named because it was over the site of Adam's grave gave this story a biblical basis.[28] This is why a skull regularly appears at the base of the cross in Christian iconography of the crucifixion.

A version of these tales was entered into *The Golden Legend,* in the mid-thirteenth century. The chapter titled "The Finding of the Holy Cross" opens with the story of Seth seeking the oil of mercy from the archangel Michael, as related by the *Gospel of Nicodemus*. It then notes that other sources say the angel gave Seth a shoot from the tree, either to plant on the mount of Lebanon or to plant on Adam's grave, adding that this was a twig from the tree under which Adam had committed his sin, and that when this shoot finally bore fruit his father would be restored.

In contrast to the Gospel of Nicodemus, *The Golden Legend* continues the story of the twig beyond the death of Adam. It reports that Solomon harvested wood from the tree for his forest house (1 Kings 7), but because it could not be cut to the right size, his workmen threw it aside to be used as a footbridge over a pond (in some manuscripts, the stream of Kedron). The Queen of Sheba encountered this bridge when she came to visit Solomon and had a vision that it was not ordinary wood but the cross on which Christ would be crucified. She knelt down to worship rather than walk on it and ended up wading across the stream. When the queen returned home, she sent word to Solomon that a certain man would be hung on that wood, which would lead to the destruction of the Jewish kingdom. Solomon, fearing this outcome, buried the wood. But it would not be destroyed. At the place where Solomon buried the wood, a miraculous, healing pool, the Piscina Probatica, bubbled up. The wood ultimately became the instrument of Christ's crucifixion. The *Legend* then goes on to narrate the story of the cross's discovery by the Empress Helena three hundred years later.

Visual depictions of these legends—beginning with Seth's journey to retrieve the oil of mercy (or twig of the tree), through the incidents with Solomon and the Queen of Sheba, and ending with Helena's discovery of the relic in Jerusalem—appeared in sequenced cycles, both in manuscript illuminations and church wall paintings from the thirteenth through the fifteenth centuries. Some of these cycles start with a scene of Adam on his bed and end with the scene of Helena and Judas the Jew testing the wood of the cross to verify that it was truly Christ's.[29]

One example occurs among the illuminations in the *Hours of Catherine of Cleves* (ca. 1440). This group includes depictions of Adam sending Seth off to Paradise, the archangel Michael giving Seth a branch from the tree of mercy, Seth putting the branch in the mouth of his dead and shrouded father, and Adam's grave with the tree growing from it. Additional leaves depict scenes from the episodes of Solomon and Sheba and the miraculous pool. Another series, in a fifteenth-century edition of a work attributed to a certain early fourteenth-

6.7 “The Tree Growing on Adam’s Grave.” Illumination from the *Hours of Catherine of Cleves*, ca. 1440.

century Austrian poet named Lutwin, the *Vitae Adae et Evae (Life of Adam and Eve)*, shows Adam on his deathbed instructing Seth and Eve to gather the oil, Seth receiving the prophecy along with the branch from the archangel, Seth bringing the branch back to his dying father, Adam's burial (with the twig of the tree), and the tree growing up from the shared tomb of Adam and Eve.[30]

These stories, their parallel motifs, and related illuminations demonstrate not only a Christian fascination with the source of the sacred wood of the cross but also the firm conviction that it, as the wood upon which salvation was accomplished, must have been directly linked with the Edenic tree that figured in the fall and expulsion of humans from Paradise. In Hades, Adam can convey the good news to his descendants that the once-forbidden fruit has been transformed into life-giving food. That the tree of life should return to fulfill its original purpose completes the circuit of creation, loss, death, and resurrection.

The Cross in Medieval Drama

Veneration of the cross had been part of Holy Week activities in Jerusalem since the late fourth century, and by the early Middle Ages, the practice had spread to other parts of the Christian world. Although the Holy Week rituals initially focused on the relic of the True Cross and incorporated elements from the feasts of the cross on September 14 and May 3, the place of the cross in Good Friday liturgies gradually included new features, including involving the cross in dramatic reenactments of Christ's burial. A crucifix, veiled throughout Lent, would be uncovered on Good Friday for veneration. This occurred at the conclusion of the service, following holy communion with the reserved sacrament. Following the congregation's veneration, the cross would be ritually buried *(depositio)* in a kind of sepulcher to await its discovery *(elevatio)* on Easter morning.[31]

A fully elaborated example of these rituals comes from the English *Regularis Concordia*, a document that emerged from the Council of Winchester at the end of the tenth century. Compiled by Ethelwold, Winchester's bishop, and Dunstan, Archbishop of Canterbury, at the behest of King Edgar, who wished to standardize the practices of English Benedictine monasteries, this document included instructions for the Good Friday liturgy. Following the service of the word, which culminated in the reading of the Passion according to John and the great intercessory prayers, deacons would process the veiled cross forward and set it up on a cushion in front of the altar. These deacons then led the chanting of three antiphons, *Ecce lignum crucis*, *Crucem tuam adoramus Domine*, and *Dum fabricator mundi*, as well the verses of Venantius Fortunatus's *Pange lingua*. During this singing, the monks would come forward, beginning with the abbot, prostrate themselves three times before the cross, and sorrowfully recite the seven penitential psalms. Once everyone had completed this devotion, the deacons would then dramatically reenact Christ's deposition from the cross and his burial in the tomb:

> Now since on that day we solemnize the burial of the Body of our Saviour, if anyone should care or think fit to follow in a becoming manner certain religious men in a practice worthy to be imitated for the strengthening of the faith of unlearned common persons and neophytes, we have decreed this only: on that part of the altar where there is space for it there shall be a representation as it were of a sepulcher, hung about by a curtain, in which the holy Cross, when it has been venerated, shall be placed in the following manner: the deacons who carried the Cross before shall come forward and, having wrapped the Cross in a napkin there where it was venerated, they shall bear it thence, singing the antiphons *In pace in idipsum*, *Habitat*, and *Caro mea requiescet in spe* to the place of the sepulcher. When they have laid the cross therein, in imitation as it were of the burial of the Body of our Lord Jesus Christ, they shall sing the antiphon *Sepulto Domino, signatum est monumentum ponentes milites qui custodirent eum*. In that same place the holy Cross shall be guarded with all reverence until the night of the Lord's Resurrection. And during the night let brethren be chosen by twos and threes, if the community be large enough, who shall keep faithful watch, chanting psalms.[32]

On Easter morning, the community would similarly reenact the women's discovery of the empty tomb. In the middle of the previous night, sacristans would have discreetly removed the cross from the sepulcher, leaving the linen cloth behind. In the morning, during the reading of the story of the three women coming to the tomb, four monks would come forward, one wearing an alb and carrying a palm branch, three carrying smoking incense burners. The monk in the alb would take his place at the tomb, while the three others would pretend to be searching for Christ's dead body. They would then reconstruct the dialog between the angel and the women, revealing that the tomb was empty apart from the discarded shroud, and triumphantly voice the Easter proclamation: "Christ is risen!"

Over time, this mimetic practice spread from monasteries to secular churches and became a widely popular element of Holy Week liturgies. Although the kind of cross used for this purpose is uncertain, these rites likely were practiced most often with a crucifix. Nevertheless, the *Regularis Concordia* ambiguously specifies a *"sancta crux,"* which could refer either to a plain (empty) cross or a crucifix. In some instances, the deacons would also bury a consecrated host. Thus, the cross becomes Christ himself, in a symbolic yet striking parallel to the eucharistic bread. As the ritual became more elaborate in later centuries, a special corpus with moveable arms would have been taken off the cross prior to burial. The moveable arms allowed the figure to be fitted in a narrow coffin, while making it even more lifelike.[33]

Such observations waned in the century following the Norman Conquest. Lanfranc, the Norman Archbishop of Canterbury, tried to make the Holy Week liturgies a bit more austere. Still, the English practice, as described in the *Regularis Concordia,* seems to have influenced the liturgical innovations of a French archbishop, Jean D'Avranches of Rouen, who wrote the *Liber de officiis ecclesiasticis,* which included this instruction for the conclusion of the Good Friday service, following the veneration of the cross:

> Let the crucifix be washed with wine and water in commemoration of the blood and water flowing from the side of the Savior, which, following holy communion, the clergy and the people drink. After the response, *Sicut ovis ad occisionem* is sung, let them carry it to a different place made to look like a sepulcher, where it is buried until the Day of the Lord. Congregated there, let the antiphon *In pace in idipsum* and the response *Sepulto Domino* be sung.[34]

These dramatic reenactments rarely included a depiction of the crucifixion itself; they rather focused on Christ's deposition from the cross, burial, and resurrection. The reticence about portraying the actual crucifixion may be due to the fact that the Mass itself was understood to be a representation of the sacrifice. Nevertheless, the Good Friday and Easter events steadily evolved into even more theatrical events, including dramatization of the crucifixion, which gradually became disconnected from the ecclesial liturgy and transferred to various lay fraternities, and thus out of direct clerical control. New musical compositions also emerged to enhance these plays, including the lament of the Virgin *(Planctus Mariae)*, which initially borrowed from eastern liturgical chants but came to have widely used Latin (and even vernacular) versions.[35] The oldest known western example dates to the twelfth century and comes from the monastery of Monte Cassino. This incomplete manuscript rehearses the story from the moment of Judas's bargain with the Jewish high priest through the events of crucifixion.[36]

The Passion plays were intended to achieve the same result as the affective art of the high Middle Ages. They engaged the spectator's emotions by offering a heightened sensory experience, in this instance with the addition of dialogue, characters, costumes, props, actions, and perhaps even olfactory triggers. They included scenes that preceded and followed the crucifixion in order to intensify the plot and its emotional impact. Such elaborations of the story necessarily added extensively to the Gospel narratives and their realism would have stimulated strong responses in an audience, prompting them to weep, even cry out in outrage. The tendency to confuse the drama with reality often aroused anti-Jewish prejudice when they presented the crucifixion as a perfidious plot of Jews against Christ.[37]

Literary and representational links between the tree of life and the cross show how avidly early and medieval Christians sought ways to connect the origin and fall of humanity with the salvation they believed came through the Passion of Christ. Thus the tree in the Edenic garden continued to play a part in the human story, showing up in the key moments of salvation history, and finally providing the wood of the cross, becoming simultaneously an instrument of death and the support for the one who restored life. The cross has a story to tell in which it undergoes its own passion, death, and burial, in order to be reborn (or rediscovered) and recognized not as an artifact of suffering, or a souvenir of endurance, but a testimonial to triumph. Linking the primordial story

6.8 Apse mosaic, Basilica of St. John Lateran, Rome.

of the fall to the story of Christ's Passion, and finally to the discovery of the True Cross in more recent history, revealed that God's providential plan for salvation was in place from the beginning. Thus, this uniquely Christian symbol linked not only earth and heaven: it also joined beginning to end, Genesis to Revelation, Old Adam to New Adam, and creation to recreation.

The visual art that reflects this idea projects this optimistic image. The cross sprouts leafy branches that are twined around with vines and flowers. Its leaves will not wither and fall but remain verdant in all seasons. It bears a new sort of fruit—fruit given to the nations for their healing. This is not a cross of ordinary wood or some historic artifact that was lost and lately excavated. It was at the center of creation and a source of life. In time it came to be drenched with blood and pierced with nails, yet never ceased to produce the oil of mercy, a balm to sinners and the tool that reopens the gates of Paradise.

The apse mosaic at Rome's Lateran Basilica displays many of these themes. Although the current apse mosaic was installed at the end of the nineteenth century when the church was extended, its composition may be based on the prior mosaic, created by Jacopo Torriti along with the Franciscan Jacopo

Camerino in the late thirteenth century, which in turn may have been inspired by an underlying, late antique model. The current apse depicts a bust of Christ hovering in a dark, cloud-streaked sky over an elaborately designed golden and gem-studded cross. The Virgin and John the Baptist stand to either side, joined by Saints Peter, Paul, Francis, John, and Andrew, along with the Pope, who kneels at the Virgin's feet. An oval medallion at the cross's center shows the baptism of Christ. Above, the dove of the Holy Spirit descends and water flows from its beak. This water streams over the cross's sides to fill a pool at the cross's base and then into the four rivers of Paradise (here named Gihon, Pishon, Tigris, and Euphrates) to which deer and lambs come to drink. Below the base of the cross, a phoenix perches in a palm that rises from the jeweled and golden walls of the Heavenly Jerusalem; a cherub guards its gates with a drawn sword. A depiction of the flowing Jordan River frames the mosaic's lower border, populated by fishing and windsurfing putti. In the stream's center is the river god with his jug, a venerable figure who bridges classical and Christian iconography.

7

Crux Patiens

Medieval Devotion to the Dying Christ

For crowned with thorns
he was ordered to bend his back under the burden of the cross
and to bear his own ignominy. . . .
And then transfixed with nails,
He appeared to you as your beloved
cut through with wound upon wound
in order to heal you.
Who will grant me
that my request should come about
and that God will give me what I long for,
that having been totally transpierced
in both mind and flesh,
I may be fixed with my beloved
to the yoke of the cross?

—Bonaventure

THE IMAGE OF Christ hanging upon the cross, relatively late to appear in the catalog of Christian visual images, became a subject of controversy during the eighth- and ninth-century Byzantine disputes over the general validity and role of holy icons. Although iconoclasts allowed depictions of the empty cross as a venerable symbol of Christ's salvific sacrifice, they resisted the crucifix as idolatrous. Those who defended icons argued that the crucifix was essential in that it displayed Christ's human nature and true corporeal suffering.[1] Western church authorities, aware if not always fully cognizant of the subtleties of the Eastern controversy, also debated the question of images and, in particular, the validity of the crucifix over the empty cross, though from a different point of view and with different conclusions. Although the Western church's quarrels initially may have been prompted by a response to the Eastern declarations about the validity of holy images, the arguments were framed in distinct ways that reflected the Latin—particularly Carolingian—Church's cultural and political circumstances.

In the meantime, representations of Christ's crucifixion became more and more common. However, before the tenth or eleventh century, both Eastern and Western depictions typically refrained from showing Jesus as suffering physical agony and death. Consistent with the earliest known crucifixion images, they tended to present Christ as vigorously alive, his eyes wide open, and often robed in the purple garments of a king. An example of this living Christ type shows up in an Irish Gospel book at St. Gall, dated to around 750. Here, a rather unusual-looking, beardless Christ with curly yellow hair and staring eyes "stands" awkwardly at attention on his cross. He is swaddled in the stylized folds of a purple mantle that winds around his body. Above, two angels hold books; below, Longinus and Stephaton lift sponge and spear.

Gradually, from the ninth through the eleventh century, the depictions of Christ's triumph over death began to shift toward a visual representation of the suffering man-God, or *Christus patiens*. Evolving theological reflection on the significance of Christ's death, the growing emphasis on the purpose and value of Jesus's physical agony, and the development of guided meditation on Christ's Passion within certain early monastic communities all contributed to this transition. Viewers were prompted to meditate on the Savior's affliction, to empathize with it, to be profoundly grateful for it, and even to imitate it. Despite this emphasis on the Savior's bodily suffering, medieval devotees did not regard the crucifix as evidence of defeat or humiliation but rather as an affective depiction of Christ's redemptive and sacrificial love. Such divine love came to be understood as the source of human salvation as much as his heroic conquest of Satan and death.

This reversal from an emphasis on a victorious Christ to a suffering Savior was somewhat contradicted in a different kind of *imitatio Christi*. Christian warriors during the Crusades who saw themselves as carrying their personal

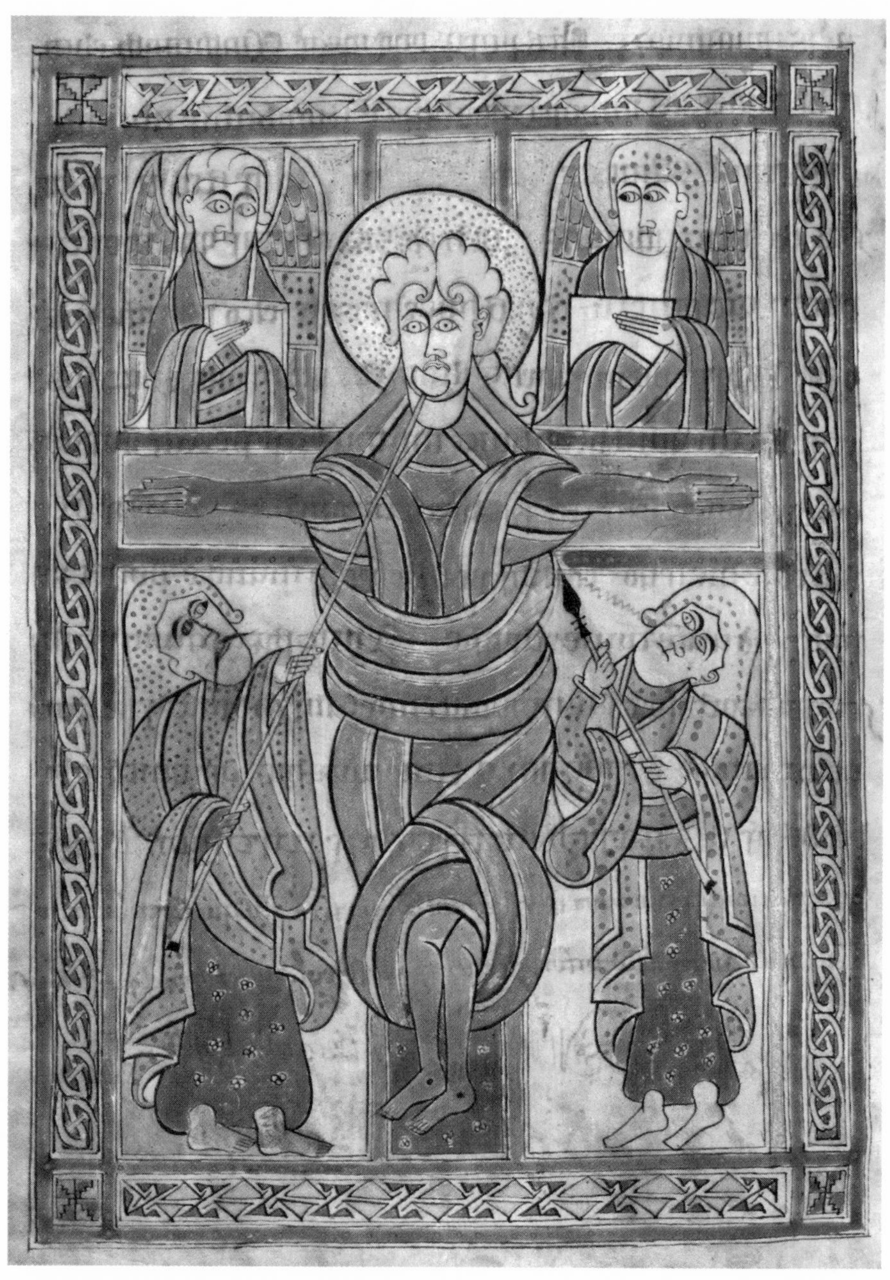

7.1 Crucifixion, St. Gall Gospel Book, ca. 750.

crosses into battle, hoping for their own version of triumph over evil. Although many, if not most, of these cross-bearing soldiers clearly aimed at earthly conquest, they also regarded their battle as a holy war and themselves as members of their Lord's anointed army. They assumed their cause was righteous: they believed they were engaging an enemy of Christ who had occupied the Holy Land. Thus, they inscribed crosses on their uniforms and banners and wore or carried them into battle.

The Cross and the Western Response to the Byzantine Image Controversy

The theological debates surrounding the image controversies that beset the Eastern Church were not fully comprehended or appreciated in the West. Shortly after the Seventh Ecumenical Council (Nicaea II) in 787 affirmed the role of images in both formal liturgy and private devotion and at least temporarily ended the official destruction of religious images, King Charlemagne ordered one of his court theologians, Theodulf of Orléans, to compose an official response to the council's decrees. Theodulf, aided by collaborators, produced the requested document, which has come to be known as the *Opus Caroli Regis* (or *Libri Carolini*).[2]

Scholars have argued that Theodulf and his colleagues misunderstood the Greek *Acta* of the council possibly because they were poorly translated (or merely summarized) and so failed to capture the subtle aspects of the debate, including the distinction between the words *latreia* (worship)—reserved to the Divinity alone—and *proskynesis* (veneration)—allowed to holy images, saints (and their relics), and the Bible. It is just as likely, however, that the issues scrutinized in the Eastern debates were identical to those that concerned Western theologians.[3] Thus, the *Opus Caroli Regis,* while provoked by the decrees of the Seventh Ecumenical Council, is better understood as a document that addressed concerns regarding the role of religious images in Frankish territories. While condemning superstitious adoration of icons, the document also decries the actual destruction of religious images that have even limited pedagogical or decorative value. Yet, although the work equally denounced both iconoclasts and iconophiles, it ultimately contributed to the condemnation of

Nicaea II at the synod of Frankfurt in 794, albeit over Pope Hadrian's official ratification of the Council's decrees.[4]

Underlying all this controversy was a characteristically Western debate over holy images. The *Opus Caroli Regis* allowed veneration to be extended to certain material objects that it termed *"res sacratae"* (holy things). Among these were the Ark of the Covenant, saints' relics, the consecrated eucharistic elements, the sign of the cross (but not its physical representation), and the Bible—objects regarded as having been sanctified by God and capable of mediating God's presence or power.[5] Although it does not refer to relics of the True Cross, the *Opus* would seem to allow for their veneration, insofar as the text asserts that human salvation was accomplished by the actual cross—though not by its human-made image. This distinction between holy reality *(res sacrata)* and artificial image made representations of the cross and crucifix alike unacceptable.

A famous incident involving a certain Claudius of Turin around 816–818 provides an illustration of this position and its consequences.[6] Charlemagne's son and coruler, Louis the Pious, put Claudius in charge of the Diocese of Turin. Soon after he arrived, Claudius noticed that members of his flock were offering some sort of veneration to images displayed in the church. Outraged at what he perceived to be idolatry, Claudius began to remove and destroy the artworks. When King Louis heard about Claudius's campaign, he sent two of his court theologians, Jonas of Orléans and the monk Dungalus from Pavia, to investigate. The image that caused the most serious contention was the crucifix. Claudius argued that while showing reverence to a crucifix was intended to honor and venerate the Savior, it was actually a false and superstitious act: referring only to Jesus's degradation and death, it denied his resurrection and ascension. Essentially, because Christ no longer suffers in the flesh, venerating such an image was tantamount to recrucifying him. He apparently also included plain crosses in his invective, as he added that adoration of ordinary wood fashioned into a cross would be like adoring any other object associated with Jesus's earthly life: a manger, a boat, or a donkey.

Both Jonas and Dungalus refuted Claudius's position, pointing out that the cross, a memorial of Christ's Passion, had been found worthy of honor from antiquity. Furthermore, they argued that rather than symbolizing death, the cross signified Jesus's triumph *over* death. Moreover, the wood was not venerated per se but only because it was the locus of Christ's crucifixion. Dungalus went on to recount the Old Testament passages that prefigure the cross, as well as the places in the New Testament epistles that affirm the significance of the cross apart from the resurrection. He even asked whether Claudius refused to make the sign of the cross when he presided at baptisms or confirmations or when he consecrated the bread and wine of the eucharist. Comparing veneration of the cross to veneration of the Bible, Jonas asked whether, when Claudius kisses the book, he understands himself to be honoring leather, ink, and paper.

Less than a decade later, a synod in Paris (825) considered the problem of holy images. The assembled bishops determined that images were permissible to a limited extent and that it was wrong to remove or destroy them, so long as they were not objects of actual worship. Yet they rejected the claim of the Eastern churches that images should be honored in the same way that the cross was venerated. Rather, they decided that the cross was altogether unique, different from other images and exclusively deserving of honor. They gave several justifications: that the cross had been revealed to Constantine as a portent of his victory; that it had clearly performed miracles when it had been discovered in Jerusalem; that making the sign of the cross was efficacious for consecrating the eucharistic elements or administering baptism; and that the cross, unlike any other image, served as a sign of salvation.[7]

Evolving Depictions of the Crucifixion in Western Art

In 1054, more than two centuries after the Paris Synod, a clash about how Jesus should be depicted on the cross arose within the controversy that resulted in the Great Schism between the Eastern and Western churches. A large contribution to this extremely complicated problem was the Roman bishop's demand that the patriarch of Constantinople recognize his claim to be head of the entire Christian Church. Additional matters of dispute included the Western use of unleavened bread as the eucharist and the Eastern emperor's refusal to provide military aid to the pope against the Norman invasion of southern Italy. On top of these more substantive ecclesial and political disputes, Pope Leo IX's legate to the East, Cardinal Humbert of Silva Candida, objected to Byzantine depictions of the crucifixion that showed Christ as dying as if he were merely mortal. He reportedly declared, "You Greeks affix the image of a man about to die to the image of Christ crucified, so that some Antichrist appears on the cross of Christ, showing himself as if to be adored like God."[8]

Humbert's complaint was well founded, at least in iconographical terms. Although earlier Byzantine depictions of the crucifixion had followed the tradition of showing Christ still alive and fully clothed on the cross (cf. Figs. 4.5 and 4.7), such images gradually had been superseded. The eighth-century Sinai icon (Fig. 4.8) was one of the earliest examples to show Christ bleeding, crowned with thorns, and dying upon the cross; by the eleventh century, eastern images had generally begun to show Christ slumped and partially nude, his eyes closed, and his head sunk upon his chest.[9]

A prominent example of a mosaic is in the Greek monastery of Hosios Loukas, which dates to the first quarter of the eleventh century. The image, one of the earliest of this type in the East, shows Christ with his eyes closed and bleeding from the wounds in his side, hands, and feet; it might be like the unidentified crucifix that scandalized Cardinal Humbert. It also is one of the earliest depictions of Mary and the Beloved Disciple expressing sorrow. Mary gestures toward her son as if calling the viewer to offer reverence. The inscription beneath the cross's arms refers to the text of John 19:26–27: "Woman, behold your son; son, behold your mother." Despite Humbert's objections, the fact that blood appears to flow from Christ's wound suggests that Christ is still living. His closed eyes may be intended to indicate only a state of repose, as if he is sleeping—the paradox of death and life, held together in the one being whose body was rendered incorruptible because of its unbreakable link with his divine nature.[10]

While we cannot know to what particular art works Humbert took offense, we can safely assume that he believed the depiction of a dead Christ was an exclusive characteristic of Eastern iconography and was unaware of Western crucifixes that—by his time—also showed Christ as dying or dead upon the cross. In fact, he seems to have assumed those earlier crucifixes that depicted the crucified Christ as alive and even wearing the long purple *colobium* were still standard.

However, by the late eighth century, Western depictions of the crucifixion had started to show Christ wearing only a loin cloth *(perizoma)* and to depict his bleeding wounds. An example appears in the Gellone Sacramentary, dated to circa 790. Here the cross becomes the *T* of the *"Te igitur"* invocation that

7.2 Crucifixion, mosaic, Monastery Church, Hosios Loukas, Greece, eleventh century.

opens the canon of the Mass.[11] A bearded Christ stands rigidly upright on the cross. His open, staring eyes and his almost blank expression are reminiscent of the Maskell Ivories, but the iconography adds a new detail: blood that flows from his side wound and trickles from his feet and hands. His chest is bare as he wears only the *perizoma*. The unusual cross (which serves also as the initial letter) is represented as almost celestial: dark blue and spangled with red and white stars. Two angels fly head downward and make a gesture of acclaim. The image unites text, image, and ritual (the Mass also being a visual presentation of Jesus's sacrifice). A similarly living Christ appears in an illumination from the Psalter of Ludwig the German (ca. 843–876). The figure of Ludwig himself embraces the cross, on which a still-robust Christ in a red loin cloth stretches out muscular arms—despite the blood trickling from the wounds in his hands and feet—and gazes calmly downwards, as if acknowledging his devotee.

Around the time that Theodulf and his colleagues were composing the *Opus Caroli Regis*, certain theologians began to produce collections of pictorial devotional poems known as *carmina figurata*. These incorporated designs were made by arranging the letters of words to form different shapes.[12] A few of these specifically combined poems about the cross with depictions of the cross or the crucified Christ. Alcuin, one of these artist-authors, gave a collection to Charlemagne. His work probably drew upon a similar series that the fourth-century poet, Publilius Optatianus Porphyrias, had dedicated to the emperor Constantine I. Thus, Alcuin apparently intended to draw comparisons between the first Christian emperor and that Carolingian king, suggesting their similar divine favor and spiritual authority.[13]

Among the most famous of these *carmina figurata* is a series by Hrabanus Maurus, the abbot of the monastery at Fulda. His work, *In Praise of the Holy Cross (In honorem Sanctae Crucis)*, written during the second decade of the ninth century, contains twenty-eight poems dedicated to the cross.[14] All include images of the cross within the grid of red and black letters; many are plain crosses combined with geometric figures, though a few contain pictorial images as well. In one instance, the cross divides the page into quadrants with cherubim and seraphim within the sections. The Lamb of God or the four living creatures are featured on others. In another example, Hrabanus Maurus shows himself kneeling before the cross.

One especially striking image shows Jesus standing upright, with arms extended, eyes wide open, and wearing only a red *perizoma*. The cross is not delineated here; rather, it is only evident in Christ's posture. His head is encircled in green by a cruciform halo that incorporates the words "King of Kings and Lord of Lords" *(Rex regum et dominus dominorum)* in the circle, while the interior cross has the letters *A*, *M*, and the Greek *omega*, indicating that Christ is the first *(alpha)*, middle *(medius)*, and last *(omega)*. His hair displays the words "This is the King of justice" *(Iste est rex iustitiae)*. Letters on his nipples and navel read *D*, *E*, and *O (Deo)*. Other parts of his body contain verses that pertain to them. For example, his right leg reads upward, "The eternal Lord guided the blessed to the stars" *(Aeternus dominus deduxit ad astra beatos)*.

The first lines accompanying his poem explain Hrabanus's concept: "Here is the image of the Savior, who through the position of his limbs, consecrates for us that most celebrated, sweetest and most beloved form of the Cross, so that, believing in his name and obeying his commandments, we may have hope of eternal life, thanks to his Passion."[15] These lines raise the question of whether

7.3 Page from Hrabanus Maurus, *In honorem Sanctae Crucis*, ca. 1170.

Hrabanus was aware of the controversy surrounding the veneration of the cross and crucifix, as the text clearly affirms the value of visually contemplating such an image. In another of his poems, Hrabanus Maurus places the letters of the name Adam in each arm of the cross, explaining in his text that the first man was the "form of the future Christ."[16]

Depictions of the Dying Christ

Almost simultaneously with the transition of iconography in the Byzantine East, from the ninth through the eleventh century the Western artistic tradition of representing a living Christ on the cross began to yield to a preference for showing Christ as dying or even dead. The *Drogo Sacramentary,* made for Drogo, Bishop of Metz in northern France, contains one of the earliest of these types (ca. 850). A small crucifixion image appears within the initial *O* that opens the Palm Sunday collect. Here, Christ hangs on the cross, his body has begun to droop, and his hips rotate to the left. His head rests on his right shoulder and, although his eyes seem to be open, his entire posture suggests that he is at the moment of death. The usual figures of Mary and the Beloved Disciple, as well as two hovering angels, are joined by two new characters: first a female, representing the personification of Ecclesia, holding a banner in one hand and a chalice to catch the blood flowing from Christ's side in the other, and then an old man, sitting on the ground, who could be either Nicodemus who helped bury Christ, or a personification of the Old Law, possibly in the guise of Moses.[17] A serpent coils around the cross below Christ's feet—alluding to the text of Psalms 91:13, "you will trample the serpent underfoot"—a reference to Christ's victory over death and Satan.[18]

Two ivory book covers, also from Metz and possibly commissioned by Drogo's successor, date to the third quarter of the ninth century. They display this emerging type of crucifixion iconography and further elaborate the scene with additional witnesses. In both instances, a half-nude Christ hangs on the cross, his body slightly twisted, and his arms stretched above to support his weight. His ribcage and belly protrude, barely suggesting his physical agony. Although his eyes are still open, his head drops slightly onto his right shoulder. Mary and the Beloved Disciple stand to his far right and left, their hands raised, and their eyes focused on high. Between them, a figure meant to be Ecclesia holds up a jug to the wound on his side, gathering his blood for the holy eucharist. Her counterpart, Synagoga, holds a banner, and though she has turned away from Christ, she still looks back toward him.

Christ's cross bears the titulus with the inscription IHS NAZARE/NVS REX IV(daeorum), "Jesus of Nazareth, King of the Jews." Above the title are roundels bearing the busts of the sun and the moon, flanked by angels who reach

7.4 Crucifixion, ivory plaque from Metz, ca. 870.

7.5 Reliquary crucifix, found in Winchester but probably made in Germany or under German influence, ca. 900–1000.

down as if to gather and transfer his soul. A serpent coils around the base of the cross. In the lower middle ground are Stephaton and Longinus, and two round mausolea with wakening dead emerging from their tombs. One of these ivory plaques includes seated figures at the bottom, intended to represent the sea (with an oar, sitting on a hippocamp) and the earth (with her babies). Together they suggest the witness of the entire cosmos to the events of the Passion.

These ivories, the *Drogo Sacramentary* crucifixion, and, in fact, most images dated before the tenth century show Jesus with his eyes still open, indicating that he is living even while representing his agony.[19] A living Christ on the cross does not disappear suddenly, however; such depictions continue into the eleventh century and beyond. Meanwhile, Christ with closed eyes (thus indicating his death) gradually became more the norm during the Ottonian era (ca. 950–1024). An especially fine example is an Anglo-Saxon ivory figure of Christ attached to a reliquary cross, now in the Victoria and Albert Museum. This object was designed to contain a relic of the True Cross, placed within the gold filigreed and enameled cross, just beneath the ivory corpus.

Perhaps the most significant and possibly the earliest depiction of Christ with closed eyes occurs on the Gero Crucifix, a gift of Archbishop Gero to the Cologne Cathedral, dated to the years 965–970. This was also one of the earliest life-sized, freestanding crucifixes. Here Christ's body slumps and twists to his left. His knees are bent and his arms rise above the level of his head; the muscles of both his chest and upper arms strain to support his weight. His swelling belly protrudes under his prominent ribcage, his chin rests upon his chest, and his eyes are closed. Even though these details suggest physical agony, Christ's expression is tranquil, as if he is at peace in death. This monumental cross probably hung over or above an altar, conceivably a centrally placed "cross-altar" in the church's nave. A legend, the so-called "Miracle of Gero of Cologne," recorded by Thietmar, bishop of Merseburg (1009–1019), reports that at some point the head of this crucifix was found to be cracked. Archbishop Gero then placed a relic of the True Cross and a consecrated host into the crack and prayed for its healing. When he rose from his prayers, the crack had miraculously closed up, leaving no trace of its ever having existed.[20] This image bears clear similarity to the Hosios Loukas mosaic and may even have been modeled on a Byzantine crucifix like it (cf. Fig. 7.2)

Devotion to the Crucifix in the Middle Ages

Depictions of Christ dying upon the cross occur in the context of the increasing focus on Christ's ordeal in the literature and devotional writing of the eleventh and twelfth centuries. While Byzantine theologians firmly argued in favor of the representation of Christ's Passion as a means of affirming his full humanity, Western theologians attended more to the reconciling work of Christ's self-sacrifice, and they encouraged the pious to regard the reality of Christ's human pain in graphic detail. One such theologian, Anselm of Canterbury (1033–1109), famously focused on the question of why God became human. In his treatise on the topic, *Cur Deus Homo (Why Did God Become Man?),* Anselm endorses the propriety of Christ's vanquishing the devil by means of a tree because the devil had conquered humanity through the eating of a tree.[21] He goes on to insist that Christ's voluntary death was necessary because humans cannot give sufficient satisfaction for their own sin; only the incarnate God could pay the infinite debt with his own life. Anselm, among others, offered prayers directed to images of the crucifixion, guided meditations on Christ's wounds, and encouraged mystical experiences of bodily pain. Anselm's *Prayer to Christ* is an especially vivid instance of a guided meditation on the Passion. He directly addresses the reader, prompting her to imagine being personally present at the scene, while lamenting the fact that she could not actually have been there:

> So, as much as I can, though not as much as I ought, I am mindful of your passion, your buffeting, your scourging, your cross, your wounds, how you were slain for me, how prepared for burial and buried. . . . Why, O my soul, were you not there to be pierced by a sword of bitter sorrow when you could not bear the piercing of the side of your Savior with a lance? Why could you not bear to see the nails violate the hands and feet of your Creator? Why could you not see with horror the blood that poured out of the side of your Redeemer? Why were you not drunk with bitter tears when they gave him bitter gall to drink?[22]

This understanding of Christ's death as an act of atonement for human sin eclipsed the earlier concentration on Christ's death as victory. Medieval theologians replaced a narrative of triumph with one of self-sacrificing love, and the *crux patiens* replaced the *crux invicta*. Devotional practices attended to Jesus's suffering, vividly imagining it, feeling sorrow and pity, and even physically experiencing pain. Visual artists began representing Christ's bodily torments, the cruel mockery of his persecutors, the crown of thorns, the wounds on his body, and other evidence of his physical and mental anguish as he hung upon the cross.

This development in theology, visual art, and personal devotional practice was particularly characteristic of monastic piety, initially among figures such as the Cistercian Bernard of Clairvaux (1090–1133) and subsequently by the mendicant orders: the Dominicans and Franciscans. All of these strove to foster a certain type of subjective—and even visceral—imaginative engagement with the narrative of Christ's life, especially his nativity and Passion. Contemporaneous with this literature was a new kind of crucifix that represented Christ's intense sorrow and pain. Such imagery underscored Jesus's full humanity, which was necessary in order to atone for human sin. But beyond assenting to the objective theological tenet, the faithful were prompted to identify personally with Jesus's suffering, even to desire to imitate it. From this emerged a new kind of piety that moved devotees to imagine themselves within the scenes and events of the life of Christ and to cultivate a deeply intimate attachment to him.

Bernard of Clairvaux's writings elaborate both the profound love of the devotee toward Christ and Christ's toward the devotee. Although he never wrote an actual treatise on the cross, Bernard, developing the ideas of earlier thinkers like Abelard, saw Christ's suffering as a revelation of his love and believed that those who returned such love would be saved. His treatise on the *Song of Songs* particularly concentrates on the way that Christ's love should provoke a response of love in the faithful after the model of Christ as bridegroom and the Church as bride.[23]

The next generation of mendicant theologians included Francis of Assisi (1181–1226), who attended so much to Christ's bodily wounds that he received similar ones on his hands, feet, and side (stigmata) in 1224. Francis's follower Bonaventure was deeply influenced by Francis's devotion to the crucified Christ. He dedicated a section of his poem "The Tree of Life" to the mystery of Christ's Passion, guiding his readers through the events and asking them to devoutly contemplate each "fruit," from his betrayal and trial to his torture and death. He concludes,

O my God, good Jesus,
although I am in every way without merit and unworthy,
grant to me,
who did not merit to be present at these events
in the body
that I may ponder them faithfully
in my mind
and experience toward you,
my God crucified and put to death for me,
that feeling of compassion
which your innocent mother and the penitent Magdalene
experienced
at the very hour of your Passion.[24]

Franciscans and Dominicans alike promoted meditation on the Passion, and in addition to the physical manifestation of the imitation in the reception of stigmata, they instituted and developed further many new devotional practices that reinforced the centrality of the cross and Christ's suffering in the prayer practice of the ordinary faithful: the stations of the cross, the rosary (especially the set of prayers known as the "sorrowful mysteries"), and various liturgical rites and feasts dedicated to commemorations of certain events of the Passion.[25]

New motifs emerged in visual art in addition to the dying Christ on the cross: representations of Christ's deposition and burial, as well as representations of the Virgin Mary with her dead son on her lap (pietá). Other popular images, included the Man of Sorrows type, which shows Christ standing in his tomb from the waist up, his arms crossed over his belly, crowned with thorns, wounded and bleeding, and gazing sorrowfully downwards or back at the viewer. In many of these instances, the instruments *(arma Christi)* of his crucifixion and deposition from the cross surround him (flagellation column, whip, ladder, nails, hammer, lance, tongs). These instruments had already appeared in earlier iconography, but in the twelfth and thirteenth centuries, they became identified as holy relics and objects for meditation in themselves as viewers contemplated the stages of Christ's suffering before and during the crucifixion.

Eucharistic piety also contributed to this focus on Christ's crucifixion. The doctrine of transubstantiation, promulgated at the Fourth Lateran Council in

1215, encouraged the faithful to believe that they were experiencing the actual sacrifice of Christ as the celebrant intoned the words of consecration. The belief in the reality of the body and blood in the eucharist had been confirmed through earlier centuries of theological debate that ultimately condemned any theologian who said that the elements were spiritually or symbolically but not *materially* transformed. Thus, the sacramental reality of Christ's body and blood on the altar not only reinforced devotion to the consecrated host but also encouraged private meditation on the Passion during the canon of the Mass and intensified the importance of seeing the host elevated at the moment of consecration.

Devotion to the consecrated bread and wine of the eucharist became a hallmark of thirteenth- and fourteenth-century mystical literature. Figures such as Gertrude of Helfta (1256–1302), Meister Eckhart (1260–1328), and Julian of Norwich (1343–1416) describe visions or experiences of special union with Christ while receiving Holy Communion.

Crucifixes were also present at the deathbed, and those *in extremis* seeking forgiveness of their sins were encouraged to focus on the image of Christ's suffering on the cross—the reassurance of the redemptive love shown by the savior and the hope of the dying.[26] Gazing at a crucifix while she was paralyzed and near death also prompted one of Julian of Norwich's visions even as it relieved her pain. As she lay in her bed, she prayed that she might experience Christ's pains and have compassion for his wounds:

> And at this, suddenly I saw the red blood running down from under the crown, hot and flowing freely and copiously, a living stream, just as it was at the time when the crown of thorns was placed on his blessed head. I perceived, truly and powerfully, that it was he who just so, both God and man, himself suffered for me, who showed it to me without any intermediary.[27]

Julian goes on to detail the rest of her experience contemplating this crucifix, not only seeing Jesus's profuse blood and bodily agony but also feeling it in her own body, understanding that her pain was diminished in comparison to his. Her compassion for him then extends to compassion for others. Through her visions, she says, she came to know the depth and universality of God's love and to anticipate the bliss of heaven, where there will be no more pain, only endless delight in the divine presence.

The foremost Dominican theologian, Thomas Aquinas (1225–1274), addressed the question of whether it was appropriate that Christ should have suffered on a cross, given that all the Old Testament sacrifices were by the sword or by fire, and moreover, that the ancient Israelites believed death on a cross to be a curse (Deut. 21:23). In his *Summa Theologica,* he offers a series of reasons why crucifixion (and the cross) was especially suited for Christ's sacrificial death, including the traditional appeal to prophetic figures such as Noah's ark and Moses's rod. Aquinas further comments that it was particularly appropriate that the crucifixion take place on a tree, as it was a tree that prompted the sin of Adam. Finally, he notes that the cross's shape, which extends in the four cardinal directions, denotes the universally dispersed power and providence of the one who hung upon it.[28]

Twelfth- through Fifteenth-Century Crucifixes

Julian of Norwich's deathly pain was eased as she gazed upon a crucifix held up by her priest. Although it is impossible to be certain, Julian's crucifix probably depicted Christ crowned with thorns, blood streaming from his wounds. Crucifixes like Julian's would have been small, personal devotional items. Others, like the large Gero Crucifix, were designed to be visual foci during the public liturgy and were therefore suspended over altars or placed in church apses.

Among the most beautiful thirteenth-century examples of such monumental crucifixes is a series painted by Giunta Pisano (1180–1250). Commissioned by both Franciscans and Dominicans, these paintings evince the mendicant Passion piety in visual form. While the crucifix that Giunta painted for the Basilica of San Francisco in Assisi no longer survives, the one he made for the Basilica of San Dominico in Bologna provides a good idea of his style. Now in a museum in Pisa, it depicts Christ in what would become conventional form: wearing only a *perizoma,* hips sharply turned toward his right, his stomach protruding, his chin dropped to his right and tucked upon his chest, his eyes closed. This crucifix, like many others painted around this time, is elaborated with bust portraits of Mary and the Beloved Disciple, incorporated within rectangles at the ends of the cross arms. Giunta's crucifix features much gold leaf and many side panels with decorative geometric designs, conceivably meant to simulate an ornately embroidered altar cloth. These rich details set off the image of the dying savior, making it as glorious as it is filled with pathos. Giunta's crucifix exerted extraordinary influence on subsequent painting, including the monumental crucifixes of Cimabue in Assisi, Florence, and Arezzo. Other examples of these types of crucifixes include narrative scenes within the panels, showing episodes from the Passion flanking Christ's body.

7.6 Crucifix, Giunta Pisano (fl. 1236–1254), Basilica of San Dominico, Bologna.

In this same vein, sequential narrative scenes framed crucifixion images that were painted on church walls. An example is the cycle of paintings from the Arena (or Scrovegni) Chapel in Padua, painted by Giotto di Bondone around 1300. This full cycle of images from Christ's life, beginning with the nativity, includes depictions of Jesus's arrest, trial, mockery, flagellation, procession toward Calvary, crucifixion, and burial. The crucifixion in particular shows Christ as dead upon the cross and his anguished mother beginning to swoon as she herself experiences pain at the sight of her son's suffering. The Beloved Disciple and another of the women support her while they too are overcome with sorrow. Mary Magdalene kneels to kiss Christ's feet, and even the angels appear to be filled with grief.

In the thirteenth and fourteenth centuries, these narrative cycles continued to include pre- and postcrucifixion scenes. Depictions of the flagellation and mockery as well as the deposition and burial often included casts of characters set in dramatic compositions meant to emphasize Christ's humiliation and physical agony. The images include both participants and witnesses, either viciously leering at him or profoundly lamenting his death. All of these often highly theatrical depictions were intended to narrate the story while also activating the viewer's imagination. The viewer, moving from panel to panel, could participate in the story as he or she was instructed by it.

Medieval Pilgrims, Crusaders, and Crosses

The motif of the heroic savior and his valiant cross who together face trials and overcome evil (as recounted in the "Dream of the Rood") has echoes in the stories of the medieval crusaders. Underlying this motif as well are the images of the cross as a victory banner, as depicted in Venantius Fortunatus's popular hymns. The Epistle to the Ephesians applies soldiering terminology to the faithful and refers explicitly to the armor of God: the breastplate of righteousness, the helmet of salvation, and the sword of the Spirit (Eph. 6:13–18). Martyrs and monks were often described as sacred warriors, going to battle against external foes or waging internal battles with physical and mental temptations.

From the age of Constantine forward, the character of the Christian soldier emerged, referring as much to those who believed themselves called to defeat political enemies or human heretics as to those battling spiritual foes. Bishop Peter II of Ravenna (494–519) commissioned a mosaic depicting Christ wearing soldier's gear and trampling on the serpent and lion of Psalms 91:13, probably meant as a challenge to the Arian Christians who had taken over the city under the Ostrogothic King Theodoric. Instead of a sword, he carries a cross in his right hand, and instead of a shield, a book with the words "I am the way, the truth and the life" *(ego sum via, veritas et vita)*.

By the eighth or ninth century, the image of the Christian knight had developed: he was not only someone engaged in spiritual warfare or battles of self-discipline but a soldier recruited to serve in an actual army.[29] Reminiscent of the christogram that the Emperor Constantine placed on his helmet, crosses appeared on the helmets of some Anglo-Saxon warriors, and apparently for the same purpose—supernatural protection in battle. The famous Benty Grange helmet, for example, had a cross inscribed on its nosepiece, and the York helmet, found in Coppergate, England, in the 1980s and dated to the mid-eighth century, was constructed to bear a cross on its crown.[30] Its inscription, "In the name of our Lord Jesus Christ, the Holy Spirit, and God; and to all we say amen, *Oshere*," ran from the nose to the neck of the wearer and ended with the Christic monogram (XRI).[31]

Crosses also decorated the uniforms and equipment of Saxon, Breton, and Norman soldiers in the tenth and eleventh centuries. The cross even turns up on the Bayeaux tapestry, emblazoned on a Norman banner, and adorning the masthead of a ship.[32] It thus became part of the standard uniform of these Christian knights following Pope Urban II's call to crusade at the Council of Clermont in 1095. Although this crusade was a response to the Byzantine emperor's appeal to help their defenses against invading Seljuk Turks, it was framed more appealingly as an effort to recapture Jerusalem and the Holy Land, occupied since the seventh century by Arab rulers.

As earlier pilgrims en route to Jerusalem had appliqued crosses onto their clothing as a symbol of their sacred journey, crusading soldiers—who considered themselves pilgrims of a certain kind—began to do the same. According to one account of the pope's speech, Urban concluded with the exhortation:

> Whoever, therefore, shall determine upon this holy pilgrimage and shall make his vow to God to that effect and shall offer himself to Him as a

> living sacrifice, holy, acceptable to God, shall wear the sign of the cross of the Lord on his forehead or on his breast. When, truly, having fulfilled his vow he wishes to return, let him place the cross on his back between his shoulders. Such, indeed, by the two-fold action will fulfill the precept of the Lord, as he commands in the Gospel: "He that taketh not his cross and followeth after me, is not worthy of me."[33]

Urban II clearly intended to incite his listeners to believe that they were liberating the cross when recapturing Jerusalem from the Turks. Thus, believing themselves to be following Christ's explicit command, those who signed up for the cause of freeing Jerusalem from Muslim control wore the cross as a symbol of commitment and a badge of identity. Because the Pope expressly described Muslims as enemies of the cross, the cross became a military standard, identifying its dedicated allies. Thus, the expression "taking up the cross" achieved a special resonance in the vocabulary of crusading in the eleventh and twelfth centuries.[34]

Taking up one's cross also came to include taking a vow of loyalty to the pope, as illustrated dramatically when King Louis VII of France took up the call. King Louis, who had been given his cross directly from the pope, was present for the fiery preaching of Bernard of Clairvaux, in which he drummed up unprecedented enthusiasm for a second crusade in 1146. According to one historian, "Such was the enthusiasm with which Bernard's sermon was received that the packet of cloth crosses which had been prepared for distribution was used up and Bernard had to tear his monastic habit into strips to provide more."[35] The long-lost twelfth-century windows of the Abbey Church of St. Denis, where Louis VII set out upon his crusade in 1147, depicted crusaders wearing crosses on their helmets and banners but, interestingly, not on their uniforms.

The cross also symbolized the crusader's allegiance as well as his progress. According to Robert of Rheims (d. 1122), a crusader put the cross on his forehead or chest when setting off on crusade and then transferred it to his back when returning, as previously described in Urban II's speech. Alan of Lille (ca. 1128–1202), by contrast, claimed that crusaders wore the cross on their shoulders when setting off for Jerusalem and on their chests when returning in order to indicate that over time its weight had become easier to bear.[36]

7.7 Emperor Frederick I, called Barbarossa, as crusader. Illuminated manuscript page.

Distinctive crusader crosses also distinguished national contingents. According to Jonathan Riley-Smith, at the planning meeting for the Third Crusade (1189–1192), the French decided to wear red crosses, the English white, and the Flemish green. The cross was more than a badge, however. It also guaranteed its wearer certain privileges. While away from home, those wearing the cross were ensured of some level of protection, not only for themselves but also for their families and property in the interim. Some crusaders apparently even tattooed crosses upon their bodies. Moreover, the cross was supposed to be worn on the clothing for the entire duration of a crusader's vow. To take off one's cross prematurely was the equivalent of desertion.

The relics of the True Cross also played an important role in the ethos of crusading. Urban II had claimed that the cross required rescue from its Muslim captors. According to Byzantine chroniclers, Heraclius rerescued the remains and carried them safely back to Constantinople in the seventh century, although another record describes their presence in Jerusalem in the eleventh century. According to these later accounts, in 1009, the Fatimid caliph ordered the destruction of the Church of the Holy Sepulcher. Certain Orthodox priests secretly rescued the relic and kept it safe until 1099, when the first Latin patriarch of Jerusalem, Arnulf Malecorne, ordered them under torture to reveal its whereabouts so that he could return it to the Holy Sepulcher.[37]

Fragments of the cross were also carried into battle as spiritual shields against human enemies, who were themselves clearly aware of the symbolic importance of the relics. This is recorded during the Battle of Montgisard, when the young King Baldwin IV ordered that the cross be displayed before the troops and then credited it for the victory. A different outcome marked the fateful Battle of Hattin (1187) between the crusader King of Jerusalem, Guy of Lusignan, and the Kurdish Sultan, Saladin. The Turks captured a relic of the cross that had been carried as a standard into battle by the bishop of Acre, conceivably the relic that Bishop Arnulf had seized almost a century earlier. Saladin brought this trophy back to Damascus, where the holy relic was tied to the tail of his horse and paraded triumphantly through the streets. This loss dealt a severe blow to the crusaders' confidence in their divine protection. The contemporary Kurdish historian Ali ibn al-Athir recorded the event and comments on its significance, as well as the crusaders' sense of desperation and the consequential defeat:

> At the same time as the King was taken, the "True Cross" was also captured, and the idolaters who were trying to defend it were routed. It was this cross, brought into position and raised on high, to which all Christians prostrated themselves and bowed their heads. Indeed, they maintain that it is made of the wood of the cross on which, they say, he whom they adore was hung, and so they venerate it and prostrate themselves before it. . . . Its capture was for them more important than the loss of the King and was the gravest blow that they sustained in that battle. The cross was a prize without equal for it was the supreme object of their faith. . . . So when the great cross was taken great was the calamity that befell them, and the strength drained from their loins. . . . It seemed as if, once they knew of the capture of the Cross, none of them would survive the day of ill-omen.[38]

During the Third Crusade, Richard I of England (the Lionheart) vowed to recover the relic from Saladin and negotiated a prisoner swap in exchange for its return. Richard offered to free three thousand Muslim men, women, and children that he held captive if Saladin would return the cross, release a number of Christian prisoners, and pay a ransom of 200,000 pieces of gold. Saladin, stalling for time, failed to cooperate, and as a consequence, Richard cruelly massacred the three thousand Muslims on Ayyadieh, a small hill near Acre. In retaliation, Saladin executed his Christian prisoners and the cross relic was never seen again.[39]

The Crusades, the Cross, and the Jews

Although Pope Urban called for a crusade in order to free the Holy Land from the control of Muslim Turks, one of the tragic results of the call to crusade was the persecution of the Jews who lived near or along the routes to Jerusalem. Presumably, the crusaders, impatient to vent their hostility against distant religious enemies, chose those near to hand as they went on their way. For Jews who found themselves attacked as convenient (and more vulnerable) Christ-killers, the cross was a symbol of Christian hatred. Despite efforts by some secular and religious leaders, Jews, particularly those in the Rhineland, were violently massacred or forcibly baptized by crusaders seeking to avenge the death of Christ on those they found closer to home. Thus, the war against the infidel was fought before the crusaders ever reached the Holy Land, and the first and perhaps most tragic casualties were the Jews living in their own cities and towns.[40]

The label "Christ-killer" did not appear suddenly in the Middle Ages; it had been applied to Jews from the earliest Christian centuries. In the second century, Justin Martyr declared that the destruction of the Jerusalem Temple was a just punishment for the Jews, whom he blamed for the crucifixion of the innocent Jesus.[41] One of the most blatant examples from the fourth century comes from John Chrysostom, who railed against Christians who attended Jewish festival services while he was a presbyter in Antioch. Calling the Jews the enemies of truth, both pitiable and miserable, John declares that because they crucified Christ, they have been forsaken by God and are fit only for killing.[42]

Appalling rumors of Jews desecrating the consecrated eucharistic bread—or worse, plotting the ritual murder of Christian children—often fueled persecutions.[43] Possibly the earliest and most famous instance of this "blood libel" unfolded in Norwich, England, in 1144. As recounted some years later by a Benedictine monk, Thomas of Monmouth, the Jews of Norwich were accused of murdering a Christian boy in a ritual sacrifice allegedly aimed at avenging their treatment at Christian hands and hastening Israel's return to Jews.[44] Official councils of the Church, in particular a canon included in the acts of the Fourth Lateran Council, supported ongoing discrimination.[45] This canon decreed that Jews and Muslims must be distinguished by their dress and that on Palm Sunday and through the last three days of Holy Week they were to be prohibited from going out in public, lest they mock Christians who mourn the death of Christ or perform other disgraceful deeds that might be an insult to Christ. Thus, the crusades contributed to the long history of Christian anti-Jewish actions, and the cross began to be regarded as an emblem of oppression and violence as well as divine love and human deliverance.

Although from the ninth through the eleventh century depictions of the crucifixion shifted from showing Christ as alive to emphasizing his human suffering and death, not all Christian thinkers agreed that the cross—or the crucifix—was a fitting object of adoration. Some even denounced its veneration as denying the resurrection and recrucifying Christ. Although this position would find a sympathetic hearing during the time of the Protestant Reformation, attention to Christ's agony on the cross became a characteristic feature of late medieval piety. Viewers were encouraged to meditate upon it and to respond emotionally to its display of pathos, with responses ranging from deep sorrow to actual empathetic physical pain. This was reinforced in iconography, hymnody, devotional tracts, visionary narratives, and theological treatises.

Understanding what prompted the change from a glorious and victorious depiction of Christ's Passion to a representation of his human torment and death is a subject of much debate, but it must have been rooted at least partially in the desire for (or belief in) a compassionate and merciful deity who comprehends and even experiences human physical pain. The example of the Isenheim

7.8 Crucifixion, Matthias Grünewald, interior panel from the Isenheim Altarpiece, 1512–1516.

Altarpiece by Matthias Grünewald is a case in point. Painted to adorn the chapel of a hospital that served those suffering from a deadly illness that caused their bodies to break out in excruciating sores, the artist chose to show Christ suffering from similar outbreak.

As the inmates of the hospital gazed upon the figure of Christ with his rib cage jutting out over a sunken belly and his hand and face contorted in pain, they may have been consoled by the assurance that God was not oblivious to their misery. It may also have served as focus for the monks' meditation on Christ in the form of their diseased and suffering patients. Although the image of Christ as co-sufferer might not have alleviated the patients' physical and mental anguish, it could have assured the patients and their caregivers alike that they were not alone, nor had they been abandoned by a loving God who had himself undergone similar torments. At the same time, in back of this horrific portrayal of Christ's Passion was a glorious image of his resurrection: his body perfect, glowing, and restored. Hope overcomes despair, and Christ, after all, conquers death in the way that the early Christians understood it. Despite the intense interest in Jesus's suffering, the claim that suffering was not the end (nor even a virtue) was not utterly eclipsed.

In a different way, medieval crusaders who took up the cross and marched off to war in a distant land must have found courage and reassurance in their leaders' declarations that by doing so they were following the way of Christ, engaging his enemies, and seeking glory for his church. While they could have had other motivations for participating in a holy war (including glory for themselves), and while some may even have become disillusioned and disappointed in the outcome, no matter how their actions are judged by modern readers, it seems undeniable that many confidently and authentically believed they were trying to imitate the divine and heroic warrior of their Christian narrative. Nevertheless, in a parallel to the Emperor Constantine's adoption of the cross with the motto "by this conquer," the cross moved from being a memorial of Christ's suffering and a sign of his Second Coming to a symbol of military conquest abroad and persecution of Jews and other non-Christians at home.

8

Crux Invicta

The Cross and Crucifix in the Reformation Period

> We say without hesitation that the one who contemplates God's sufferings for a day, an hour, yes, only a quarter of an hour, does better than to fast a whole year, pray a psalm daily, yes, better than to hear a hundred masses. . . . Here the passion of Christ performs its natural and noble work, strangling the old Adam and banishing all joy, delight, and confidence, which one could derive from other creatures, even as Christ was forsaken by all, even by God.
>
> —Martin Luther

By the late Middle Ages, recounting Christ's Passion story had become an occasion for the faithful's empathetic participation. Dramatic reenactments of Christ's crucifixion, burial, and resurrection were becoming more and more widespread, both in official liturgy and more secular venues. Images of crucifixion had evolved from showing Christ as a living and victorious hero to a suffering and dying victim. These graphic depictions of Jesus's agony and death were meant to arouse viewers' mixed emotions of love, sorrow, and gratitude. They were reminder of the profundity of God's love, as well as the enormity of their sins that had to be expiated through Christ's terrible ordeal. Meanwhile, veneration of the cross continued to be observed on Good Friday and the annual feast of the cross, and the freestanding crucifix had become an essential part of church décor, taking its place on the altar as a visual memorial of the sacrifice reenacted there.

8.1 Destruction of religious images in Zurich, 1524.

This deeply physical and material form of devotion was expressly challenged in the sixteenth century, as Protestant reformers renewed concerns about whether the honor given to visual images and holy relics was idolatrous. Much as in the East in the eighth and ninth centuries, authorized delegations and local mobs alike tore down, smashed, or whitewashed depictions of Christ, the Virgin Mary, and the saints in order to cleanse the church from these alleged idols. Most Protestant groups replaced their crucifixes with plain crosses, and more ardent reformers even banned crosses altogether.

Yet, as in the earlier Byzantine iconoclastic controversy, Protestant iconoclasts regularly spared plain crosses from destruction, believing them fundamentally different from the kind of pictorial art that prompted idolatrous veneration of human-made objects. And though Protestants often removed the cross from sight, they continued to envision it in their hymns and prayers. Reformers regarded the cross as an abstract symbol of Christ's atoning sacrifice, authorized by scripture and long tradition of the church. In some instances, even the crucifix was neither automatically nor inevitably condemned—though relics of the Holy Cross usually were regarded as specious. Still, one of the visible and still-evident consequences of the Protestant movement is the loss of much medieval religious art and the continuing lack of pictorial art in reformed churches—an austerity that characterizes many Protestant worship spaces to this day.

Meanwhile, in direct response to the Protestant movement, the Roman Catholic Church reaffirmed the centrality of the crucifix, along with images of the saints, in worship and popular piety. Scenes of crucifixion continued to be painted and sculpted in a manner intended to provoke strong emotional responses from viewers and to prompt prayer and veneration. Christ was once again portrayed as heroic and even triumphant upon his cross, his body displaying a physical perfection that reflected its unbreakable unity with his divine nature. Rituals of the cross also persisted. Catholics continued to make the sign of the cross in prayer, to acknowledge the crucifix with a pious bow when they entered the church, and to kneel before it and offer it a kiss on Good Friday. They continued to pay homage to the relics of the True Cross, dispersed as they were throughout the world. Specific devotions like the stations of the cross found their place in most Catholic churches, and the faithful who participated in them received indulgences along with their spiritual edification.

The Cross and Crucifix in the Protestant Reformation

The Isenheim Altarpiece (cf. Fig. 7.8) had exemplified late medieval iconography, particularly in northern Europe, and the artist's fixation with the gruesome details of Christ's suffering did not disappear overnight in art associated with the Protestant Reformation. It was echoed in early works of Lucas Cranach the Elder (1472–1553), who had produced several dark images of the crucifixion in the first decade of the sixteenth century. Cranach depicts the crucifixion as a horrific event, with Christ dead and bleeding upon the cross, the two thieves near him often twisting or bent over, the witnesses expressing fear and emotional distress. Through perspective, angle of view, color, and composition, Cranach stressed the physical and psychological anguish of the crucifixion, as well as the terrible grief of the onlookers.

Cranach was one of Martin Luther's close allies and, in the mid-sixteenth century, he produced altarpieces for Lutheran churches in Wittenburg, Weimar, Schneeburg, Kemberg, Regensburg, and Dessau. Unlike other reformers,

8.2 *Crucifixion*, Lucas Cranach the Elder, 1506–1520.

Luther never forbade images, especially of the crucifixion, and many of Cranach's paintings and altarpieces functioned as didactic exercises, almost schematic diagrams of Lutheran soteriology. Cranach often divides the panel (or central painting of an altarpiece) into two parts by a tree, dead on one side and living on the other. This reprisal of the ancient tree of life / tree of death theme directs the viewer (as well as the figure in the painting who represents "everyman") to recognize that the depiction of Moses and the Israelites on the left indicates the Law (damnation), while the representation of the crucifixion and resurrection on the right signifies the Gospel (salvation). In the background are the figures of Eve passing the forbidden fruit to Adam, and Moses elevating the brazen serpent on a crosslike pole (Num. 21:9).

In the Stadtkirch (City Church) of Wittenburg, where Luther often preached, another of Cranach's altarpieces depicts a triptych that displays the Lutheran interpretation of the sacraments (baptism, the Lord's Supper, and confession of sin). In the altarpiece's predella, Cranach depicts Luther himself, preaching in an elevated pulpit and pointing to a crucifix that has materialized before a small gathering of congregants, implying that the words of his sermon successfully conjure the image in the imaginations of his listeners.[1] The scene alludes to a central tenet in Luther's theology—that the preached word has a sacramental dimension—but also to the fact that Christ's Passion was one of Luther's favorite subjects. Moreover, this painting is an exact illustration of Luther's own words, written to justify allowing actual crucifixes like the one on church altars:

> Of this I am certain, that God desires to have his works heard and read, especially the passion of our Lord. But it is impossible for me to hear and bear it in mind without forming mental images of it in my heart. For whether I will or not, when I hear of Christ, an image of a man hanging upon a cross takes form in my heart, just as the reflection of my face appears in the water when I look into it. If it is not a sin, but good to have the image of Christ in my heart, why should it be a sin to have it in my eyes?[2]

Luther's theology of the cross drew upon medieval themes of satisfaction and atonement, emphasizing the need for the faithful to attend to Christ's suffering

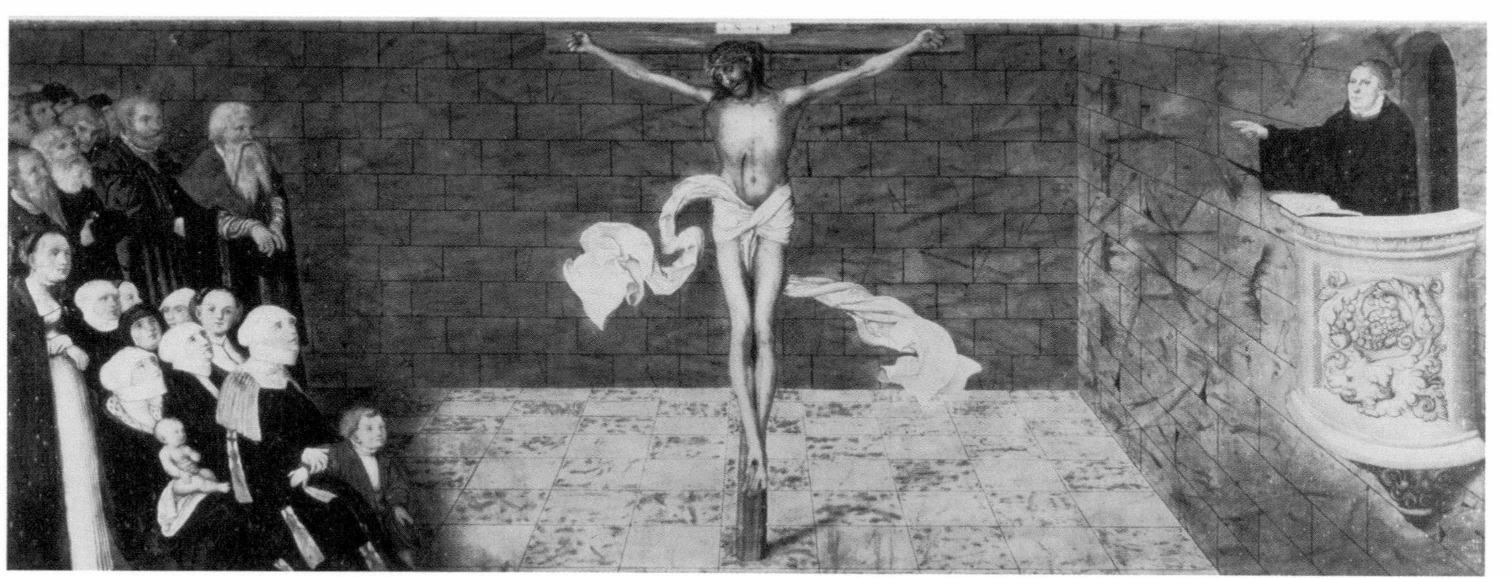

8.3 *Luther Preaching*, Lucas Cranach the Elder, 1547. From the Wittenberg Altarpiece (predella), Marienkirch, Wittenberg.

and sacrifice and to accept it in their own lives. But because he stressed the teaching that Christ's crucifixion overcomes human servitude to sin, Luther revived the ancient motif of Christ as victorious over death and Satan. Thus, Luther and his followers continued to allow crucifixes that accentuated Christ's suffering, while also depicting him trampling on Satan and harrowing Hell.[3]

Other reformers were not as liberal as Luther in their attitudes toward religious iconography in general or toward crucifixes in particular. Although they never denied the centrality of the crucifixion in the story of salvation and continued to encourage their followers to mediate on the Passion, they insisted that the only true sacrifice had taken place once for all on the hill of Calvary. Images of the cross or crucifix would therefore prompt believers to think that Christ's death was still occurring—that it had not been overcome by the resurrection and ascension.

Although he tolerated narrative religious art in domestic and secular settings, Ulrich Zwingli (1484–1531) condemned the inclusion of images in churches because he was convinced that they would prompt veneration and thereby lead to idolatry. Initially, he urged the town council to take steps that their removal be undertaken peacefully and supported the retention of crucifixes in churches insofar as they were merely signs of the humanity and suffering of the human Christ and not representations of the invisible deity.[4] Within a few months, however, the Zurich leaders moved to eradicate the images more thoroughly and swiftly. Zwingli himself appeared to have a change of heart; he spoke specifically against images of Christ and crucifixes, using the long-standing argument that images could not display the truth of Jesus, who was both human and divine.[5] Other reformers followed suit, including Heinrich Bullinger, who followed Zwingli's argument about the impossibility of depicting divinity.[6]

More radical opponents of images, such as Andreas Karlstadt (1486–1541), argued that the crucifix depicted only Christ's human suffering and neglected to display his resurrection and redemptive power. He urged his followers to abandon their superstitious attachment to crucifixes, even in their sickrooms and deathbeds.[7] He asserted that nothing could be learned and no benefits gained from gazing at a crucifix, which focused only on Christ's suffering in the body, and he pointedly cited Jesus's own words as proof: "It is the spirit that gives life; the flesh is of no avail" (John 6:63).[8]

John Calvin (1509–1564) strongly disapproved of figurative images in churches, and while he allowed that crucifixes were tolerable, he still insisted they should be removed. In his *Institutes of the Christian Religion*, Calvin reminded his readers that Paul's preaching was vivid enough to make the crucifixion appear as if before the eyes of his audience (Gal. 3:13), and he notes that if this had been faithfully practiced, there would have been no need for crosses of wood, stone, silver, or gold. Perhaps, he suggests, without the temptation of material adornments, people would become less covetous and more attendant upon the word of God.[9] Contrary to Luther, he concluded that good sermonizing requires no supplementary visual aids. Crosses and crucifixes served no useful purpose, but rather indicated a failure by the clergy to rightly explicate the sacred word. Calvin was even more contemptuous of relics of the cross, famously saying that "if we were to collect all these pieces of the True Cross exhibited in various parts, they would form a whole ship's cargo."[10]

Lutherans and those on the more "liberal" end of the reforming movement (including members of the Anglican churches) continued to use the sign of the cross in their liturgies, although with far less frequency than had become the practice in medieval Catholicism. Thus "crossing oneself" remained acceptable in certain congregations, mainly as a memorial of one's baptismal signing, whereas other reformed churches eschewed the gesture as an artifact of medieval or "papist" ceremony. Such liturgical austerity was paralleled in the removal of images, statuary, decorative vessels, and candlesticks from churches in what was viewed as a work of purification. But even the most determined iconophobes would sometimes allow a "reformed" cross to remain—a cross without corpus as a memorial of Christ's death—so long as it was not likely to be an object of veneration.

Protestant Iconoclasm and Crucifixes

As during the image controversies of the seventh through ninth centuries in both East and West, the cross and crucifix became controversial subjects among the various groups of Protestants. Lutherans continued to place crucifixes on their altars, just as they continued to allow painted altarpieces like those of Lucas Cranach, most of which included depictions of Christ's crucifixion. As noted earlier, some reformers, like the Byzantine iconoclasts, rejected crucifixes as idolatrous, while allowing plain crosses as acceptably nonfigurative (and therefore not idols). Others argued that, as the crucifix symbolized the humanity of Christ and was a long-standing sign of the Church, it could be retained and even expressly protected from acts of iconoclasm. For example, in 1524, Zurich's civic leaders initially allowed a special exemption for crucifixes in their policy of image removal. This exemption allowed crucifixes to remain in place so long as they did not "signify divinity" as such, but rather signified "alone the humanity and the suffering of Christ." Furthermore, they recognized the crucifix as a universal sign of the Church through the ages and in all places of the world.[11] In Lent of 1525, members of the Strasbourg town council even replaced a statue of the Virgin on the altar of the Cathedral's Marian chapel with a crucifix.[12]

This moderate and restrained removal of images gradually gave way to more active iconoclasm. Inevitably, the crucifix became targeted for destruction. As an object used for personal devotion and veneration, it was—to certain reformers' minds—particularly inclined to lead the faithful into idolatrous acts and so especially deserving of desecration (or perhaps more aptly, ritual purification). In Advent of 1526, the gilded cross—possibly a gift from Charlemagne—that had been a prominent adornment of the Strasbourg Cathedral was removed and probably melted down to provide alms for the city's poor.[13]

Illustrations from contemporary and later chronicles of the period show townspeople hauling crucifixes out of churches to smash and burn them. In satirical reenactments of the events of the Passion, crucifixes were personified by being mocked, flogged, or commanded to drink, just as Christ had been, in order to demonstrate the impotence of the images and even to punish them.[14] A famous instance of this kind of abuse comes from Basel in 1529, when a mob carried a crucifix from the church, through the streets, and into the marketplace, tossing it onto a bonfire while a particularly zealous citizen exclaimed, "If you are God, help yourself; if you are man, then bleed!"[15] In other instances, crucifixes were simply torn down, decapitated, smashed into pieces, or dumped into trash heaps, lakes, or latrines.

The famous case of Klaus Hottinger illuminates the often-vacillating sides of this controversy. In 1524, possibly on September 14, the Feast of the Elevation of the Cross, Hottinger, a Swiss shoemaker and follower of Ulrich Zwingli,

8.4 *Klaus Hottinger and Party Take Down the Stadelhofen Crucifix*. Drawing attributed to Heinrich Thomann (1748–1794), from a copy of Heinrich Bullinger's *Reformationgeschichte*.

took part in a demonstration that included tearing down and destroying the Stadelhofen crucifix, which stood in front of Zurich's town gates. Hottinger was banished from Zurich and subsequently arrested and tried for blasphemy in the neighboring Roman Catholic city of Lucerne. At his trial, he refused to venerate a crucifix brought out for the purpose of testing him and declared it to be a mockery of religion. He was condemned to be burned at the stake, thus becoming one of the first Protestant martyrs.[16]

Iconoclasm in Reformation England

The English reformers were no less zealous for the removal of images, and the historical record shows parallel incidents of initially tolerating and then despising images of the crucifix and even plain crosses. They had predecessors in the Lollards, who lived in the fourteenth century and espoused many Reformation precepts well before Luther and his colleagues began their own movements. Among their principles was that veneration of the cross was a form of idolatry. They also insisted that the story of the True Cross's discovery could not be authenticated, and that its supposed relics were certain to be specious.[17]

The destruction of the Cheapside Cross is an illustrative case. In 1643, iconoclasts destroyed this large, freestanding stone monument, which had been standing in the City of London since King Edward I had it set up in the thirteenth century, as part of a group of eleven others across the east of England. Among all these crosses, the Cheapside Cross achieved particular notoriety.[18] Those on the Protestant side considered it to be both an idol and—partly because it was adorned with images of saints—an abhorrent memorial to the hated Catholic faith. A nonconformist minister, William Greenhill, believed it was attracting veneration and preached a sermon in which he decried the sin of idolatry and claimed that God would punish those who spared such crosses, urging them to lay the axe to their roots and "hew them down."[19]

The Cheapside Cross's razing had been a goal of iconoclasts intermittently in the Reformation period, and so suffered recurring assaults. In 1581, for example, a gang of youths tied ropes around the Cross's lower figures, including a Madonna and Child, and while they succeeded in defacing the Virgin and pulling the infant off her lap, they failed to do more harm to the monument. In 1641 it was the subject of a dialogue with the Charing Cross, in which the two crosses console and commiserate with each other as they anticipate their destruction.[20] In 1642 it was the centerpiece of a series of riots, during which some townspeople tried to pull it down and others rallied to protect it. The monument's final demolition may have been provoked by Richard Overton's publication of a satirical tract, *The Articles of High Treason Exhibited against the Cheapside Cross*, which accused the cross of having provoked "tumultuous political and national disturbances," and wielding an almost demonic power to seduce good English Protestants to backslide into the papist religion. Earlier the cross even had been compared to the idol of Dagon (1 Sam. 5), which toppled over when the Philistines tried to install the Ark of the Covenant in their temple. According to Overton, a member of the rebellious English political group known as the Levellers, the cross also was a primary catalyst for the English Civil War. Although that is likely an overstatement, its removal did stimulate a wider movement to remove religious images from both churches and the public square, including the Long Parliament's creation of a committee to oversee the demolition of monuments of "superstition and idolatry" in 1643.[21]

A popular subject for tractarians and illustrated in mass-produced woodcuts, the Cheapside Cross had champions as well as detractors. The cross's defenders responded to works like Overton's with their own publications, including a tract titled *A Vindication of Cheapside Crosse against the Roundheads*, printed shortly after the cross had been demolished. This document contained the following lines, written as if in the Cross's own voice, decrying the iconoclasts' destruction not only of the Cheapside Cross but also of crosses generally:

> They say they'le pluck the tower of Babel down,
> All things go right when there's no Cross i'th' Towne.
> But who can live without them? Crosses are
> The good man's blessings, and his certain share.
> He that would win an everlasting Crowne,
> Must elevate his Crosse, not throw it downe.[22]

Like the Ruthwell Cross, the Cheapside Cross came to be personified with a voice and a narrative, and like the Ruthwell Cross, the Cheapside Cross was destroyed by Protestant iconoclasts who objected to its attracting veneration.[23] While it was not later excavated, restored, and reerected as a historical and religious monument, its story survives as a testimony to the controversial symbolism of the cross.

The Cross in the Catholic Reformation

Protestant iconoclasm prompted a strong reaction among traditional Roman Catholics; the more reformers removed and destroyed sacred images, the more Catholics were moved to love, defend, and protect them. Along with defending images, the Roman church reiterated its long-standing beliefs regarding the benefits to humanity through Christ's death on the cross, in response to the Lutheran position that sinners were justified by faith alone. Following medieval theologians' formulations, Catholic teaching continued to insist that the crucifixion overcame human captivity to Satan and sin and satisfied the debt owed to God. Christ's death assuaged divine wrath and rescued humanity from eternal death. In order to appropriate these merits, however, humans had to cooperate with God's gift of grace, strive to live a virtuous life, and participate in the sacraments. Justification was not simply imputed; sinners needed to respond to God's offer of salvation and show the fruits of their conversion: striving to live a virtuous life, performing good works, and being faithful followers of Jesus.

This reaffirmation of Catholic traditional teaching naturally endorsed pious devotion to the image of the crucifix and emphasized the centrality of the cross in liturgy as well as ecclesial art and architecture. In particular, the Roman church ratified the valid use of images and relics in a decree promulgated at the twenty-fifth session of the Council of Trent (1563). This decree specifically upheld the value of depictions of Christ, the Virgin Mary, and the saints, while reiterating the traditional assertion that images are not of themselves worthy of veneration and that honor shown to them is rather referred to the holy persons they represent.[24] The council specified that certain images were to be rejected, particularly any that could be judged erroneous, profane, superstitious, indecorous, or unusual.

The place of the cross and crucifix were not directly addressed in this decree, however. They may have been simply taken for granted. Although crucifixes were clearly common adornments of Catholic churches and altars, little canonical legislation survives regarding their composition, placement, or portability. In the early thirteenth century, Pope Innocent III declared that an altar cross should be set between two candles for the duration of the Mass, but did not explicitly indicate a crucifix. The 1570 *Missale Romanum* promulgated under Pope Pius V prescribes that clergy approach the altar and offer a profound bow to the altar or the crucifix.[25] The earliest known mandate *requiring* a crucifix on or near the altar during Mass shows up in the constitution *Accepimus* of Benedict XIV (1746). The most explicit instruction regarding the form of the crucifix turns up much later, in a 1947 encyclical of Pius XII, which states that a crucifix that does not display the signs of Christ's suffering is unacceptable.[26]

The Council of Trent's affirmation of visual art in the church was aimed at encouraging devotion among the faithful by fostering an affective piety as well as appealing to their appreciation of beauty. Subsequent Catholic theologians, including the Jesuit Cardinal Robert Bellarmine (1542–1621), produced treatises that pointedly critiqued Protestant arguments against images and defended the use of images as doctrinally and biblically instructive and inspirational.[27] Bellarmine was influenced by the meditations prescribed by the Jesuit founder, Ignatius of Loyola. Ignatius's *Spiritual Exercises* prescribed the third and fourth weeks of a month-long retreat to introspective and imaginative contemplation of Christ's Passion in order to prompt sorrow over personal sin, sincere conversion, and strengthened commitment to an apostolic mission (that is, "taking up one's cross"). These writings promoted a distinctly Catholic aesthetic: one that intentionally addressed the viewer's emotions and produced an affective response, even more perhaps than the suffering and bleeding crucifixes of the High Middle Ages.

Ignatian affectivity often developed into a highly mystical form of meditation on the Passion, as in the writings of the Spanish Carmelite mystics, Teresa of Avila (1515–1582) and John of the Cross (1542–1591). Teresa's work, *The Interior Castle,* imagines the human soul as divided into seven mansions and guides the reader through each on a journey toward God. In the second of the mansions, she encourages her sisters to "embrace the cross which your spouse bore upon his shoulders and realize that this cross is yours to carry too," for the one who is capable of the greatest suffering for him "will have the most perfect freedom."[28] Like Teresa, John of the Cross is best known for his guided spiritual meditations, but he also created an extraordinary drawing of the crucifixion that was based on a vision he had while at prayer. The unusual composition represents Christ on the cross as if seen from above, perhaps as if from God the Father's perspective.[29]

The art that emerged from the time around and just after the Council of Trent thus focused on the centrality of the sacraments, the Passion of Christ, and the role of the saints in a style that was highly sensual, tending toward dramatic lighting and sumptuous colors. The aim was not only to communicate doctrine but also to promote the spiritual and devotional function of religious art. Figures—especially that of Christ—were rendered as heroic and vigorous, their postures typically exaggerated and expressive. Subjects were supernaturally illuminated and set off against dark backgrounds, their gestures and faces often indicating mystical rapture. The splendid decorations of churches included gilded crosses surrounded by radiant beams that symbolized the triumph of the cross and made the transcendent sign of Christ a palpable and glorious presence.

The figure of the crucifix was particularly transformed from late medieval sagging and suffering depictions. Instead, it is as if the triumphant crucifixes of earlier centuries were revived. Rather than slumping on his chest, Christ's head is often thrown back as if in an ecstatic state or perhaps looking up toward his Father in heaven. His body is rendered as powerfully muscular rather than emaciated, his arms even start to straighten out as if they are able to support his weight, his wounds are less pronounced, and there is often very little evident blood. Compared to Cranach's extremely didactic and crowded compositions, artists working for Catholic patrons tended to simplify and show only three figures: Christ, the Virgin, and the Beloved Disciple.[30] Such edited groupings left out certain scriptural details such as the two thieves or the lance and sponge bearers, along with common insertions of saints or patrons, and thus emphasized devotional focus over narrative or didactic purposes. Most of all, they transformed the crucifixion scene from a portrayal of a gruesome reality to a representation of divine beauty.

Although probably the most renowned (and prototypical) painter of the Catholic Reformation was Peter Paul Rubens (1577–1640), who created numerous paintings depicting Christ's Passion in a profoundly dramatic style, the mannerist painter El Greco (1541–1614) and famed Spanish baroque artists Diego Velázquez (1559–1600), Francisco de Zurbarán (1598–1664), and Bartolomé Esteban Murillo (1617–1682) developed an even more emotional style in their representations of Christ's death. Probably modeled on late medieval processional sculptures that depicted an eerily lifelike and life-sized Christ upon the cross, seventeenth-century Spanish artists produced particularly affecting artworks that focused the viewer's attention once again on Jesus's physical agony. In many instances, Christ's eyes are open, and he looks upward as if supplicating his heavenly Father. The composition and style of both painting and sculpture were similar to other Catholic Reformation works, while also echoing medieval depictions of the Man of Sorrows. Compositions feature minimal narrative context, shallow depth, and few figures. Both sculpture and painting were made to be exceptionally realistic and were clearly designed to prompt devotees to experience intense feelings of sorrow.

While mannerist and baroque representations of the crucifixion emphasized Jesus's physical pain, the Council of Trent's instructions included an admonition that works of art for the church should not be indecent or overtly sensual, which raised the problem of nude figures in ecclesiastical art. Church authorities, motivated by this proscription, went about covering nudes or removing them from churches, including those in Michelangelo's famous *ignudi* in the Sistine Chapel's *Last Judgment* (1535–1541). Although the council never addressed the

8.5 Francisco de Zurbarán, *Christ Crucified*, ca. 1665.

work of any specific artist, depictions of Christ as nude may have touched an especially sensitive nerve. Although the historical record suggests that ancient victims of crucifixion were likely nude, visual representations of his crucifixion virtually never show Christ depicted without some kind of covering, either a full *colobium* or at least a minimal loincloth.[31]

Nevertheless, in the fifteenth and sixteenth centuries, sculptors chose to show Christ as nude (or nearly so). One of these controversial images, Filippo Brunelleschi's wooden crucifix, now in the Gondi chapel of Santa Maria Novella in Florence, predated the council's work (and thus its reproach) by a nearly century and a half, as it was carved between 1410 and 1415. According to the sixteenth-century historian Giorgio Vasari, a crucifix sculpted by Brunelleschi's colleague and friend, Donatello, which he judged to show Christ as if he were a rough peasant, offended Brunelleschi. His work aimed rather to show Christ as the ideal human form. Another example, Michelangelo's polychrome wooden sculpture, intended for the high altar of Florence's Santa Maria del Santo Spirito, was completed around 1492. However, Benevenuto Cellini's similar crucifix, sculpted in 1562 and also intended for Florence's church of Santa Maria Novella (and for his own tomb), was subject to much criticism. It subsequently was given by Francesco I de' Medici to Philip II of Spain and is currently housed in the Escorial.[32]

These artists did not intend to show Christ immodestly, or even to emphasize his maleness (or humanity), but more likely were attempting to represent him as sublimely beautiful, in the classical style revived during the Renaissance. The fact that Christ's genitals are not rendered in any detail indicated that the artists probably did not intend that Christ be shown utterly nude, but that they planned to drape Christ's loins with an actual fabric *perizoma*.[33]

Stations of the Cross

During the sixteenth and seventeenth centuries, the meditation known as the stations of the cross grew in popularity, largely out of the Roman church's continued interest in inspiring and guiding imaginative and even dramatized spiritual practices among the laity. Based on an early Christian practice, evident already in the fourth-century pilgrim Egeria's diary, pilgrims reconstructed Christ's movements on Good Friday along Jerusalem's "Via Dolorosa." By the early Middle Ages, the devout would stop at designated spots (such as Pilate's and Herod's houses), where they would read the relevant passages from the biblical accounts of Christ's Passion and added special prayers.

This "way of the cross" was gradually transported to chapels outside of the Holy Land in order to reconstruct the experience of pilgrimage for those who could not make the trip. By the twelfth century, once Turks had taken Jerusalem and had control of the Christian shrines, the need for a comparable activity to actual pilgrimage to Jerusalem was even greater, although some pilgrims still made the journey. Franciscan friars, who by the mid-fourteenth century had become the official guardians of the holy sites, devised a fixed circuit there and were allowed to grant special indulgences to those who completed the devotion. By the middle of the fifteenth century, these stops came to be known as "stations," a term apparently used for the first time by William Wey, an English pilgrim who visited the Holy Land between 1458 and 1462. By the time the Turks actively suppressed Christian veneration of the holy sites in the sixteenth century, the activity had been successfully transferred abroad.[34]

Throughout the next centuries, the practice spread to churches across Europe and the British Isles. Around 1521 appeared a printed German devotional book titled *Geystlich Strass (Spiritual Road),* which included illustrations of the stations from the Holy Land. Another book, composed by a Dutch cleric, Christian Adrichomius, in the 1580s, set the number of stations at twelve. Translated into a variety of languages, it included a set of readings and prayers that soon became a standard.[35] Adrichomius's series more or less conforms to the first twelve of the fourteen now-standard stations: Jesus condemned in Pilate's palace, the imposition of the cross, Jesus's first fall, Jesus meets his mother, Simon of Cyrene takes the cross, Veronica wipes Jesus's face with her veil, Jesus's second fall, Jesus meets the women of Jerusalem, Jesus's third fall, Jesus stripped of his garments, the nailing to the cross, and Jesus raised upon the cross.

By the seventeenth century, the stations were spreading quickly to more churches in Europe. In 1686, Pope Innocent XI granted Franciscans the exclusive privilege of erecting stations in any of their churches and extending the same indulgences to any religious associated with the order who completed the devotion. Franciscans initially promoted the practice and were responsible for building replicas of the holy sites, usually a series of small oratories or outdoor shrines in the vicinity of a church. The number and designations of the particular stations nevertheless still varied, sometime as few as seven and at other times as many as forty-three, although the usual number fell between twelve and fourteen.

In 1726, Pope Benedict XIII then extended the earning of indulgences to any Christian. In 1731, Pope Clement XII allowed stations to be set up in non-Franciscan churches, so long as Franciscans supervised their construction and the local bishop gave his consent. Clement also fixed their number at fourteen. In 1742, Pope Benedict XIV encouraged all parishes to have stations, usually accompanied by pictorial renderings of the scenes. One productive Franciscan, St. Leonard of Port Maurice, set up more than five hundred and seventy sets of stations between 1731 and 1750. In 1751, St. Leonard also erected an enormous wooden cross surrounded by fourteen stations in the center of Rome's Coliseum.

The stations gradually moved inside churches and were set up in aisles or narthexes. Today the devotion, including readings, prayers, and hymns, is practiced particularly during the Lenten season and especially on Good Friday. The stations begin with Pilate's condemnation and end with Jesus's burial, but traditionally include some episodes that are not found in the New Testament. Because of this variance from scripture, in 1975, Pope Paul VI authorized a new set of stations based more closely on the Gospels, beginning at the last supper and ending with the resurrection. While the stations are ordinarily accompanied by pictorial illustrations, an absolute requirement is that each includes the figure of the cross.

The Cross in Protestant Hymnody

Protestant Reformation theology upheld the importance of Jesus's death on the cross, even as it repudiated visual images of the crucifixion in its liturgical environments. The locus for meditation on Christ's sacrificial and salvific death simply migrated from graphic depictions in visual art to vivid descriptions in sermons, literature, and perhaps most of all in hymn texts. Thus, the kind of affective piety fostered by Catholic Reformation art also found its way into the devotion of the Protestant faithful, to a large extent through the lyrics they sang in church.

Congregational hymn singing became one of the primary modes of Protestant worship, although the lyrics were often restricted to psalms or paraphrases of other biblical texts. Some reformation groups, including Lutherans, allowed nonscriptural texts, and often adapted earlier Latin hymns and poetry.

One of the earliest of these is based on the last stanzas of the Latin poem *"Salve mundi salutare"* (Hail, Savior of the World), often attributed to Bernard of Clairvaux (1091–1153), but now usually assigned to Arnulf of Leuven (1200–1251). The text, which focuses its seven stanzas on Christ's feet, knees, hands, side, breast, heart, and face, was translated into German by the Lutheran hymnist Paul Gerhardt in the mid-seventeenth century as *"O Haupt voll Blut und Wunden"* (O Head Full of Blood and Wounds) and set to a popular secular tune that Johann Sebastian Bach later arranged and included in his *Saint Matthew Passion* (1757). The text, translated into English in the mid-eighteenth century, was revised several times in the nineteenth. Its stanzas, still based on the structure of the medieval poem, came to be most widely known in the version by the poet Robert Bridges that appeared in the 1940 Episcopal hymnal:

O sacred head sore wounded, defiled and put to scorn;
O kingly head surrounded with mocking crown of thorn.
What sorrow mars thy grandeur? Can death thy bloom deflower?
O countenance whose splendor, the hosts of heaven adore!

Thy beauty long desired, hath vanished from our sight;
Thy power is all expired, and quench'd the light of light.
Ah me! For whom thou diest, hide not so far thy grace:
Show me, O Love most highest, the brightness of thy face.

In thy most bitter passion, my heart to share doth cry,
With thee for my salvation upon the cross to die.
Ah, keep my heart thus moved to stand thy cross beneath.
To mourn thee, well beloved, yet thank thee for thy death.

My days are few, O fail not, with thine immortal power,
To hold me that I quail not in death's most fearful hour;
That I may fight befriended and see in my last strife
To me thine arms extended upon the cross of life.[36]

Thus the centrality of the Passion was a constituent part of Protestant piety from the sixteenth century onward, but it emerged more graphically in hymn texts than in visual art. Yet, like visual art, the texts of these hymns invited imaginative contemplation of an image of Christ on the cross. The individualistic dimension of Protestant devotion is particularly evident in many of these hymn texts, which urge the singer to mentally and affectively participate in the scene as if actually present. This kind of devotional engagement is clearly encouraged in the title and opening lines to Isaac Watts's 1707 hymn, "When I Survey the Wondrous Cross." The third verse is particularly intended to encourage and guide visualization:

> See, from his hands, his feet,
> sorrow and love flow mingled down
> Did e'er such love and sorrow meet,
> or thorns compose so rich a crown?[37]

Charles Wesley (1707–1788), arguably the most famous Methodist hymn writer, was particularly gifted at composing texts that aroused and fostered individual piety, including attention to the self-sacrificial and redemptive love displayed by Christ on the cross. In its second verse, Wesley's 1742 hymn "O Love Divine, What Hast Thou Done!" offers a vivid example of Wesley's urging an individual encounter with the figure of Christ crucified—in a manner not altogether different from contemplative exercises of the Middle Ages:

> Behold him all ye that pass by,
> The bleeding Prince of life and peace,
> Come see ye worms, your Maker die,
> and say, was ever grief like his!
> Come feel with me his blood applied:
> My Lord, my love, is crucified![38]

In this case, the singer becomes a spectator, and the crucifix cannot but be vividly imagined in the mind's eye, even if it is not physically present. The realism of the descriptions is no less gripping than any late medieval or baroque painting. Likewise, the effects of these hymns and their accompanying melodies were no less powerful than those of the statuary and paintings that filled the great churches after the Council of Trent affirmed the value of visual art for fostering devotion.

These engrossing images continue to multiply in Protestant hymnody. They are especially palpable in the works of the American Gospel hymn writer Ira Sankey (1840–1908), who wrote hymns to accompany the evangelistic revivals of Dwight L. Moody (1837–1899). Moody was renowned for sermons in which he emphasized the power of Jesus's blood for salvation. One of Sankey's best-known hymns, "Are You Washed in the Blood?" draws from the text of Revelation 12:11 by adding the vivid image of being washed clean from sin in the blood of the lamb:

> Have you been to Jesus for the cleansing power?
> Are you washed in the blood of the Lamb?
> Are you full trusting in his grace this hour?
> Are you washed in the blood of the Lamb?[39]

Sankey's fourth verse speaks of a fountain of blood, an evocation of an earlier hymn by William Cowper, "There Is a Fountain Filled with Blood."

Arguably, the most beloved of Protestant hymns about the cross is "The Old Rugged Cross," written by the Methodist evangelist George Bennard in 1913, reportedly in response to being heckled by youths at an earlier revival meeting. Bennard, identifying with Christ being mocked as he was led to crucifixion, wrote the hymn as a personal witness to the power of an image:[40]

> On a hill far away stood an old rugged cross,
> The emblem of suffering and shame;
> And I love that old cross where the dearest and best
> For a world of lost sinners was slain.
>
> Refrain:
> So I'll cherish the old rugged cross
> Till my trophies at last I lay down;
> I will cling to the old rugged cross
> And exchange it someday for a crown.

Oh, that old rugged cross, so despised by the world,
Has a wondrous attraction for me;
For the dear Lamb of God left His glory above
To bear it to dark Calvary.

In that old rugged cross, stained with blood so divine,
A wondrous beauty I see,
For 'twas on that old cross Jesus suffered and died,
To pardon and sanctify me.

To the old rugged cross I will ever be true;
Its shame and reproach gladly bear;
Then He'll call me someday to my home far away,
Where His glory forever I'll share.[41]

The Reformation of the sixteenth century brought about changes in the theology, imagery, and popular attitudes regarding the cross and crucifix in both Protestant and Catholic communions. The story, however, is not a simple one in which Protestants rejected and Catholics promoted imagery of and devotion to the representation of Christ on the cross. Rather, as Luther explained, an image of Christ's crucifixion is not easily eradicated from the mind or even from the eye. Lutherans, of course, retained both cross and crucifix in their religious iconography. Yet, even for Lutherans, the crucifix was adapted to serve an evangelical theology that did not allow overt demonstrations of reverence or adoration.

One image that survived in both Lutheran and Catholic iconography is an allegorical figure of Jesus, pressed down under the weight of a wooden cross that was attached to a wooden screw and reconceived as part of a wine press. The blood that streams from his wounds mixes with the grape juice to become the eucharistic wine. In some depictions the vine grows from Christ's body, and in others he squeezes the grapes with his own hands, making him both victim and vintner. In many of these depictions, Christ stands within the actual chalice. These images were featured on the frontispieces of Lutheran Bibles, as well as engravings, paintings, and sculptures from the Catholic Reformation period.

The motif itself dates back to the eleventh century and is based on several biblical texts, including Isaiah 63:3, "I have trodden the winepress alone,

8.6 Hieronymous Wierix, *Christ in the Wine Press*, before 1619.

and from the peoples no one was with me; I trod them in my anger and trampled them in my wrath." The story of the spies returning from the Promised Land bearing a huge bunch of grapes (Num. 13:23) is also part of the context, as well as Jesus's statement that he is the "True Vine" (John 15:1). Thus the vine is a figure of the cross and Christ is the grape whose blood (juice) is extracted at his Passion. Those who share in it through the Eucharistic sacrament will thereby earn access to the true Promised Land.[42]

From the sixteenth century onward, the image's interpretation depends on whether it was displayed in a Catholic or Protestant context. During the Reformation, Catholics understood it to affirm the doctrine of transubstantiation, the literal identity of Christ's blood with the eucharistic wine, against Protestant denial of the corporal presence of Christ in the Lord's Supper. Catholics also insisted on a sacrificial understanding of the Mass. Lutherans, however, would have viewed the image not only as a confirmation of their particular belief in Christ's real, sacramental presence in contradiction to other reformation groups who believed that the bread and the wine were merely symbols. Since almost all reformed groups believed that all the faithful should receive the wine, the depiction of Christ as the vintner as well as the source of the wine could also have signified that position against the Catholic practice of withholding the cup from the laity.

9

Crux Perdurans

The Cross in the New World, Islam, and the Modern Era

The Tree of Life grows
In the land of mystery;
There we were created;
There we were born.
There He-by-whom-all-things-live
Spins the thread of our lives . . .
You have become the Tree of Life.
Dying, you have been born again.
Swaying, you spread your branches
And stand before the Giver-of-all-life.
In your boughs our home shall be:
We will be your flowers.

—Angel María Garibay

THE CROSS WAS a disturbing symbol for Jews from the beginning and eventually also came to be for Muslims and other non-Christians. Crusaders fought in the Holy Land under its banner and carried its relic into battle. The relic was captured by Saladin and carried off to Damascus where it disappeared, but it continued to be an emblem around which Christian armies would rally. In the fifteenth and sixteenth centuries, Christian missionaries carried the cross with them on their voyages of discovery and conquest, through which its message was by turns imposed, accepted, and resisted.

Christian preoccupation with Christ's suffering on the cross is bewildering to members of other faith traditions, including Buddhists who seek to rise above bodily existence and transcend all forms of physical suffering. Jews, of course, reject Jesus's identification as the Messiah, largely because they believe he did not fulfill messianic prophecies but also, according to scripture, his form of death was accursed (Deut. 21:22–23). Although Muslims regard the cross as a symbol of Christianity and may connect it with historical instances of Christian aggression, unlike Jews, they accept Jesus as a prophet. In addition, while their sacred texts recount the story of Christ's condemnation to die on the cross, Muslims deny that he actually underwent crucifixion. In contrast to docetic Christians, they do not believe that he escaped suffering insofar as he was a divine being; they rather assert that Allah raised him up to heaven as a reward, perhaps even evading his human death.

In recent years, theological, political, and social critics alike have objected to the cross's symbolism, arguing that it has been historically identified with colonizing nations or supremacist groups. In secular contexts, the cross has become a controversial object, whether displayed in a municipal building, along a state highway, or in a publically funded museum. Those who advocate the exclusion of religion from civic affairs and public spaces have pointed out its unambiguous identity as a symbol of the Christian faith. Its predominant place in the history of Western art has guaranteed its exhibition in art museums and galleries, but even when viewed as a cultural artifact, it has drawn objections, sometimes by those who believe it to be disrespected in the manner of its presentation. In the final analysis, all this demonstrates the power and tenacity of the symbol. Whether it is beloved or feared, revered or denigrated, misconstrued or mystical, the cross endures.

The Cross and the Crucifix in the New World

The cross, a symbol of the Crusades in both the Middle East and Spain, sailed with the colonizing Europeans to the Americas and to Africa, where it was paraded ashore by clerics and conquistadors as an emblem of both Christian faith and secular power. Along with these European armies—mostly from Spain and Portugal—came the style of religious painting that emerged and developed in the Catholic territories during the Reformation period, in particular the works of Spanish artists. Depictions of Christ's Passion were characterized by the sensuousness that had become the hallmark of that sacred art. At the same time, the cultures that these Europeans encountered had their own sacred iconography and in them actually recognized some parallels in the material artifacts and ritual practices of these native religions. In some cases, the process of colonization aimed at supplanting the indigenous cults and their imagery with specifically Christian signs and symbols. In other instances, it was more pragmatic for the missionaries and colonizers simply to adapt the native visual vocabulary in order to make conversion appear to be a more or less seamless transition from the old to the new belief system. What may have been overlooked was the endurance of the pre-Christian religious cultures and the ways it survived even under the guise of having been displaced.

The Cross and the Crucifix in Mesoamerica

While both Muslims and Jews in the Old World recognized the cross as a unique—and negatively charged—emblem of Christian political and religious power, the indigenous peoples of the Americas, specifically those living in central Mexico, possessed a symbol that looked quite similar to the cross and shared some of its positive significations, insofar as it represented the four cardinal directions of the cosmos and functioned as a sign of life. This symbol eventually became merged with the Christian cross, though in a kind of syncretized way, retaining much of its original cultural and religious significance.

The first episode of this story begins with Christopher Columbus, who understood his voyage, at least partly, in religious terms: as a crusade whose aim was to find enough gold to finance a new attempt to retake Jerusalem, with himself as an agent (or bearer of) Christ along the way. Columbus believed the end of the world was approaching, and that part of his mission was to find the biblical Garden of Eden by sailing across the ocean to the unexplored landmass to the west.[1] Among other evidence of Columbus's particular sense of religious mission, he emblazoned a large cross on the sails of his ships and remarked that he first sighted land on a Friday (the day of Christ's Passion) in 1492. In eerily similar fashion, Hernán Cortés and his conquering Spanish army fled from Cuba and landed on the east coast of Mexico on Good Friday, 1519. Perhaps because of that auspicious date, Cortés named his first colonial settlement the City of the True Cross (Veracruz).

The figure of the cross and depictions of Christ's crucifixion went on to play a central role in the evangelization of the natives by Christian missionaries (Augustinians, Dominicans, Franciscans, and—eventually—Jesuits). Seeking a means to make their religion comprehensible, the missionaries found that they could adapt extant symbolic systems to fit their own. For example, Aztec religion practiced human sacrifice, understanding it to be both a form of oblation to the gods and a means of deification for the victims. The crucifixion therefore made a certain kind of sense by analogy and the cross was thus incorporated into this sacrificial narrative. Nahua (Aztec) converts could comprehend a crucified god, self-offered to a yet-higher deity.[2]

Holy violence was not difficult for them to understand, and the cross, an already common symbol in their religious iconography, was effectively incorporated into the blended pictorial language that undergirded and advanced the conversion process. One of the central symbols of early Mexican churches was a large stone cross, set upon a stepped pedestal, and placed in the center of a large open courtyard or patio in front of the church. These atrial crosses normally lacked a body of Christ, although they usually depicted the instruments of the Passion, carved on the upright and crosspiece, as well as the title, and the face of Christ at the center. Often a skull or the image of a human heart appears at the pedestal's base. Some crosses incorporated pieces of polished obsidian in place of the face of Christ—a stone that had sacred significance for both Christians and Aztecs.[3] The representation of the heart is both a visual reference to the part of the Aztec human sacrifice ritual in which the victim's heart was removed while still beating, and a traditional Christian image of the sacred heart of Jesus.[4]

The missionaries' work of conversion was not benign. More often than not conversions were forced, and those who obstinately refused to acknowledge the "true cross" (and deny their native symbols) were dealt with as heretics. The Inquisition came to New Spain in the 1520s in order to seek out and punish those who disrespected the Christian faith, including those who refused to venerate the cross. As in Spain, many of those accused were Jews, but natives were also charged with blasphemy. One example is the 1528 case of Diego de

9.1 Atrial cross with Face of Christ, surmounting a small sepulcher attended by the Virgin Mary.

Morales, his brother Gonzalo de Morales, and Hernando Alonso, who were charged with being Judaizers and blasphemers. Diego, said to have taken a cross and trampled upon it, was forced to do public penance. His brother, Gonzalo, admitted to flogging and urinating on a crucifix and was burned at the stake.[5]

The Mayan people had a different kind of encounter with the Christian cross. According to a legendary Mayan prophet, Chilam Balam, the arrival of white conquerors would be presaged by a cross symbol. The conquerors naturally interpreted this prophecy as a divine message that the Maya should renounce their own gods, convert to Christianity, and submit to Spanish rule. Analysis of the authenticity of this prophecy (and of the existence of Chilam Balam) has suggested that the claim, rather than a wholly fabricated justification for colonial subjugation of the natives, contains a kernel of truth.[6]

An image of a sacred tree existed in the religious iconography of nearly all native groups in preconquest Mesoamerica. One of the central images of the ancient Maya was a "world tree," an *axis mundi* that linked the three layers of the cosmos: upperworld, earth, and underworld. An intersecting horizontal bar divided the heavenly and earthly realms and represented the source of life. A famous depiction of this was carved on the seventh-century tomb of King Pacal at Planenque, Yucatan. The king is depicted in a sitting position, leaning back with his knees bent at the base of the tree, as if he is being drawn down into the underworld. The crosslike tree rises from the center of his torso.[7] The parallels between this and the crucifix (and even more to the Christian images of the tree of Jesse) are striking, and would have suggested to the Spanish invaders that their conquest was foreordained and guided by divine providence. In native traditions, the sacred trees were fed and fertilized by human blood, so the links between the human sacrificial victim, the blood-nourished world tree, Jesus's blood-drenched cross, and the sacred blood of Christ at the eucharist were relatively intuitive. A severed head often shown at the base of the world tree even had similarities to the skull of Adam, notably shown at the base of the crucifix in Christian iconography.[8] To some extent, then, this was more a process of assimilation or adaptation than of conversion.

Some Christian missionaries evidently believed that the similarities in their religious rituals and iconography demonstrated that the indigenous people had actually been converted to Christianity at some distant time in the past and had

9.2 *Cruz de ánimas* with two carved kneeling figures, ca. 1820.

fallen away again into polytheistic idolatry. According to a 1545 report of Francisco Hernandez, when he and his Spanish settlers arrived on the Yucatan peninsula, they found crosses, including one very large, standing near a temple and adored as a god of water or rain. When the Spanish asked how they came to know of this sign, they answered that a very handsome man had passed through and left it as his memorial. Others replied that a man more dazzling than the sun had died upon it.[9] Despite their subsequent slide back into (perceived) paganism, the cross survived as a testament to their apostasy. Thus, by European reckoning, the process of conversion was actually a reconversion, reviving symbols that had been perverted or misunderstood through the centuries.[10]

In the eighteenth century, painted crosses became popular in the regions of Querétaro and Guanajuato in central Mexico. These crosses commonly included the image of Christ crucified surrounded by the instruments of the Passion, the face of God the Father, the Holy Spirit (normally imaged as a hummingbird), the sun and moon, and a sorrowing Virgin Mary. In most cases, St. Michael appears below, judging souls, some of whom are shown at the bottom of the base burning in Purgatory. Praying figures, probably representing the souls for whom the votive cross was made, sit on either side and just above are small scenes of Adam and Eve, a monstrance displaying the consecrated host, and the devil shooting a dying person. Widely made for personal devotion, these *cruces de ánimas* were banned by church authorities in the nineteenth century, as they were concerned that such crosses might have been used for sorcery or witchcraft.

The Cross in Kongo

Like the crosses that Europeans found in Mesoamerica and took to be precolonial indications of indigenous Christianity, the Portuguese who arrived at the mouth of the Zaire River in the late fifteenth century also discovered crosslike symbols among the native Bakongo people. Cruciform designs were painted onto rock faces, impressed into ceramics, woven into textiles, and engraved in ivory.[11] The religious significance of these images is uncertain, but it seems that the simple cross (two intersecting lines) may have symbolized the four directions of the universe, depicted the connection between upper and lower worlds, inscribed a line of communication between the living and the dead, or represented the intersection of the mundane and spiritual realms.[12] However, rather than was the case in Mesoamerica, the local leaders embraced the symbol of the cross as a means of establishing their authority among their own people and—to a degree—exercising autonomy in spite of the European colonists.[13]

In 1491, a year before Columbus reached the New World and less than a decade after the first Portuguese landed in the region, chronicler Rui de Pina reports that the king of Kongo, Nzinga a Nkuwu, was baptized along with six members of his court and received the new Christian name of João I. Some days after this event, the Virgin Mary appeared to two of the newly baptized and one of them subsequently found a cross carved on a black stone outside his front door. Considered a heaven-sent sign of the Christian God's special endorsement, the object was ceremonially processed to a newly constructed church and installed there as a sacred relic.[14]

The Constantinian echoes in this story would have been evident to the European arrivals.[15] In fact, a second story of a supernatural apparition reportedly came to João's son, Afonso. Following a battle against his brother for control of the kingdom, Afonso recounted how he and his outnumbered army had prayed to St. James for aid. He attributed his surprising victory to the saint, who appeared in the sky, wielding the cross and joined by a heavenly host mounted for battle. The opposing army was so terrified that they broke ranks and fled. A later story about Afonso tells of yet another stone cross that materialized shortly after Afonso executed his mother for refusing to forsake her pagan idols.[16] Thus, in Kongo, the figure of the cross became a means of legitimizing both colonial and local power, as the rulers both embraced and manipulated the Christianity of their Portuguese allies. Like Constantine, who emblazoned the christogram on the helmets and shields of his troops, Afonso presented crucifixes to his chosen representatives—tribal chiefs who were empowered to act as judges as well as spiritual healers.[17]

Following Afonso's victory, crosses and crucifixes were produced in large numbers. Although they were clearly inspired by imports from western Europe, the appearance of these artifacts was distinctive and reflected a kind of hybrid iconography that merged Christian with African motifs.[18] In the sixteenth century, Kongo artists began to cast brass crucifixes in which Jesus is depicted in a stylized fashion, with African facial features and extremely large

9.3 Brass crucifix, Angola, Republic of the Congo, sixteenth to seventeenth century.

hands. The feet are flattened and overlapped as if they form a single appendage. His loincloth appears to be made from the local raffia textile, with an X-shaped cross woven into it. The crucifixes often include additional characters, including the Virgin Mary as well as unidentified kneeling figures that are attached to either the base or the arms. These may represent saints, souls of the dead, mourners, intercessory petitioners, or even captives or criminals. An unusual triple crucifix now in the Metropolitan Museum may be a reference to the Holy Trinity.

The Cross in Islam

Muslims, like many Protestants, object to pictorial iconography in their places of prayer, although most take an even stronger position against figurative art generally, whether in religious or secular contexts. Yet, despite their long-standing condemnation of idols and their opposition to representational art historically, Muslims have rarely attacked or destroyed Christian images, unless they were blatantly blasphemous or doctrinally incorrect.

Since a simple cross (without a corpus) was often acceptable even to those opposed to images, crosses have never been significant targets for destruction by Muslims. The occasional incidents in which Islamic leaders of the past ordered the removal of crosses from conspicuous public display were most likely prompted by the cross's role as a Christian emblem, rather than by antipathy to the cross as a figure in itself.[19] Nevertheless, evidence exists to show that Christians themselves often took care not to display, possess, or venerate holy images—including crosses—when they lived in Muslim territories, lest they bring trouble with religious authorities upon themselves.[20]

Islam particularly denounces depictions of God or the Prophet as blasphemous. They judge depictions of Jesus similarly, yet regard images of the crucifixion as especially problematic, not because Muslims view Jesus as God but because representations of him dying on the cross contradict their own teachings about his death. Although Muslims deny that Jesus was the incarnate Son of God—and absolutely reject the Christian doctrine of the Holy Trinity—they accept Jesus as a prophet who was persecuted and condemned to die by crucifixion. Yet, they do not claim that Jesus actually died on the cross. Islam's sacred text asserts that God was able to save Jesus from death (cf. Heb. 5:7) and raise him into heaven. Yet, the writing is ambiguous about whether he somehow survived his attempted execution or whether someone else took his place on the cross:

> They [the Jews] said (in boast), "We killed Christ Jesus, the Son of Mary, the Messenger of God." But they did not kill him, nor crucify him, rather it only was made to appear so to them. And those who differ in regard to this are full of doubt, with no (certain) knowledge, but only follow conjecture. For surely they did not kill him. Rather, God took him up unto Himself; for God is Mighty and Wise. (Qur'an Sura 4.157–158)

A particular problem arises around the meaning of the words "made to appear so to them." Muslim scholars have considered the implications: If Jesus only appeared to be crucified, what actually happened? The classical commentaries contain conflicting interpretations.[21] Several of these recount the legend that someone whom God made to look like Jesus was crucified in Jesus's place, either voluntarily or mistakenly. In one case, this was a faithful disciple. In another, Jesus's likeness was given to Judas, making him pay the ultimate price for his betrayal.[22] This story of a substitute victim has some parallels with early gnostic traditions that Simon of Cyrene died in Christ's stead.[23]

Many Muslims hold that Jesus did not die on the cross but merely lost consciousness. This tradition belongs to the Ahmadiyyah movement, named for its founder Mirzā Ghulām Ahmad, which emerged in the late nineteenth century as a self-styled renewal of Islam that included direct criticism of Christianity and its New Testament narratives about Jesus. According to this version of events, while Jesus was actually nailed to the cross, he was taken down and buried while still alive. He revived in the tomb, escaped, traveled to the East, and eventually died in Kashmir. According to Ahmad, a shrine in Srinagar is his tomb.[24] A more recent South Asian Muslim missionary Ahmed Deedat (1918–2005) promoted this story, and the tomb became a modern-day tourist attraction.

The Qur'an never actually denies that Jesus died, either on the cross or at some other time and place. In fact, several other passages allude either directly to his death or to his being "taken up" by God (S. 3.55, 5.117, 19.15, and 19.33). Thus, the Qur'an at very least says that at some point in time (and not necessarily on the cross), God (rather than the Jews) caused Jesus to die and then raised him up to heaven.[25] According to one tradition, when Jesus returns—a righteous Imam—at the end time, he will kill all swine, forcibly convert all Christians to Islam . . . and destroy all crosses.[26] Thus, although the Qur'an accepts the virgin birth of Christ, they do not accept his crucifixion and regard the belief that God would allow such a death of his prophet to be unthinkable.

Epilogue: The Cross in Contemporary Culture

The cross's story continues, of course, into the present day. Perhaps today's story is no more complex than that of the previous two millennia; still, it would fill another volume to tell in any depth. Nevertheless, a few trajectories can be outlined.

Both ubiquitous and tenacious, the cross turns up in the most mundane contexts. Roadside crosses set up by private citizens compete with advertising billboards and mark the sites of traffic casualties—a sobering reminder of the death toll on highways.[27] Shrines with crosses fill the landscape in some parts of the world. A hill in northern Lithuania, completely covered with votive crosses and crucifixes is a testimony to the persistence of Catholic Christianity in this former Soviet-occupied country. The subject of an extraordinarily popular cult, pilgrims flock to this place, climbing the hill on their knees and praying the stations of the cross.[28] At the other end of the spectrum, gaudy rhinestone crosses turn up on denim jeans, handbags, or leather jackets—a fashion trend that may have little to do with religion.

Crosses in the public square can be perceived as communicating Christian triumphalism or religious intolerance. The fiery crosses of the Ku Klux Klan are an extreme example of the symbol being used to terrorize victims, incite racial hatred, and widely regarded as an emblem of hate-based terrorism, especially (although not exclusively) against African Americans. Klan spokespersons have argued, however, that the lighted cross (versus the "burning cross") is not intended as an act of desecration but rather as a show of allegiance to Christ.[29] This intimidating symbol may have been borrowed from the fiery crosses burned by Scottish clansmen, used to rouse their countrymen to repel the English armies during the Jacobite rising. Its sympathetic portrayal in D. W. Griffith's 1915 epic film, *The Birth of a Nation*, may have encouraged the Klan's embrace of the figure. Despite the Klan's justification of its use, recent Supreme Court decisions have judged the display of a burning cross to be a hate crime rather than an instance of freedom of expression when expressly used to intimidate or if motivated by racial, religious, or gender bias.[30] James Cone's important work, *The Cross and the Lynching Tree*, looks at the conflicted connections between the two powerful images of the cross and the tree, noting that some African Americans may find the cross to be a symbol of God's solidarity with their suffering in the face of the terrifying history of racial violence, perpetrated upon the "lynching tree."[31]

Jews objected to the placement of crosses at the site of the Auschwitz concentration camp in the 1980s, as they evoked painful memories of both ancient and modern persecution. Although the large cross at Auschwitz was originally set up for a convent of Carmelite nuns, and the subsequent placement of smaller crosses may have been intended to commemorate the death of Christians—including many Christian Roma—at that camp, Jews perceived their installation as profoundly disrespectful and demanded their removal.[32] Conversely, the Chinese government's removal of crosses from the exteriors of Chinese Christian churches, ostensibly only enforcing zoning ordinances, arguably has a different motivation. Journalists have reported that the authorities are targeting Christian churches because they regard their display of religious affiliation as too excessive or "overly popular."[33]

Feminist critique of the cross as a symbol has been a hallmark of modern theology, as writers have argued that the image of the crucifixion has been used as a justification for abuse and even violence against women and marginalized peoples. The argument focuses on the way that the traditional Christian emphasis on Christ's suffering has been used to encourage meek and submissive self-sacrifice (especially of women) or simply to validate and even glorify suffering more generally. Some even take the position that the cross and the medieval atonement theory that lauded it are sadomasochistic.[34] A more widespread view among feminist theologians is that Christian theology has been suffused with patriarchal values and often used to oppress women and that Jesus's admonition to "take up your cross" could be understood as a justification for tolerating abuse.[35]

The idea that human guilt is absolved by a violent death, or that a loving God should require such propitiation, is abhorrent to many Christians. Others hold a different view and identify Jesus's suffering with that of oppressed communities, a view that characterizes the work of certain liberation theologians and prompts a call to solidarity with those who suffer from poverty, injustice, or hate-based crimes. In addition, theologians have argued that to neglect the suffering of Christ is to deny his true humanity. Christ does not suffer because suffering is beneficial, justified, or even justifying, but because he fully participates in and has compassion for the inevitable suffering of human existence.[36]

Perceiving Christ's crucifixion as God's identification with the suffering, abused, or oppressed has inspired artists to depict Christ as a martyred Russian Jew, a naked female, a battered African slave, a Nicaraguan peasant, or a freedom fighter. Marc Chagall's *White Crucifixion* (1938) was painted shortly after Kristallnacht—the horrifying, widespread Nazi raid on German Jews. The painting shows a world swallowed up by violence, including the figure of Christ on the cross with a Jewish prayer shawl draped around his loins. Critics have condemned Edwina Sandys's *Christa* (1975), an image that depicted Christ as a crucified female, for apparently denying that Jesus was a historic, human male.[37] Her supporters commended the work for its implication that Christ, as God, transcends the particularity of gender, while as both divine and human, he truly experienced the totality of human experience, including physical, mental, and emotional torment. Some feminists have argued, however, that the image unintentionally reinforces violence against women and emphasizes the figure's vulnerability and sexuality.[38]

Other artists, eschewing traditional Eurocentric iconography, have incorporated distinctively ethnic symbols or figures into their representations of the crucifixion or cross. Showing Christ as African, Asian, or Central American underlines the universality of his humanity. The depiction of the Holy Spirit as a hummingbird rather than a dove on the Mexican *cruz de ánimas* (Fig. 9.2) is a modest but striking instance of using meaningful visual language for a particular culture. A more monumental example is the Totem Cross (1975), carved by First Nations artist Stanley Peters. Peters placed a thunderbird on the cross in place of a human male corpus. The artist chose the thunderbird to represent Christ because natives of the Northwest Coast believe the bird to be a messenger of the Great Spirit. In a letter to the Canadian Council of Catholic Bishops, Peters described his work:

9.4 *The Yellow Crucifixion*, Marc Chagall, 1942.

9.5 *Christa*, Edwina Sandys, 1975.

God's eyes watch from the four directions, from above and below, from both wings, saying that God is all around us at all times. All races, black and yellow, red and white, are represented in the four colours taken from nature and found in the earth-circle and all over Thunderbird. Christ-as-Thunderbird, in dying for us, restores happiness and understanding; he fills us with new dignity and great richness.[39]

A number of contemporary artists have produced notably controversial depictions of the cross or crucifixion, and many of them have been accused of being intentionally insulting or blasphemous. Cosimo Cavallaro's crucifix, *My Sweet Lord* (1985), sculpted entirely out of chocolate, was labeled as hate speech by the president of the Catholic League. Sarah Lucas's *Christ You Know It Ain't Easy* (2003) was a crucifix made entirely from cigarettes. Andres Serrano's *Piss Christ* (1987), a large-format color photograph of a crucifix submerged in urine, is a more famous (or infamous) example. Some viewers regarded Serrano's work as a powerful—even sacramental—allusion to the life-giving and death-dealing aspects of human bodily fluids, especially at the height of the AIDS crisis in the United States. Others, including Senator Jesse Helms of North Carolina, called it abhorrent and sickening, and used the storm of indignation to challenge taxpayer support for artists.[40] In many cases, the artists were not attempting to make religious statements, or even deliberately offensive ones. Rather, they chose a subject so deeply embedded in Western visual consciousness that it instantly communicated a powerful message, whether sacred or profane. To the extent that such a message might cause outrage actually confirms its continued power and relevance. So long as Christians continue to ponder the meaning of Christ's crucifixion and to sing about it, wear images of it, or install it in their worship environments, the cross will never become irrelevant or trivial. Rather, the cross will continue to project significant valence, both positive and negative depending on where or when it turns up, how it is used, what it looks like, and who sees it.

Notes

Abbreviations—Ancient Authors and Works

Act. Pionii	*Acts of the Martyr Pionius*
Acts Pet.	*Acts of Peter*
Agnellus	
Max.	*Maximianus* (from the *Book of Pontiffs of Ravenna*)
Amalarius of Metz	
Lib. off.	*On the Liturgy*
Ambrose	
Obit. Theo.	*On the Death of Theodosius*
Apoc. Elij.	*Apocalypse of Elijah*
Apoc. Pet	*Apocalypse of Peter*
Apuleus	
Met.	*Metamorphoses (The Golden Ass)*
Arnobius	
Nat.	*Against the Nations*
Athanasius	
Inc.	*On the Incarnation*
Vit. Ant.	*The Life of Anthony*
Augustine of Hippo	
Civ.	*The City of God*
C. Jul.	*Contra Julianum*
Catech.	*Catechizing the Uninstructed*
Doct. chr.	*On Christian Doctrine*
Ennarat. Ps.	*Expositions of the Psalms*
Ep.	*Epistle*
Faust.	*Against Faustus the Manichee*

Abbreviations

Serm.	*Sermons*
Tract. Ev. Jo.	*Homilies on the Gospel of John*
Babylonian Talmid, sanh.	*Sanhedrin*
Basil of Caesarea	
Bapt.	*On Baptism*
Bede	
Hist. ecc.	*Church History*
Bordeaux Pilgrim	
Itin.	*Pilgrimage Itinerary*
Cicero	
Pro. Rab. perd.	*For Rabirius on a Charge of Treason*
Verr.	*Against Verres*
Clement of Alexandria	
Paed.	*Christ the Teacher*
Protr.	*Exhortation to the Greeks*
Cyprian	
Carm.	*Poems*
Test.	*Testimonies against the Jews (To Quirinius)*
Cyril of Alexandria	
Cont. Jul.	*Against Julian*
Cyril of Jerusalem	
Cat.	*Catecheses*
Ep. Const.	*Letter to Emperor Constantius*
Myst.	*On the Mysteries*
Dionysius of Halicarnassus	
Ant. rom.	*Roman antiquities*
Egeria	
Itin.	*Pilgrimage Itinerary*
Epiphanius	
Adv. haer.	*Against Heresies*
Ep. Theod.	*Letter to Theodosius*
Epis. Apos.	*Epistle to the Apostles*
Eusebius	
Hist.	*Church History*
Vit. Const.	*Life of Constantine*
Firmicus Maternus	
Err. prof. rel.	*The error of the pagan religions*
Gos. Thom.	*Gospel of Thomas*
Gos. Pet.	*Gospel of Peter*
Gos. Phil.	*Gospel of Philip*

Abbreviations

Gos. Truth	*Gospel of Truth*
Gregory I (the Great)	
Ep.	*Letter*
Gregory of Nazianzus	
Or. c. Jul.	*Against Julian*
Gregory of Nyssa	
Cont. Eun.	*Against Eunomius*
Diem lum.	*On the Day of Lights (Epiphany)*
In Christ. res. or. 1	*On the Resurrection of Christ, Oration 1*
Or. cat.	*Catechetical Oration*
Vita Mac.	*Life of Macrina*
Gregory of Tours	
Lib. Hist.	*History of the Franks*
Mart.	*Glory of the Martyrs*
Hippolytus	
Antichr.	*On Christ and Antichrist*
Ref.	*Refutation of All Heresies*
Hrabanus Maurus	
Hom.	*Sermon.*
Ignatius of Antioch	
Eph.	*To the Ephesians*
Rom.	*To the Romans*
Smyr.	*To the Smyrnaeans*
Trall.	*To the Trallians*
Irenaeus	
Haer.	*Against Heresies*
Jerome	
Comm. Eph.	*Commentary on Ephesians*
Comm. Matt.	*Commentary on Matthew*
Comm. Zech.	*Commentary on Zechariah*
Ep.	*Letter*
John Chrysostom	
Adv. Jud.	*Against Judaizing Christians*
Bapt. Inst.	*Baptismal Instructions*
Cont. Jud. et Gent.	*That Christ is God, Addressed to Jews and Greeks*
Hom. 1 Cor.	*Homily on 1 Corinthians*
Hom. Jo.	*Homily on Gospel of John*
Hom. Matt.	*Homily on Gospel of Matthew*

Abbreviations

John of Damascus	
Fide	*The Orthodox Faith*
Orat.	*Orations against Those Who Oppose Images*
Josephus	
B.J.	*Jewish Wars*
A.J.	*Jewish Antiquities*
C. Ap.	*Against Apion*
Justin Martyr	
1 Apol.	*First Apology*
Dial.	*Dialogue with Trypho the Jew*
Lactantius	
Inst.	*Divine Institutes*
Mort.	*Deaths of the Persecutors*
Leo I	
Serm.	*Sermon*
Lib. pont.	*Liber pontificalis*
Lucan	
Bell.	*Civil Wars*
Melito of Sardis	
Pasch.	*On Pasch*
Minucius Felix	
Oct.	*Octavius*
Origen	
Cels.	*Against Celsus*
Comm. Matt.	*Commentary on the Gospel of Matthew*
Sel. Ezech.	*Homilies on Ezekiel*
Pan. Lat.	*Latin Panegyrics*
Paulinus	
Carm.	*Poem*
Ep.	*Epistle*
Piacenza Pilgrim	
Itin.	*Pilgrimage Itinerary*
Pliny the Elder	
Nat.	*Natural History*
Plutarch	
Sera	*On the Delays of Divine Vengeance*
Procopius	
Bell. Pers.	*Persian Wars*
Prudentius	
Perist.	*On the Martyrs' Crowns*

Note to Page viii

Pseudo-Alcuin

Div. off. lib.	*On Divine Offices*

Pseudo-Bonaventure

Medit.	*Meditations on the Life of Christ*

Pseudo-Hippolytus

De Pasch. Hom.	*Homily on Pascha*

Rufinus

Hist.	*Church History*

Seneca

Marc.	*To Marcia on Consolation*
Ep.	*Epistle*

Suetonius

Cal.	*Life of Caligula*
Dom.	*Life of Domitian*

Sulpicius Severus

Chron.	*Chronicle*

Tacitus

Ann.	*Annals*
Hist.	*Histories*

Tertullian

Adv. Jud.	*Against the Jews*
Apol.	*Apology*
Cor.	*On the Soldier's Crown*
Marc.	*Against Marcion*
Nat.	*Against the Gentiles*
Orat.	*On Prayer*
Praesc.	*Prescription against Heretics*

Theodore of Mopsuestia

Bapt. hom.	*Homily on Baptism*

Theodoret

Hist.	*Church History*

Theophanes

Chron.	*Chronicle*

Preface

1. Much of this information has been reported in the popular media, but details are taken from the story by Rick Hampson, "Ground Zero Cross a Powerful Symbol for 9/11 Museum," *USA Today*, May 15, 2014, http://www.usatoday.com/story/news/nation/2014/05/13/911-ground-zero-museum-cross-world-trade-center/8907003.

1. *Scandalum Crucis*

Epigraph: Justin Martyr, *1 Apol.* 13, trans. A. Roberts and J. Donaldson, *The Ante-Nicene Fathers* (hereafter ANF) 1.167.

1. See discussion of this "curse" later in this chapter.

2. Ignatius of Antioch, *Eph.* 18:1.

3. Plutarch, *Sera* 9, cited in Raymond E. Brown, *The Death of the Messiah*, vol. 2 (New York: Doubleday, 1994), 914.

4. Melito of Sardis, *Pasch*, 97, cited in Brown, *Death of the Messiah*, 952–954.

5. See Chapter 4 for a discussion of Christ's garments (or lack of them) in Christian iconography.

6. See, e.g., Col. 2:14, which speaks of Jesus erasing the record of human sins by "nailing it to the cross." Also, *Gos. Pet.* 21; Ignatius of Antioch, *Smyrn.* 1.2. On the use of nails in crucifixions generally, see discussion later in this chapter.

7. Brown, *Death of the Messiah*, 2.1178–1182.

8. Suetonius, *Cal.* 32.2; *Dom.* 10.1.

9. Tacitus, *Hist.* 2.72.1–2. Brown, *Death of the Messiah*, 946, suggests this might lie behind the identification of Jesus "taking on the form of a slave" in the Philippians hymn (Phil. 2:7–8).

10. John Granger Cook, *Crucifixion in the Mediterranean World* (Tübingen: Mohr Siebeck, 2014) and Gunnar Samuelsson, *Crucifixion in Antiquity* (Tübingen: Mohr Siebeck, 2011) for extensive references, helpful summaries, and markedly different interpretations of the ancient literary data.

11. Josephus, *B.J.* 1.4.6.

12. Josephus, *A.J.* 17.10.10.

13. Josephus, *B.J.* 5.11.1, also 5.6.5.

14. Cicero, *Pro. Rab. Perd.* 16, trans. H. Grose Hodge, Loeb Classical Library (hereafter LCL) 198. See also Cicero, *Verr.* 2.5.165, where he describes crucifixion as a cruel and disgusting punishment.

15. E.g., the Jehovah's Witnesses, who maintain that the cross was actually only an upright stake.

16. Josephus, *B.J.* 5.11.1.

17. Seneca, *Marc.* (*Dial.* 6) 20.3.

18. Seneca, *Ep.* 101.14.

19. On crucifixion with nails generally, see Joseph William Lewitt, "Use of Nails in Crucifixion," *Harvard Theological Review* 25 (1932): 29–45.

20. Textual evidence for this scourging in Dionysius of Halicarnassus (b. 60 BCE), *Ant. rom.* 5.51.3 and 12.6.7.

21. Augustine, *Tract. Jo.* 36.4, trans. author, Corpus Christianorum Series Latina (hereafter CCL) 36.326.

22. See Joseph Zias and Eliezer Sekeles, "The Crucified Man at Giv'at ha-Mivtar: A Reappraisal," *Israel Exploration Journal* 35 (1985): 22–27. Additionally, see some graffiti images of crucifixion discussed later in this chapter.

23. John Granger Cook, "Crucifixion as Spectacle in Roman Campania," *Novum Testamentum* 54 (2012): 68–100.

24. See Josephus, *C. Ap.* 2.7.80–88; Tertullian, *Apol.* 16; *Nat.* 1.11.

25. Tacitus, *Hist.* 5.304.

26. Tertullian, *Nat.* 1.14.

27. Minucius Felix, *Oct.* 28.7–8

28. Justin Martyr, *1 Apol.* 21–22, 46, 55.

29. See Chapter 2 for a discussion of these signs.

30. See Chapter 2 for a discussion of the cross as evident in everyday objects.

31. Origen, *Cels.* 1.68.

32. Ibid., 2.47, 7.16–17, 7.53, 6.34–39.

33. Tertullian, *Apol.* 16; *Nat.* 1.12.

34. A parallel comparison appears in Tertullian, *Apol.* 16.8; *Nat.* 1.12.

35. Minucius Felix, *Oct.* 29.7–8. Other arguments from Christian apologists along these lines include works of Arnobius, *Nat.* 1.36; Firmicus Maternus, *Err. prof. rel.* 27.

36. Augustine, *Civ.* 19.23.

37. David Chapman, *Ancient Jewish and Christian Perceptions of Crucifixion* (Tübingen: Mohr Siebeck, 2008), 117–154.

38. Max Wilcox, "Upon the Tree—Deut. 21:22–23 in the New Testament," *Journal of Biblical Literature* 96 (1977): 85–99.

39. Chapman, *Ancient Jewish and Christian Perceptions*, 36–37, 119–120, 241–253.

40. Justin Martyr, *Dial.* 32, 89.

41. Ibid., 86, 90–107.

42. Ibid., 40.

43. Tertullian, *Adv. Jud.* 10.1–5.

44. Also see Tertullian, *Marc.* 3.18.4–7, 5.11.8; *Adv. Jud.* 13.

45. Babylonian Talmud, *Sanh.* 43a. On this subject, see Marc Saperstein, "Jewish Responses to the Passion Narrative," in *The Passion Story: From Visual Representation to Social Drama*, ed. Marcia Kupfer (University Park: Penn State University Press), 194–195.

46. For references and bibliography, see Chapman, *Ancient Jewish and Christian Perceptions*, 250–251.

47. For more on this document, see Herbert Basser, "The Trial of Jesus," in the *Frank Talmage Memorial*, ed. Barry Walfish, vol. 1 (Haifa: Haifa University Press, 1993), 273–282.

48. Hippolytus, *Ref.* 8.3.25; Irenaeus, *Haer.* 1.24.2, 3.11.3. See also Ignatius of Antioch, *Smyrn.* 2.1, 8.2; *Eph.* 1:1; *Rom.* 6:6; *Trall.* 10.

49. *Gos. Truth* 34.10–38, 36:11–31.

50. *Apoc. Pet.* 83.1–3.

51. *Acts John* 97. See also the *Second Treatise of the Great Seth,* which maintains that it was Simon of Cyrene who was crucified, while Jesus stood by and laughed at those who believe he died on the cross. Similarities between this and later Muslim interpretations of the crucifixion are discussed in Chapter 8.

52. *Gos. Phil.* 64.

53. See Augustine, *Faust.* 14.2–4, for a brief summary of Manichaean teaching on the crucifixion.

54. Iain Gardner and Samuel S. N. Lieu, *Manichaean Texts from the Roman Empire* (Cambridge: Cambridge University Press, 2004), 94–95.

55. Augustine, *Enarrat. Ps.* 140.120; also *Faust.* 20.2–11. This cross of light seems to be confirmed by the Greek Cologne Mani-Codex, discovered in Egypt and dated to the fifth century, which includes some of the teachings of Mani.

56. A cross of light also appears in *Acts John* 98.

57. The fourth-century Alexander of Lycopolis described the way that Christ's crucifixion gave knowledge of this cross of light in his anti-Manichaean treatise. On this topic, see Pieter Willem van der Horst and Jaap Mansfield, *An Alexandrian Platonist against Dualism: Alexander of Lycopolis' Treatise "Critique of the Doctrines of Manichaeus"* (Leiden: Brill, 1974).

58. Hans-Joachim Klimkeit, *Iconography of Religions, Manichaeism, Manichaean Art and Calligraphy* (Leiden: Brill, 1982); and more recently, Zsuzsanna Gulácsi, *Mani's Pictures: The Didactic Images of the Manichaeans from Sasanian Mesopotamia to Uygur Central Asia and Tang-Ming China* (Leiden: Brill, 2015), esp. 385–386.

2. *Signum Crucis*

Epigraph: John Chrysostom, *Hom. Matt.* 76.3, trans. G. Prevost, *Nicene and Post-Nicene Fathers* (hereafter NPNF), ser. 2, 10:459.

1. Matthew's image here could allude to passages in Daniel 7:13, which also mentions a "sign." See also Revelation 1:7 for a similar New Testament image.

2. Cyril of Jerusalem, *Cat.* 15.22.

3. Origen, *Comm. Matt* 10.17. Some editions of Origen's text, however, do not include the section of the manuscript that was discovered in the 1880s, which contains only a Passion narrative.

4. Eusebius, *Hist.* 3.3.2 and 6.12, in which Eusebius cites a letter circulated by Serapion, Bishop of Antioch, who discourages its liturgical use at a neighboring church because he judged it to contain elements compatible with the docetic heresy.

5. *Gos. Pet.* 34–42. On this passage, see Jason Combs, "A Walking, Talking Cross: The Polymorphic Christology of the Gospel of Peter," *Early Christianity* 5 (2014): 198–219.

6. The date is based on its being cited by such writers as Clement of Alexandria and Theophilus of Antioch.

7. *Apoc. Pet.* 1, trans. J. K. Elliott, *The Apocryphal New Testament* (Oxford: Clarendon Press, 1993), 600.

8. *Apoc. Elij.* 87.32; *Epis. Apos.* 16.

9. *Acts John* 97–98; Elliott, *Apocryphal New Testament*, 320.

10. *Acts John* 99; Elliott, *Apocryphal New Testament*, 320.

11. On the tradition of the two Edenic trees and their links to the cross, see F. Young, *Construing the Cross: Type, Sign, Symbol, Word, Action* (Eugene, OR: Cascade Books, 2015), 48–57.

12. *Acts Pet.* 37–39.

13. *Gos. Phil.* 80.

14. Irenaeus, *Haer.* 5.16.3, 5.19.1.

15. Tertullian, *Adv. Jud.* 13. Here Tertullian also cites Psalm 96:10, including the words "from a tree" to the first line, "The Lord reigns!"

16. Cyril of Jerusalem, *Cat.* 13.19, 35, trans. L. P. McCauley, S.J., *The Works of Saint Cyril of Jerusalem*, vol. 2, Fathers of the Church 64 (Washington, DC: Catholic University Press, 1970), 16–17, 28. See also a homily attributed to Hippolytus, Pseudo-Hippolytus, *De Pasch. hom.* 6 (Patrologia Graeca 59.743), cited by Young, *Construing the Cross*, 56, from a translation by J. Danièlou in *Theology of Jewish Christianity* (London: Darton, Longman, and Todd, 1964), 287.

17. Ephrem, *Hymn* 16.9–10 (On Virginity), trans. K. McVey, *Ephrem the Syrian: Hymns* (Mahwah, NJ: Paulist Press, 1989), 331–332.

18. Leo, *Serm.* 57.4, CCL 138A.

19. This tradition is related to medieval legends and visual art that depict the tree planted upon Adam's grave. See discussion in Chapter 6.

20. See Origen, *Comm. Matt.* 27.32; Epiphanius, *Adv. haer.* 46.5; John Chrysostom, *Hom. Jo.* 85.1; and Jerome, *Comm. Matt.* 27.33 and *Comm. Eph.* 5.14.

21. Justin Martyr, *1 Apol.* 55; Tertullian, *Apol.* 12.3, 16.7, and *Nat.* 1.12; *Marc.* 4.20.2–4; Minucius Felix, *Oct.* 29.7–8. See discussion in Chapter 1.

22. Hippolytus, *Antichr.*, 59, trans. author, Patrologia Graeca (hereafter PG) 10.781–783.

23. Gregory of Nyssa, *Or. cat.* 32.

24. Gregory of Nyssa, *In Christ. res. or.* 1 and *Cont. Eun.* 3.3.40. See Gerhard Ladner, "St. Gregory of Nyssa and St. Augustine on the Symbolism of the Cross," in *Images and Ideas in the Middle Ages: Selected Studies in History and Art* (Rome: Edizioni di Storia e Letteratura, 1983), 197–208.

25. Augustine, *Serm.* 165.3–5. See also Augustine, *Doctr. chr.* 2.62; *Ep.* 140; *Ep.* 155; *Enarrat. Ps.* 103.1.14; *Tract. Ev. Jo.* 118.5; *Serm.* 53 and 165.

26. John Chrysostom, *Cont. Jud. et Gent.* 9, trans. author, PG 48.824–825.

27. Jack Finegan, *Archeology of the New Testament* (Princeton, NJ: Princeton University Press, 1992), discusses rabbinic evidence for anointing of Jewish priests with an X on the forehead, 346–348.

28. Tertullian, *Marc.* 3.22.

29. Origen, *Sel. Ezech.* 9.

30. E.g., Cyprian, *Test.* 2.22.

31. Augustine, *Catech.* 20.4.

32. Many of the following examples discussed by Carol Neuman de Vegvar, "*In Hoc Signo:* The Cross on Secular Objects and the Process of Conversion," in *Cross and Culture in Anglo-Saxon England*, ed. Karen L. Jolly, Catherine E. Karkow, and Sarah Larratt Keefer (Morgantown: West Virginia University Press, 2007), 79–98.

33. Tertullian, *Cor.* 3, trans. author, CCL 2:1048. See also Prudentius, *Cath.* 7.

34. From the Emperor Julian's treatise *Against the Galileans*, excerpted in Cyril of Alexandria, *Cont. Jul.* 1.57.

35. Athanasius, *Vit. Ant.* 13, 35, and 80. See also Athanasius, *Inc.* 29, 47, 53, which describes the defeat of demons with the cross sign.

36. Lactantius, *Inst.* 4.27.

37. Epiphanius, *Ep. Theod.*, in *Art of the Byzantine Empire: Sources and Documents*, trans. Cyril Mango (Toronto: University of Toronto, 1986), 41–42.

38. Cyril of Jerusalem, *Cat.* 4.14.

39. Ibid., 13.22, 36.

40. John Chrysostom, *Hom. 1 Cor.* 12.13–14. Here find a long discussion of different kinds of amulets and traditional practices.

41. John Chrysostom, *Hom. Matt.* 54.7.

42. Augustine, *Enarrat. Ps.* 50.1.

43. Augustine, *Ep.* 158.2.

44. Augustine, *Tract. Ev. Jo.* 118.5, cited in Neuman de Vegvar, "*In Hoc Signo,*" 81.

45. Ibid.

46. Cyprian, *Test.* 2.22.

47. See, e.g., Justin Martyr, *Dial.* 19, where he declares that only Christian circumcision (i.e., baptism) was of any value (without mentioning the cross sign, however).

48. Cyril of Jerusalem, *Cat.* 5.6, trans., slightly adapted from McCauley, *Works of Saint Cyril of Jerusalem*, 1.142–43.

49. Augustine, *Serm.* 160.1, 6, 260A.

50. Cyril of Jerusalem, *Myst.* 4.7, where he also compares it to the engraving of a signet.

51. Gregory of Nyssa, *Diem lum.* 15. See also Basil of Caesarea, *Bapt.* 4.

52. For example Minucius Felix, *Oct.* 19; Tertullian, *Praescr.* 40.

53. John Chrysostom, *Bapt. inst.* 11.27; 22. See also *Bapt. inst.* 10.16 on the brand of the sheep, as compared to the tattoo of a soldier.

54. Theodore Mopsuestia, *Hom. bapt.* 2.17–18.

55. Ambrose, *Sac.* 6–7.

56. Tacitus, *Ann.* 15.44.4.

57. Tertullian, *Praescr.* 36—Paul was beheaded (he adds). Peter's martyrdom by crucifixion (as well as Paul's beheading) also is mentioned in Eusebius, *Hist.* 25.5–8.

58. *Acts Pet.* 37–38.

59. Eusebius of Caesarea denounces the *Acts of Andrew* as heretical, *Hist.* 3.25.6; also Epiphanius, *Adv. haer.* 1.2, 2.47, 61.1, 63.2. Augustine associates the story of Andrew's crucifixion with Manichaeans in *Faust.* 14.1 and 30.4.

60. *Acts of Andrew*, 54, trans. adapted from M. R. James in Elliott, *Apocryphal New Testament*, 262.

61. Elliott, *Apocryphal New Testament*, 272–283.

62. Francis Dvornik, *The Idea of Apostolicity in Byzantium and the Legend of the Apostle Andrew* (Cambridge, MA: Harvard University Press, 1948).

63. *Act. Pionii*, 21.

64. *Acts of the Martyrs of Lyon and Vienne*, included in Eusebius, *Hist.* 5.1.41.

65. Finegan, *Archeology of the New Testament*, 356–374. L. Y. Rahmani, in *A Catalogue of Jewish Ossuaries in the Collections of the State of Israel* (Tel Aviv: Israel Antiquities Authority, 1994), holds some of them to be later Christian additions to Jewish ossuaries.

66. William Holladay, "The Herculaneum Cross," *Journal of the American Academy of Religion* 19 (1951): 16–19; Finegan, *Archaeology*, 374.

67. A recent study by Bruce Longenecker, *The Cross before Constantine* (Minneapolis: Fortress Press, 2015), considers many of these examples more positively than this author would do. However, Longenecker's point, that there may have been more early Christian crosses than scholars generally have allowed, may be valid.

68. Larry Hurtado, "The Staurogram in Early Christian Manuscripts: The Earliest Visual Reference to the Crucified Jesus?" in *New Testament Manuscripts: Their Texts and Their World*, ed. Thomas J. Kraus and Tobias Nicklas (Leiden: Brill, 2006), 207–226.

69. Jeffrey Spier, *Late Antique and Early Christian Gems* (Wiesbaden: Richert, 2007), 30–34, 41–52.

70. *Inscriptiones Christianae Urbis Romae* 5, no. 12889.

71. Socrates, *Hist.* 5.17, trans. G. Prevost, NPNF, ser. 2, 2:127–128. See also Sozomen, *Hist.* 7.15.

72. Clement of Alexandria, *Paed.* 3.11. See Paul Corby Finney, "Images on Finger Rings and Early Christian Art," *Dumbarton Oaks Papers* 41 (1987): 181–186.

73. William Baines, "Rotas-Sator Square: A New Investigation," *New Testament Studies* 33 (1987): 469–473.

3. *Inventio Crucis*

Epigraph: Paulinus of Nola, *Ep.* 31.6, trans. P. G. Walsh, *Letters of Paulinus of Nola,* vol. 2 (Westminster, ME: Newman Press, 1967), 132–133.

1. The christogram also appears on domestic objects, personal jewelry, and liturgical vessels, as well as in the decoration of baptisteries and fonts, an allusion to the overcoming of death through the Christian ritual of initiation.

2. Lactantius, *Mort.* 44.

3. Eusebius, *Vit. Const.*1.28–31. Note that Eusebius does not mention the cross vision in his *Ecclesiastical History,* written before Constantine's death (probably before 326).

4. The term *labarum* appears to be specific to Constantine; before his time, the term for a military standard was *vexillum.* On this object, see Henri Grégoire, "L'étymologie de 'Labarum,'" *Byzantion* 4 (1927–28): 477–482; and Michael Rostotovtzeff, "Vexillum and Victory," *Journal of Roman Studies* 32 (1942): 92–106.

5. Historians of the early fifth century give slightly varied versions of Constantine's visions. Following Eusebius, both Sozomen, *Hist.* 1.3, and Socrates, *Hist.* 1.2, say that Constantine saw a cross encircled by light at midday and a dream in which Christ appeared with the pattern of the labarum at night.

6. Eusebius, *Vit. Const.* 1.32.

7. Ibid., 2.7.

8. Harold A. Drake, *In Praise of Constantine: A Historical Study and New Translation of Eusebius's Tricennial Orations* (Berkeley: University of California Press, 1976), 73–77.

9. See Jeffrey Spier, *Late Antique and Early Christian Gems* (Wiesbaden: Richert, 2007), 30–34.

10. This Apollo vision recounted in the anonymous *Pan. Lat.* 7(6).21.3–6. On the coinage, see Patrick Bruun, "The Victorious Signs of Constantine: A Reappraisal," *Numismatic Chronicle* 157 (1997): 41–59.

11. Eusebius, *Vit. Const.* 3.3. See also Robert Grigg, "Constantine the Great and the Cult without Images," *Viator* 8 (1977): 1–32.

12. Eusebius, *Vit. Const.* 3.49.

13. Ibid., 1.40.

14. Sozomen, *Hist.* 1.8.13.

15. Cyril of Jerusalem, *Ep. Const.* 3.

16. Gregory of Nazianzus, *Or. c. Jul.* 5.4–7.

17. Rufinus, *Hist.* 10.40.

18. Cyril of Jerusalem, *Cat.* 13.4. See also *Cat.* 4.10 and 10.19.

19. Eusebius, *Vit. Const.* 3.41–43.

20. Ibid., 3.30.

21. Ibid., 3.25–29.

22. Jan Willem Drijvers, *Helena Augusta: The Mother of Constantine the Great and the Legend of Her Finding of the True Cross* (Leiden: Brill, 1992), 84–85; Harold A. Drake, "Eusebius on the True Cross," *Journal of Ecclesiastical History* 36 (1985): 1–22.

23. For more discussion of these theories, see Stephen Borgehammar, *How the Holy Cross Was Found* (Stockholm: Almquist and Wiksell, 1991), chap. 6, "The Silence of Eusebius," 93–122, and his speculative conclusion that Eusebius is not actually silent about this after all. See also P. W. L. Walker, *Holy City, Holy Places?: Christian Attitudes to Jerusalem and the Holy Land in the Fourth Century* (Oxford: Oxford University Press, 1990), 128–129.

24. Pilgrim of Bordeaux, *Itin.* 593.

25. Ambrose, *Obit. Theo.* 40–51. Ambrose says he sees the gift of the nails as fulfilling a prophecy of Zechariah (14:20): "What is placed in the mouths of horses shall be holy." Jerome, *Comm. Zech.* 3.14.20, expresses skepticism about the nails. Ambrose is careful to insist that Helena did not actually venerate the wood because to do so would have been pagan idolatry; rather, she intended to adore Christ who had been crucified upon it. On Helena's presentations of cross fragments and nails to Constantine, see discussion later in this chapter.

26. John Chrysostom, *Hom. Jo.* 85. He adds that thieves' crosses would not have had titles.

27. Rufinus, *Hist.* 10.7–8.

28. Borgehammar, *Holy Cross,* 11–17.

29. Paulinus of Nola, *Ep.* 31.5–6.

30. Sulpicius Severus, *Chron.* 2.34.

31. Sozomen, *Hist.* 2.1; Socrates, *Hist.* 1.17; and Theodoret, *Hist.* 1.17.

32. Sozomen, *Hist.* 2.1.

33. On this topic, see H. J. W. Drijvers and Jan Willem Drijvers, *The Finding of the True Cross: The Judas Kyriakos Legend in Syriac* (Leuven: Peeters, 1997).

34. Gregory of Tours, *Lib. Hist.* 1.35.

35. See Jan Willem Drijvers, "The Protonike Legend and the *Doctrine Addai,*" *Studia Patristica* 33 (1996): 517–523.

36. *Golden Legend (Legenda aurea),* chap. 64, covers the story of the finding of the Cross.

37. The most comprehensive work on the legend of the discovery is by Barbara Baert, *A Heritage of Holy Wood: The Legend of the True Cross in Text and Image,* trans. Lee Preedy (Leiden: Brill, 2004). Another version is included in Syriac Dormition of the Virgin literature. See Stephen Shoemaker, "A Peculiar Version of the *Inventio Crucis* in the Early Syriac Dormition Traditions," *Studia Patristica* 41 (2009): 75–81.

38. Egeria, *Itin.* 48.

39. Ibid., 37.2.

40. Ibid., 24.7, 25.9, 27.6, 37 passim.

41. Ibid., 25.8–9.

42. Paulinus of Nola, *Ep.* 31.6. He himself receives one of these gifts; see discussion later in this chapter and *Ep.* 32.11.

43. Jerome, *Ep.* 108.9.

44. Piacenza Pilgrim, *Itin.* 20.

45. Egeria, *Itin.* 37.2.

46. On the subject of the long-lost Constantine statue, see Garth Fowden, "Constantine's Porphyry Column: The Earliest Literary Allusions," *Journal of Roman Studies* 81 (1991): 119–131; John Wortley, "The Legend of Constantine the Relic Provider," in *Studies on the Cult of Relics in Byzantium up to 1204* (Aldershot: Ashgate, 2009), 492–496. Also see discussion later in this chapter.

47. Rufinus, *Hist.* 10.7–8; Socrates, *Hist.* 1.17; Sozomen, *Hist.* 2.1; and Theodoret, *Hist.* 1.17, all mention the nails incorporated into Constantine's bridal bits and helmet. Sozomen implies that the headpiece was for the horse, not for Constantine. Only Socrates mentions the relics' being inserted into Constantine's statue in Constantinople, while the others say that the cross relics simply went to Constantine (Sozomen, Rufinus) or the palace (Theodoret). Both Sozomen and Theodoret cite the prophecy of Zechariah, perhaps influenced by Ambrose (see note 25 in this chapter).

48. Gregory of Tours, *Mart.* 8.

49. Cyril of Jerusalem, *Cat.* 13.4.

50. Paulinus of Nola, *Ep.* 31.1–2, 32.11.

51. Ibid., 31.6.

52. Gregory of Tours, *Mart.* 5. See Lynn Jones, "Perceptions of Byzantium: Radegund of Poitiers and Relics of the True Cross," in *Byzantine Images and Their Afterlives: Essays in Honor of Annemarie Weyl Carr*, ed. L. Jones (Burlington, VT: Ashgate, 2014), 105–124.

53. See discussion on hymns in Chapter 5.

54. Gregory I, *Ep.* 14.12.

55. Gregory of Tours, *Mart.* 5. In chapters 6 and 7, Gregory also recounts miracles associated with the lance, the crown of thorns, and Christ's tunic.

56. Procopius, *Bell. Pers.* 2.11.14–30. See further discussion in Chapter 5.

57. Gregory of Nyssa, *Vit. Mac.* 30.

58. See discussion in Chapter 2.

59. De Blaauw, "Jerusalem in Rome," following the *Lib. pont.* 22 (Silvester).

60. Klein, "Constantine, Helena, and the Cult of the True Cross," 37.

61. *Lib. pont.* 34 (Silvester) asserts that the Constantine built the basilica in the Sessorian Palace, named it "Jerusalem," and put a gold and gemmed casket containing some of the holy wood there.

62. Modern historians have suggested that Leo received the relic from Juvenal on the basis of his reference to the cross in *Ep.* 138 (to Juvenal), but the text is not overly clear on that point. On Hilarius and Symmachus, see *Lib Pont.* 48 (Hilarius) and 53 (Symmachus).

63. See Chapter 5 for more discussion of this Holy Week ritual.

64. The authenticity of these relics has been tested, most recently by a team from the Università di Roma, "Roma Tre," which dated the titulus to the early Middle Ages. See the publication of their results in an article by Francesco Bella and Carlo Azzi, "C Dating of the 'Titulus Crucis,'" in *Radiocarbon* 44, no. 3 (2002): 685–689.

65. The christogram alone also appeared on coinage of mid-fourth-century emperors, in particular on the reverses of coins issued by the "usurper" emperors, Magnentius and Decentius, possibly as an attempt to appropriate the iconography of the Constantinian dynasty.

66. Justin Martyr, *1 Apol.* 55; Tertullian, *Apol.* 16.7, *Nat.* 1.12; Minucius Felix, *Oct.* 29.7.

67. See Chapter 4.

4. *Crux Abscondita*

Epigraph: Athanasius, *Inc.* 26, trans. Archibald Robinson, NPNF, ser. 2, 4:50.

1. Jeffrey Spier argues for an earlier date—the early fourth century, on the basis that their engraving, letterform, and inscriptions compare with other Christian gems from eastern workshops of around 300. See *Picturing the Bible: The Earliest Christian Art* (New Haven, CT: Yale University Press, 2007), 73–74. See also Jeffrey Spier, *Late Antique and Early Christian Gems* (Wiesbaden: Reichert Verlag, 2007), 73–75.

2. Felicity Harley, "The Constanza Carnelian and the Development of Crucifixion Iconography in Late Antiquity," in *Gems of Heaven: Recent Research on Engraved Gemstones in Late Antiquity, c. AD 200–600*, ed. Chris Entwhistle and Noel Adams (London: British Museum, 2011), 214–220.

3. Other gems dated to the same approximate time period make use of the *tau*-shaped cross without a corpus. See Spier, *Late Antique and Early Christian Gems*, 73–75.

4. Ibid., 74.

5. Ibid. 74–75; Harley, "Constanza Carnelian," 217–218.

6. Spier, *Late Antique and Early Christian Gems*, 178 (cat. no. X94). See also Francesco Carotta with Arne Eickenberg, "Orpheus Bakkikos—the Missing Cross," originally published as "Orfeo Báquico—La Cruz Desaparecida," *Isidorianum* 35 (2009): 179–217; Miguel Herrero de Jáuregui, *Orphism and Christianity in Late Antiquity* (Berlin: De Gruyter, 2010), esp. 122–126.

7. See Clement of Alexandria, *Protr.* 1, where he calls Christ a singer who takes human souls, or 7, where he says that Orpheus sings about the Word. Early Christian images of Orpheus in Christian contexts (so-called Christ-Orpheus figures) are found in the Catacombs of Priscilla, Domitilla, and Peter and Marcellinus, and on a number of sarcophagi as well as at least one ivory pyxis. See Paul Corby Finney, "Orpheus-David: A Connection in Iconography between Greco-Roman Judaism and Early Christianity," *Journal of Jewish Art* 5 (1978): 6–15.

8. For more on this object and additional bibliography, see Carotta, "Orfeo Bakkikos"; de Jáuregui, *Orphism and Christianity in Late Antiquity,* 122–126, esp. 123n83.

9. Pliny the Elder, *Nat.* 28.11.46.

10. Lucan, *Bell.* 6.543–549; Apuleius, *Met.* 3.17.4–5. See also Cook, *Crucifixion in the Mediterranean World,* 130, 336; Chapman, *Ancient Jewish and Christian Perceptions of Crucifixion,* 182–185 (with evidence also from the Cairo Geniza).

11. Recently, Jutta Dresken-Weiland proposed that a fourth-century sarcophagus fragment, now in the Vatican Museum, might show witnesses to the crucifixion. See Dresken-Weiland, "A New Iconography in the Face of Death? A Sarcophagus Fragment with a Possible Crucifixion Scene in the Museo Pio Cristiano," in *The Face of the Dead in the Early Christian World,* ed. Ivan Foletti (Vielly: Studia Artium Medievalium Brunensia, 2013), 133–148.

12. For a reading of the classical prototypes of this image, see Felicity Harley McGowan (same as F. Harley, note 2 above), "The Maskell Passion Ivories and Greco-Roman Art," in *Envisioning Christ on the Cross: Ireland and the Early Medieval West,* ed. Juliet Mullins, Jenifer Ní Ghrádaigh, and Richard Hawtree (Dublin: Four Courts Press, 2013), 13–33.

13. Tertullian and Minucius Felix both note that the prayer stance recalls the image of crucifixion; Tertullian, *Orat.* 14; Minucius Felix, *Oct.* 29.8.

14. For a different interpretation, see Allyson Everingham Schekler and Mary Joan Winn Leith, "The Crucifixion Conundrum and the Santa Sabina Doors," *Harvard Theological Review* 103 (2010): 67–88. These authors also compare the three figures (Christ and the two thieves) to the iconography of three youths in the fiery furnace.

15. Gregory of Tours, *Mart.* 22, in *Gregory of Tours: Glory of the Martyrs,* trans. Raymond Van Dam (Liverpool: Liverpool University Press, 1988), 41. For some theories about the date and context of this image and this story, see K. Wessel, "Der nackte Crucifixus von Narbonne," *Rivista di archeological cristiana* 43 (1967): 333–345.

16. Mary's veil is mentioned in Pseudo-Bonaventure, *Medit.* 78. The *Gospel of Nicodemus* (or *Acts of Pilate*) 10.1 mentions the guards covering Jesus with a linen cloth *(perizoma).*

17. Recall the story of the oil from the Piacenza Pilgrim, *Itin.* 20; see Chapter 3.

18. Gary Vikan, *Early Byzantine Pilgrimage Art* (Washington, DC: Dumbarton Oaks Byzantine Collection Publications, 2010), 38; Robert Ousterhout, *The Blessings of Pilgrimage* (Urbana: University of Illinois Press, 1990); Kurt Weitzman, "Loca Sancta and the Representational Arts of Palestine," *Dumbarton Oaks Papers* 28 (1974): 31–55; André Grabar, *Ampoules de Terre Sainte* (Paris: C. Klincksieck, 1958).

19. The pilgrimage function of these objects is emphasized in their iconography because the women coming to the tomb often carry censers rather than ointment jars and the tomb itself appears to depict the aedicule at the Anastasis Rotunda of the Holy Sepulcher rather than a reconstruction of Jesus's actual tomb.

20. See the discussion of the cross as tree of life in Chapter 2.

21. Gary Vikan, *Byzantine Pilgrimage Art*, 39–40.

22. ACCIPE QUAESO A DOMINA MEA REGINA MUNDI HOC VEXILLUM CRUCIS QUOD TIBI PASCHALIS EPISCOPUS OPTULIT. See Erik Thunø, *Image and Relic: Mediating the Sacred in Early Medieval Rome* (Rome: Bretschneider, 2002), 25–51.

23. Glenn Peers, *Sacred Shock: Framing Visual Experience in Byzantium* (University Park: Penn State University Press, 2004), 12–34; Cynthia Hahn, *Strange Beauty: Issues in the Making and Meaning of Reliquaries, 400–ca. 1204* (University Park: Penn State University Press, 2012), 81–84. On the cross as phylactery, see Chapter 3.

24. Peers, *Sacred Shock*, 24–25, for an example of devotional prayer to such a crucifix.

25. John A. Cotsonis, *Byzantine Figural Processional Crosses*, vol. 10 (Washington, DC: Dumbarton Oaks Byzantine Collection Publications, 1994).

26. Bede, *Ecc. Hist.* 1.25.

27. Cotsonis, *Byzantine Processional Crosses*, 40–46.

28. Anna Kartsonis, *Anastasis: The Making of an Image* (Cambridge: Cambridge University Press, 1986), 40–63; also Anna Kartsonis, "The Emancipation of the Crucifixion," in *Byzance et les images: Cycle dé conférences organisé au musée du Louvre par le Service culturel du 5 octobre au 7*, ed. André Guillou and Jannic Durand (Paris: La Documentation Française, 1994), 166–168.

29. See examples of these scenes in Chapter 6.

30. Regarding Leo III's attitude toward holy images, see the work of Leslie Brubaker, *Inventing Byzantine Iconoclasm* (London: Bristol Classical Press, 2012), 28–29; also Leslie Brubaker and John F. Heldon, *Byzantium in the Iconoclast Era, c. 680–850: A History* (Cambridge: Cambridge University Press, 2011), 128–135. Older works on the controversy often take Theophanes's history as factually accurate.

31. Interestingly, this nonrepresentational style would have been consistent with the church's original decoration in Justinian's reign, as the surviving sixth-century mosaics seem only to consist of plain crosses and simple, geometric designs.

32. Brubaker, *Inventing Byzantine Iconoclasm*, 35–36.

33. The iconoclasts' use of the cross and its theological and political implications are summarized in Charles Barber, *Figure and Likeness: On the Limits of Representation in Byzantine Iconoclasm* (Princeton, NJ: Princeton University Press, 2002), 83–105.

34. Brubaker and Heldon, *Byzantium in the Iconoclast Era*, 141–143.

35. John of Damascus, *Orat.* 1.54–55, 2.19; *Fide* 4.16.

36. See, e.g., Theodore the Studite, *Refutation of the Iconoclasts*, 1.15, 2.16. On the argument for the superiority of the crucifix, see Charles Barber, "The Body within the Frame: A Use of Word and Image in Iconoclasm," *Word and Image* 9 (1993): 140–153.

37. See translated excerpt in Mango, *Art of the Byzantine Empire*, 176.

38. Kathleen Corrigan, "Text and Image on an Icon of the Crucifixion at Mount Sinai," in *The Sacred Image East and West*, ed. Robert Ousterhout and Leslie Brubaker (Urbana: University of Illinois Press, 1995), 45–62.

39. E. J. Tinsley, "The Coming of a Dead and Naked Christ," *Religion* 2 (1972): 24–36; Peter G. Moore, "Cross and Crucifixion in Christian Iconography: A reply to E. J. Tinsley," *Religion* 4 (1974): 104–113.

40. Athanasius, *Inc.* 21–26. See also Lactantius, *Inst.* 4.26, in which he makes a similar statement that Christ needed to be lifted up on the cross to be conspicuous, so that all the nations should see his majesty and his outstretched arms to embrace the world.

5. *Adoratio Crucis*

Epilogue: Ps. Theophilus, *Sermon on the Cross and the Good Thief*, trans. and discussion of the full text in Alin Suciu, "Ps.-Theophili Alexandrini Sermo de Cruce et Latrone (CPG 2622): Edition of M595 with Parallels and Translation," *Zeitschrift für Antikes Christentum* 16 (2012): 181–225.

1. Eusebius, *Vit. Const.* 1.30–31. See earlier discussion of this object in Chapter 3.

2. Eusebius, *Vit. Const.* 3.49.

3. Egeria, *Itin.* 24 and 27 (Sundays), 36–37 (Good Friday). Text and trans., John Wilkinson, *Egeria's Travels* (Warminster: Aris and Phillips, 1981), 124, 128–129, 135–138. Note: I have chosen not to capitalize terms like "Before the Cross," although Wilkinson does.

4. Jerome, *Ep.* 108.9.

5. John Wilkinson, *Jerusalem Pilgrims* (Oxford: Oxbow Books, 2002), 93. See a close reading of this text with a different conclusion by Christine Milner, "*'Lignum Vitae'* or *'Crux Gemmata'?* The Cross of Golgotha in the Early Byzantine Period," *Byzantine and Modern Greek Studies* 12 (1996): 86.

6. See discussion in Chapter 4.

7. Christa Belting-Ihm, *Die Programme der christlichen Apsismalerei*, 4.–8. Jahrhundert (Wiesbaden: Franz Steiner Verlag, 1960), 90–91, 194, fig. 24.

8. Theophanes, *Chron.* 86. The date of 421 is suggested by K. Holum, "Pulcheria's Crusade AD 421–22 and the Ideology of Imperial Victory," *Greek, Roman and Byzantine Studies* 18 (1977): 163n46. See the contrary arguments by Milner, who asserts that Theophanes's story is a medieval fabrication; "*'Lignum Vitae,'*" 77–99.

9. Milner, "*'Lignum Vitae,'*" 97. The story of Heraclius's rescue of the cross from the Persians is recounted later in this chapter.

10. See Chapter 3.

11. Bianca Kühnel, *From the Earthly to the Heavenly Jerusalem: Representations of Christian Art in the First Millennium* (Freiburg: Herder, 1987), 187n34.

12. Paulinus of Nola, *Ep.* 32.10–11.

13. Hugo Brandenburg, *Ancient Churches of Rome from the Fourth to Seventh Century: The Dawn of Christian Architecture in the West* (Turnhout: Brepols, 2004), 200–213.

14. See Chapter 4.

15. Deborah Mauskopf Deliyannis, *Ravenna in Late Antiquity* (Cambridge: Cambridge University Press, 2010), 74–84.

16. For example, Otto von Simson, *Sacred Fortress: Byzantine Art and Statecraft in Ravenna* (Princeton, NJ: Princeton University Press, 1978), 42–43; André Grabar, *Martyrium Recherches sur le culte des reliques et l'art Chrétien antique II: Iconographie* (Paris: Collège de France, 1946), 111; Gillian Mackie, *Early Christian Chapels in the West: Decoration, Function, and Patronage* (Toronto: University of Toronto Press, 2003), 181.

17. By contrast, Gillian Mackie, "New Light on the So-Called Saint Lawrence Panel at the Mausoleum of Galla Placidia, Ravenna," *Gesta* 26 (1990): 54–60, identifies him as Vincent of Saragossa.

18. Egeria, *Itin.* 37.1.

19. *Brev.* c.

20. *Lib. pont.* 53.7.

21. Agnellus, *Max.* 37.

22. In the Middle Ages, similar processional crosses, richly encrusted with precious stones and even ancient cameos, came to be known as the crosses of Desiderius (ca. 760) and Lothair (ca. 1000).

23. Egeria, *Itin.* 48.1–49.3.

24. *Armenian Lectionary*, 67–68.

25. Noted in Louis van Tongeren, *Exaltation of the Cross: Toward the Origins of the Feast of the Cross and the Meaning of the Cross in Early Medieval Liturgy* (Leuven: Peeters, 2000), 18.

26. Ibid., 50–55.

27. *Lib. pont.* 86.10.

28. On this story, see Chapter 3.

29. In the Greek text, this is identified as the third day of the third month, which was transmitted into Latin as *quinto nonarum maiorum*, as the western liturgical year began in the month of March. See Stephen Borgehammar, *How the Holy Cross Was Found: From Event to Medieval Legend* (Stockholm: Almqvist and Wiskell, 1991), 271.

30. *Lib. pont.* 31.

31. Egeria, *Itin.* 36–37.

32. Paulinus of Nola, *Ep.* 31.6.

33. Irénée-Henri Dalmais, "L'Adoration de la Croix," *La Maison-Dieu* 45 (1956): 77.

34. Gregory of Tours, *Glor. mart.* 1.5.

35. Louis van Tongeren, "Imagining the Cross on Good Friday: Rubric, Ritual and Relic in Early Medieval Roman Gallican and Hispanic Liturgical Traditions," in *Envisioning Christ on the Cross: Ireland and the Early Medieval West*, ed. Juliet Mullins, Jenifer Ní Ghrádaigh, and Richard Hawtree (Dublin: Four Courts Press, 2013), 34–51.

36. Patrick Regan, "Veneration of the Cross," *Worship* 52 (1978): 4.

37. See discussion in Chapter 7.

38. Louis van Tongeren, "A Sign of Resurrection on Good Friday: The Role of the People in the Good Friday Liturgy until 1000," in *Omnes Circumadstantes: Contributions towards a History of the Role of the People in the Liturgy Presented to Herman Wegman*, ed. Charles Caspers and Manfred Schneides (Leuven: Peeters, 1990), 101–120; also Regan, "Veneration," 6.

39. Amalarius of Metz, *Lib. off.* 1.14.10.

40. Pseudo-Alcuin, *Div. off. lib.* 28. Regan's work includes these texts to make this argument; "Veneration," 12.

41. Summarized effectively (with primary sources noted) by B. Baert, *Heritage of Holy Wood*, 149–152.

42. Anatole Frolow, "La Vrai Croix et les expeditions d'Héraclius en Perse," *Revue des Études Byzantines* 11 (1953): 89–105, esp. 97–98.

43. Hrabanus Maurus, *Hom.* 70. More discussion of works of Hrabanus Maurus are found in Chapter 7.

44. On these other feasts, see Joseph Hallit, "La croix dans le rite byzantine: Histoire et théologie," *Parole de l'orient* 3 (1972): 261–311; esp. 286–302.

45. Other dates in the Orthodox calendar include May 7 (a commemoration of the day when the cross appeared in the sky above Jerusalem in 351). See Hallit, "La croix dans le rite byzantine," 286n114.

46. Holger Klein, "Constantine, Helena, and the Cult of the True Cross in Constantinople," in *Byzance et les reliques du Christ*, ed. Jannic Durand and Bernard Flusin (Paris: Monographies du Centre d'histoire et civilisation de Byzance, 2004), 31–59.

47. John Wortley, "The Wood of the True Cross," in *Studies on the Cult of Relics in Byzantium up to 1204* (Farnham, UK: Ashgate, 2009), 12.

48. See Arculf's story earlier in the chapter. The account is preserved in both Adamnanus, *De locis sanctis* I, v. 1; Bede, *Ecc. hist.* 5.15. See Wortley, "Wood of the True Cross," 6, 12.

49. See discussion of this episode in Chapter 7. Also Steven Runciman, *A History of the Crusades*, vol. 1, *The First Crusade and the Foundation of the Kingdom of Jerusalem* (Cambridge: Cambridge University Press, 1951), 294.

50. Robert de Clari, *La Prise de Constantinople*, as cited in Wortley, "Wood of the True Cross," 18.

51. The dispersion of the True Cross is discussed in Wortley, "Wood of the True Cross," 18–19.

6. *Carmina Crucis*

Epigraph: Venantius Fortunatus, *Sing, My Tongue of the Engagement*, Peter G. Walsh, ed. and trans., *One Hundred Latin Hymns: Ambrose to Aquinas* (Cambridge, MA: Harvard University Press, 2012), 97.

1. Joseph Szövérffy, *Hymns of the Holy Cross: An Annotated Edition with Introduction* (Leiden: Brill, 1976).

2. Paulinus of Nola, *Carm.* 19.724–730, trans. author, *Corpus Scriptorum Ecclesiasticorum Latinorum* (hereafter CSEL) 29:143.

3. Latin text in Hartel, Cyprian, *Opera* 3.3.305–308, and attributed by E. Dekkers, *Clavis,* no. 1458 to "Victorinus Poeta" and roughly dated "saec. V?."

4. See the discussion of this motif in early Christian texts, Chapter 2.

5. In Cyprian, *Carm.* 5, trans. author, CSEL 3.3.305. See translation of the full text in Carolinne White, *Early Christian Latin Poets* (London: Routledge, 2000), 136–139.

6. Romanos the Melodist, *Kontakion* 22.3.16, in *Sacred Song from the Byzantine Pulpit, Romanos the Melodist,* trans. R. J. Schork (Gainesville: University of Florida Press 1995), 133.

7. Gregory of Tours's account of Radegund and the True Cross is in his history of the Franks *(Hist. Lib.)* 10. It appears also in Venantius Fortunatus, *De vita Sanctae Radegundis.* See the essay of Jennifer C. Edwards, "Their Cross to Bear: Controversy and the Relic of the True Cross in Poitiers," *Essays in Medieval Studies* 24 (2007): 65–77; Isabel Moreira, "Provisatrix optima: St. Radegund of Poitiers's Relic Petitions to the East," *Journal of Medieval History* 19 (1993): 285–305.

8. Two of the six were, apparently, *carmina figurata,* and so possibly not meant to be orally delivered (chanted) = the "only work on the page." On the ordering of these hymns and their liturgical context, see Inge B. Millfull, "Hymns to the Cross: Contexts for the Reception of *Vexilla regis proderunt,*" in *The Place of the Cross in Anglo-Saxon England,* ed. Catherine Karkov, Sarah Larratt Keefer, and Karen Louise Jolly (Woodbridge: Boydell and Brewer, 2006), 43–57.

9. Venantius Fortunatus, *Sing, My Tongue of the Engagement,* 8–10, trans. Peter Walsh, *One Hundred Latin Hymns,* 99–101. Venantius's text was influential on Thomas Aquinas's later version of the *Pange lingua,* which is more often sung during the transfer of the eucharist to the altar of repose on Holy Thursday.

10. Venantius Fortunatus, *Vexilla regis prodeunt* 1, 5–7, trans. P. G. Walsh, *One Hundred Latin Poems,* 101–103.

11. Bonaventure, *Tree of Life,* in *Bonaventure: The Soul's Journey into God; The Tree of Life; The Life of St. Francis,* trans. Ewert Cousins (New York: Paulist Press, 1978), 121. The original poem is quoted in other works of Bonaventure and has been reconstructed in the critical edition, *S. Bonaventurae opera omnia,* 8, 86–87. On Bonaventure's imagery see Rab Hatfield, "The Tree of Life and the Holy Cross: Franciscan Spirituality in the Trecento and the Quattrocento," in *Christianity and the Renaissance, Image and Religious Imagination in the Quattrocento,* ed. Timothy Verdon and John Henderson (Syracuse, NY: Syracuse University Press, 1990), 132–159.

12. Christopher Irvine, "The Iconography of the Cross as the Green Tree," in *The Edinburgh Companion to the Bible and the Arts,* ed. Stephen Prickett (Edinburgh: Edinburgh University Press, 2014), 195–207.

13. See Chapter 4. The oil most likely had been poured over a fragment of the wood of the cross.

14. This object is widely published, but most comprehensive is Elizabeth Parker and Charles T. Little, *The Cloisters Cross: Its Art and Meaning* (New York: Metropolitan Museum of Art, 1994).

15. *Ecclesiam Cristi viti similabimus isti quam lex arentem set crux facit esse virentem.*

16. Christopher Chase, "'Christ III,' 'The Dream of the Rood,' and Early Christian Passion Piety," *Viator* 11 (1980): 11–33; Graham Holderness, "The Sign of the Cross: Culture and Belief in The Dream of the Rood," *Literature and Theology: An International Journal of Theory, Criticism, and Culture* 11, no. 4 (1997): 347–375.

17. Holderness, "The Sign of the Cross," 360.

18. "Dream of the Rood," in *Anglo-Saxon Spirituality: Selected Writings,* trans. Robert Boenig (New York: Paulist Press, 2000), 262–263.

19. John V. Fleming, "The Dream of the Rood and Anglo-Saxon Monasticism," *Traditio* 22 (1966): 43–72.

20. Helen Roe, "The Irish High Cross: Morphology and Iconography," *Journal of the Royal Society of Antiquaries of Ireland* 95 (1965): 213–226; also Martin Werner, "On the Origin and Form of the Irish High Cross," *Gesta* 29 (1990): 98–110. On the wreathed christogram, see Chapter 3.

21. The identification of the figure as Christ in majesty has been convincingly argued by Paul Mayvaert, "Reclaiming the Apocalypse *Majestas* Panel for the Ruthwell Cross," in *Insular and Anglo-Saxon Art and Thought in the Early Medieval Period,* ed. Colum Hourihane (University Park: Penn State University Press, 2001), 109–132.

22. Éamonn Ó Carragáin, *Ritual and the Rood: Liturgical Images and the Poems of the Dream of the Rood Tradition* (London: University of Toronto Press, 2005).

23. Paul Mayvaert, "A New Perspective on the Ruthwell Cross: *Ecclesia* and *Vita Monastica,*" in *The Ruthwell Cross,* ed. Brendan Cassidy (Princeton, NJ: Princeton University Press, 1992), 95–166, on the problem of the reconstruction.

24. Parallel texts in Gary Anderson and Michael Stone, *A Synopsis of the Books of Adam and Eve* (Atlanta: Scholars Press, 1999). Summary of the textual problem in Michael Stone, *A History of the Literature of Adam and Eve* (Atlanta: Scholars Press, 1992); Johannes Tromp, *The Life and Adam and Eve and Related Literature* (Sheffield: Sheffield Academic Press, 1997), 11–44. See also Gary Anderson, "The Original Form of the Life of Adam and Eve: A Proposal"; Marinus de Jonge, "The Literary Development of the Life of Adam and Eve," in *Literature on Adam and Eve: Collected Essays,* ed. Gary Anderson, Michael Stone, and Johannes Tromp (Leiden: Brill, 2000), 215–231 and 239–249.

25. These and related stories are extensively summarized, discussed, and compared in Barbara Baert, *A Heritage of Holy Wood: The Legend of the True Cross in Text and Image* (Leiden: Brill, 2004), 310–349.

26. Synopsis based on Anderson and Stone, *Synopsis of the Books of Adam and Eve,* 33–47. Also see Michael Stone, *The Penitence of Adam,* Corpus Scriptorum Christianorum Orientalium (hereafter CSCO), 429–430 (Leuven: Peeters, 1981).

27. *Gospel of Nicodemus (Acts of Pilate)* 3.19. Both Baert, *Heritage of Holy Wood,* and Stone, *Penitence of Adam,* call attention to the Nag Hammadi document, the *Apocalypse of Adam,* which gives a different version of Adam's instructions (or revelations) to Seth.

28. See discussion of Golgotha as the site of Adam's grave in Chapter 2.

29. Baert, *Heritage of Holy Wood,* 350–451.

30. Mary-Bess Halford, *Illustration and Text in Lutwin's Eva und Adam: Codex Vindob. 2980* (Stuttgart: Kummerle Verlag, 1980).

31. Sarah Larrett Keefer, "The Performance of the Cross in Anglo-Saxon England," in *Cross and Culture in Anglo-Saxon England,* ed. Karen Louise Jolly, Catherine E. Karkov, and Sarah Larrett Keefer (Morgantown: West Virginia University Press, 2007), 203–241; Nathan Mitchell, "The Cross That Spoke," in *The Cross in Christian Tradition,* ed. Elizabeth Dreyer (New York: Paulist Press, 2000), 72–92; also Karl Young, "The Burial of Cross and Host," in *The Drama of the Medieval Church,* vol. 1 (Oxford: Clarendon Press, 1933), 112–147.

32. *Regularis Concordia: The Monastic Agreement of the Monks and Nuns of the English Nation,* trans. Dom T. Symons (London: Thomas Nelson and Sons, 1953), 44–46; also cited in Pamela Sheingorn, *The Easter Sepulchre in England* (Kalamazoo: Western Michigan University Medieval Studies, 1987), 21.

33. Ulla Haasrup, "Medieval Props in the Liturgical Drama," *Hafnia: Copenhagen Papers in the History of Art* 11 (1987): 133–70; and Amy Powell, "A Machine for Souls: Allegory before and after Trent," in *The Sensuous in the Counter-Reformation,* ed. Marcia B. Hall and Tracy E. Cooper (Cambridge: Cambridge University Press, 2013), 263–284.

34. *Lib. off. eccl.,* trans. author, *Patrologia Latina* (hereafter PL) 147, cols. 51–52. See also Karl Young, *Drama of the Medieval Church,* vol. 1 (Oxford: Oxford University Press, 1933), 555.

35. Sandro Sticca, *The Latin Passion Play: Its Origins and Development* (Albany: State University of New York Press, 1970), 51–83 (on the Monte Cassino play). Here Sticca summarizes the arguments for and against seeing the *Planctus Mariae* incorporated into Good Friday liturgies as the source of the Passion play.

36. First published by Mauro Inguanez, "Un dramma delle Passione del secolo XII," in *Miscellanea Cassinese* 12 (1936): 7–38; repr. with an additional fragment in *Miscellanea Cassinese* 17 (1939): 7–50. Also Robert Edwards, *The Montecassino Passion Play and the Poetics of Medieval Drama* (Berkeley: University of California Press, 1977).

37. James Shapiro, *Oberammergau: The Troubling Story of the World's Most Famous Passion Play* (New York: Pantheon Books, 2000); also Marc Saperstein, "Jewish Responses to the Passion Narratives," in *The Passion Story: From Visual Representation to Social Drama,* ed. Marcia Kupfer (University Park: Penn State University Press, 2008), 191–202.

7. *Crux Patiens*

Epigraph: Bonaventure, *Tree of Life* 26, trans. Ewert Cousins, *Bonaventure* (New York: Paulist Press, 1978), 149.

1. See the discussion of this controversy in Chapter 5.

2. See Chapter 5 for a discussion of iconoclasm in the East.

3. Thomas F. X. Noble, *Images, Iconoclasm, and the Carolingians* (Philadelphia: University of Pennsylvania Press, 2009), 162–169.

4. Ann Freeman, "Carolingian Orthodoxy and the Fate of the *Libri Carolini*," *Viator* 16 (1985): 65–108.

5. Celia Chazelle, "Matter, Spirit, and Image in the Libri Carolini," *Recherches Augustiennes* 21 (1986): 163–184. See also Celia Chazelle, *The Crucified God in the Carolingian Era: Theology and Art of Christ's Passion* (Cambridge: University of Cambridge Press, 2001), 50.

6. Summarized in Noble, *Images, Iconoclasm, and the Carolingians*, 288–294. See also Richard Viladesau, *The Beauty of the Cross: The Passion of Christ in Theology and the Arts—from the Catacombs to the Eve of the Renaissance* (Oxford: Oxford University Press, 2006), 63–64, with translated excerpt from Claudius's *Apology*.

7. Noble, *Images, Iconoclasm, and the Carolingians*, 276 and 369.

8. *Humbertus Silvae Candidae Adversus Graecorum Calumnias*, PL 143, 973 *(Hominis morituri imaginem affigitis crucifixae imagini Christi, ita ut quidam Antichristus in cruce Christi sedeat ostendens se adorandum tanquam si Deus)*.

9. See discussion in Chapter 4. John R. Marten, "The Dead Christ on the Cross in Byzantine Art," in *Late Classical and Mediaeval Studies in Honor of Albert Mathias Friend, Jr.*, ed. Kurt Weitzmann (Princeton, NJ: Princeton University Press, 1955), 189–196.

10. Viladesau, *Beauty of the Cross*, 50–55.

11. Fol. 143v, now in the Bibliothèque nationale de France. See discussion of the *Te Igitur* page in Chapter 6.

12. Bianca Kühnel, "Carolingian Diagrams, Images of the Invisible," in *Seeing the Invisible in Late Antiquity and the Early Middle Ages*, ed. Giselle de Nie, Karl F. Morrison, and Marco Mostert (Turnhout: Brepols, 2005), 359–389.

13. Chazelle, *Crucified God*, 20.

14. For a modern critical edition of the text and translation, see Michel Perrin, *Hrabanus Maurus, In honorem sanctae crucis, Corpus Christianorum Continuatio Mediaevalis*, 100–100A (Turhout: Brepols, 1997); Noble, *Images, Iconoclasm, and the Carolingians*, 347. According to Perrin, there are eighty-one surviving manuscripts and manuscript fragments along with many additional copies made under Hrabanus's supervision.

15. Hrabanus Maurus, *In honorem laudibus Sanctae Crucis*, trans. author, Lib. 1, fig. 1.

16. Ibid., fig. 12, PL 107, col. 197A; and Perrin, *Hrabanus Maurus*, 26–33. See Kühnel, "Carolingian Diagrams," 373–374.

17. Celia Chazelle, "An Exemplum of Humility: The Crucifixion Image in the Drogo Sacramentary," in *Reading Medieval Images: The Art Historian and the Object*, ed. Elizabeth Sears and Thelma Thomas (Ann Arbor: University of Michigan Press, 2002), 2–35. Here Chazelle argues for the personification of the Old Law partly on the basis of the parallel with later juxtaposed figures of Ecclesia and Synagoga in crucifixion iconography. Chazelle also supports and elaborates the identification with Nicodemus.

18. Chazelle, "Exemplum," 30, suggests two other possibilities: the biblical passages heard before the reading of the Passion narrative on Good Friday: Habbakuk 3:5 and Psalms 139. She also suggests a parallel with the Numbers 21:9 / John 3:14–15 typology.

19. Exceptions may be the Sinai icon and the Utrecht Psalter. See Chazelle, *Crucified God*, 246.

20. Annika E. Fisher, "Cross Altar and Crucifix in Ottonian Cologne," in *Decorating the Lord's Table: On the Dynamics between Image and Altar in the Middle Ages*, ed. Soren Kaspersen and Erik Thunø (Copenhagen: Museum Tusculanum Press, 2006), 43–62, esp. 45n12. The tradition that the Gero Crucifix was actually a reliquary has been disproven by investigation.

21. Anselm of Canterbury, *Cur Deus Homo*, 3.

22. Anselm, *Prayer to Christ*, *Oratio* 2, *Opera Omnia*, 3.9–7, in *The Prayers and Meditations of St. Anselm*, trans. Benedicta Ward (Harmondsworth: Penguin Books, 1973), 95–97.

23. Bernard of Clairvaux, *Song of Songs*, 11.7.

24. Trans. Cousins, *Bonaventure*, 158.

25. On the stations of the cross, see Chapter 8.

26. On this subject, see Mary Catherine O'Connor, *The Art of Dying Well: The Development of the Ars Moriendi* (New York: Columbia University Press, 1942); Eamon Duffy, *The Stripping of the Altars: Traditional Religion in England, 1400–1580* (New Haven, CT: Yale University Press, 1992), 314–327.

27. Julian of Norwich, *Showings* (long text) 4, in *Julian of Norwich, Showings*, trans. Edmund Colledge and James Walsh (New York: Paulist Press, 1978), 181.

28. Thomas Aquinas, *Summa Theologica*, pt. 3, Q. 46, a. 4, Ans. to Objection 3; cited in Viladesau, *Beauty of the Cross*, 95. Here Viladesau also quotes Augustine's reading of Ephesians 3:18.

29. Thomas F. X. Noble and Thomas Head, eds., *Soldiers of Christ: Saints and Saints Lives from Late Antiquity and the Early Middle Ages* (University Park: Penn State University Press, 2011), xxxv–xl.

30. Neuman de Vegvar, "*In Hoc Signo*," 101–105.

31. *Oshere* was apparently the name of the helmet's owner. See Dominic Tweddle, "The Anglican Helmet from Coppergate," *The Archaeology of York: Small Finds* 17, no. 8 (1992): 1015, 1082, fig. 597.

32. Giles Constable, *Crusaders and Crusading in the Twelfth Century* (Burlington, VT: Ashgate, 2008), 54–55; David Wilson, *The Bayeaux Tapestry* (New York: Thames and Hudson, 1985), pl. 42, 49–50, cited in Constable.

33. The version of Robert the Monk, in *The First Crusade: The Chronicle of Fulcher of Chartres and Other Source Materials,* ed. Edward Peters (Philadelphia: University of Pennsylvania Press, 1971), 5.

34. Constable, *Crusaders and Crusading,* 63–91.

35. Jonathan Riley-Smith, *The First Crusade and the Idea of Crusading* (Philadelphia: University of Pennsylvania Press, 1986), 67–68. This was also true of the armies of the Reconquista in Iberia and the colonizers of the New World, discussed in Chapter 9.

36. Constable, 81, citing Robert the Monk, *Hist. Ihero.* 1.2, in *RHC Hist. Occ.* 3.730; Marie-Thérèse d'Alverny, *Alain de Lille: Textes inédits avec un introduction sur sa vie et ses ouvres* (Paris: J. Vrin, 1965), 281n50.

37. See discussion of Heraclius's restoration in Chapter 5. Regarding Arnulf's role in recovering the cross, see the version of Raymond of Aguilers, in *The Chronicle of Fulcher of Chartres and Other Source Materials,* ed. Edward Peters, 2nd ed. (Philadelphia: University of Pennsylvania Press, 1998), 217–218. Also see Steven Runciman, *A History of the Crusades,* vol. 1, *The First Crusade and the Foundation of the Kingdom of Jerusalem* (Cambridge: Cambridge University Press, 1951), 294–295.

38. In Francesco Gabrieli, *Arab Historians of the Crusades,* trans. E. J. Costello (Berkeley: University of California Press, 1984), 136–137.

39. Again here see Gabrieli, *Arab Historians,* 218–224.

40. Shmuel Shepkaru, "The Preaching of the First Crusade and the Persecutions of the Jews," *Medieval Encounters* 18 (2012): 93–135.

41. Justin Martyr, *Dial.* 17.

42. John Chrysostom, *Adv. Jud.* 1, esp. 7.2. On the history of Christian anti-Jewish diatribes, see John Gager, *The Origins of Anti-Semitism: Attitudes toward Judaism in Pagan and Christian Antiquity* (Oxford: Oxford University Press, 1983); Jeremy Cohen, *Christ Killers: The Jews and the Passion from the Bible to the Big Screen* (Oxford: Oxford University Press, 2007).

43. Miri Rubin, *Gentile Tales: The Narrative Assault on Late-Medieval Jews* (New Haven, CT: Yale University Press, 1999).

44. Thomas of Monmouth, *Life and Miracles of St. William of Norwich,* ed. and trans. Miri Rubin (London: Penguin Classics, 2015).

45. Fourth Lateran Council, *Can.* 68.

8. *Crux Invicta*

Epigraph: Martin Luther, "A Meditation on Christ's Passion," in *Luther's Works,* vol. 42 (Devotional Writings), ed. Martin O. Dietrich, trans. Martin H. Bertram (Philadelphia: Fortress Press, 1969), 7.

1. See the extended analysis of this image in Joseph Leo Koerner, *The Reformation of the Image* (Chicago: University of Chicago Press, 2004), 171–190.

2. Martin Luther, *Against the Heavenly Prophets*, trans. Bemhard Erling in *Luther's Works*, vol. 40 (Philadelphia: Fortress Press, 1958), 98–99.

3. Sergiusz Michalski, *The Reformation in the Visual Arts: The Protestant Image Question in Western and Eastern Europe* (London: Routledge, 1993), 32–33.

4. Ulrich Zwingli, *Werke* 3, 120, 1–123, cited in Lee Palmer Wandel, *Voracious Idols and Violent Hands* (Cambridge: Cambridge University Press, 1994), 95.

5. Zwingli, *Werke* 4, 119, cited in Michalski, *Reformation and the Visual Arts*, 56–57.

6. Charles Garside Jr., *Zwingli and the Arts* (New York: Da Capo Press, 1981), 179–180.

7. Koerner, *Reformation of the Image*, 138–140.

8. Andreas Karlstadt, *On the Abolition of Images*. Text cited in *A Reformation Debate: Karlstadt, Emser, and Eck on Sacred Images: Three Treatiests in Translation*, vol. 1, ed. and trans. Bryan Mangrum and Giuseppe Scavizzi (Toronto: Center for Reformation and Renaissance, 1991), 28.

9. John Calvin, *Institutes* 1.11.7

10. John Calvin, *Treatise on Relics*, trans. Valerian Krasinski (Edinburgh: Johnstone, Hunter, 1870).

11. Palmer Wandel, *Voracious Idols and Violent Hands*, 94–96.

12. Ibid., 121–122.

13. Ibid., 123–124, 138, noting two other crosses removed in Strasbourg.

14. Koerner, *Reformation of the Image*, 128–132; Palmer Wandel, *Voracious Idols and Violent Hands*, 72–80.

15. Recounted by Robert Scribner, "Reformation, Carnival, and the World Turned Upside-Down," in *Popular Culture and Popular Movements in Reformation Germany* (London: Bloomsbury Academic, 2003), 76 (with citations of several contemporary sources). Other examples in Koerner, *Reformation of the Image*, 132–134.

16. Koerner, *Reformation of the Image*, 129–131, citing Bullinger, *Chronicle of the Reformation*. The illustration (Fig. 8.4) shows a plain cross and not a crucifix, which may reflect the later illustrator's confusion.

17. Margaret Aston, *Broken Idols of the English Reformation* (Cambridge: Cambridge University Press, 2016), 707–720. See also Aston's chapter, "The Cross," 707–882, for a superb summary of the cross and crucifix in this period.

18. Julie Spraggon, *Puritan Iconoclasm during the English Civil War* (Woodbridge: Boydell and Brewer, 2003), 50. See also David Cressy, *Travesties and Transgressions in Tudor and Stuart England* (Oxford: Oxford University Press, 2000), esp. chap. 14, "The Downfall of the Cheapside Cross," 234–250; and most recently, Aston, *Broken Idols*, 854–882.

19. Greenhill quoted in Spraggon, *Puritan Iconoclasm*, 50.

20. Henry Peacham, *A Dialogue between the Crosses in Cheap, and Charing Crosse* (1641).

21. Cited in Spraggon, *Puritan Iconoclasm*, 83–84.

22. Quoted in Spraggon, *Puritan Iconoclasm*, in Richard Overton, *Articles of High Treason Exhibited against Cheap-side Cross* (1642), 43.

23. On the Ruthwell Cross, see Chapter 6.

24. Council of Trent, Session 25 (December 3–4, 1563); decree on invocation, veneration, and relics of the saints, and on sacred images.

25. *Missale Romanian* 2.2 *(De ingressu sacerdotis ad altare)*.

26. Pius XII, *Mediator Dei* 62.

27. On the Catholic Reformation's position on iconography and, especially, on some of its most prominent theologians and major works of art, see Viladesau, *Triumph of the Cross*, 192–281.

28. Teresa of Avila, *Interior Castle, Second Mansion* 7, in *Teresa of Avila: The Interior Castle*, trans. Kieran Kavanaugh (New York: Paulist Press, 1979), 52.

29. This image inspired the title of the famous painting of Salvador Dali, *Christ of Saint John of the Cross* (1951) that depicts the scene also from above. Dali claimed to have based his painting on a dream vision. The painting is now in the Kelvingrove Art Gallery and Museum, Glasgow.

30. Viladesau, *Triumph of the Cross*, 228. See also John W. O'Malley, "Trent, Sacred Images, and Catholics' Senses of the Sensuous," in *The Sensuous in the Counter Reformation Church*, ed. Marcia B. Hall and Tracy E. Cooper (Cambridge: Cambridge University Press, 2013), 28–48.

31. See Chapter 4 for a discussion of the scandal of the nearly nude Christ reported by Gregory of Tours.

32. Viladesau, *Triumph of the Cross*, 55–56, 229.

33. See Victor M. Schmidt, "Statues, Idols, and Nudity," in *Antiquity Renewed: Late Classical and Early Modern Themes*, ed. Zweder von Martels and Victor M. Schmidt (Leuven: Peeters, 2003), 211–229, esp. 220–225. See also Philip Fehl, "The Naked Christ in Santa Maria Novella in Florence: Reflections on an Exhibition and the Consequences," *Storia dell'arte* 45 (1982): 161–164.

34. Herbert Thurston, *The Stations of the Cross: An Account of Their History and Devotional Practice* (London: Burns and Gates, 1906), 45–61.

35. Christianus Adrichomius (also Christian Kruik van Adrichem), *Jerusalem sicut Christi tempore floruit* (later incorporated into *Theatrum Terrae Sanctae et Biblicarum Historiarum*), posthumously published in 1590. Thurston, *Stations of the Cross*, 76–95 (where he argues that Adrichomius was indebted to a Carmelite named Jan Pascha who wrote a meditation on his journey to Jerusalem around 1530).

36. Robert Bridges, trans., "O Sacred Head Sore Wounded," https://www.hymnary.org/text/o_sacred_head_sore_wounded (accessed January 15, 2016).

37. Isaac Watts, "When I Survey the Wondrous Cross," https://www.hymnary.org/text/when_i_survey_the_wondrous_cross_watts (accessed January 16, 2016).

38. Charles Wesley, *Hymns and Sacred Poems*, https://divinity.duke.edu/sites/divinity.duke.edu/files/documents/cswt/10_Hymns_and_Sacred_Poems_%281742%29.pdf (accessed January 20, 2016).

39. Ira Sankey, "Are You Washed in the Blood?" http://www.traditionalmusic.co.uk/ira-sankey/are-you-washed-in-the-blood-ira-sankey.htmfount (accessed January 16, 2016).

40. Story recounted in the *South Bend Tribune*, September 14, 2013, http://www.southbendtribune.com/news/local/keynews/community/article_cb3d78ae-1d28-11e3-8156-0019bb30f31a.html (accessed January 16, 2016).

41. George Bennard, "The Old Rugged Cross," http://www.hymnsite.com/lyrics/umh504 (accessed January 14, 2016).

42. Horst Wenzel, "The Logos in the Press: Christ in the Wine-Press and the Discovery of Printmaking," in *Visual Culture and the German Middle Ages*, ed. Kathryn Starkey and Horst Wenzel (New York: Palgrave Macmillan, 2005), 223–249; Elina Gertsman, "Multiple Impressions: Christ in the Winepress and the Semiotics of the Printed Image," *Art History* 36 (2013): 310–337.

9. *Crux Perdurans*

Epigraph: Angel María Garibay, *La literature de los aztecas* (Mexico City: J. Moritz, 1964), 55.

1. Delno West, "Christopher Columbus, Lost Biblical Scenes, and the Last Crusade," *Catholic Historical Review* 78 (1992): 519–541.

2. Jaime Lara, *Christian Texts for Aztecs: Art and Liturgy in Colonial Mexico* (Notre Dame, IN: University of Notre Dame Press, 2008), esp. chap. 9, "Holy Blood: The Rehabilitation of Human Sacrifice," 229–253.

3. Jaime Lara, *City, Temple, Stage: Eschatological Architecture and Liturgical Theatrics in New Spain* (Notre Dame, IN: University of Notre Dame Press), 168–174.

4. Lara, *Christian Texts for Aztecs*, 239–246.

5. Richard Greenleaf, *The Mexican Inquisition of the Sixteenth Century* (Albuquerque: University of New Mexico Press, 1969), 7–44.

6. Timothy W. Knowlton, *Maya Creation Myths: Words and Worlds of the Chilam Balam* (Boulder: University Press of Colorado, 2010).

7. Illustrated in Lara, *City, Temple, Stage*, 154.

8. Samuel Edgerton, "Christian Cross as Indigenous 'World Tree' in Sixteenth-Century Mexico: The 'Atrio' Cross in the Frederick and Jan Mayer Collection," *Exploring New World Imagery: Spanish Colonial Papers from the 2002 Mayer Center Symposium*, ed. Donna Pierce (Denver: Denver Art Museum, 2005), 17–30.

9. Francisco Hernandez, "Of the Religious Beliefs of the Indians of Yucatan in 1545," reprinted in *Reports on the Maya Indians of Yucatan*, vol. 9, Indian Notes and Monographs, ed. Marshall Saville (New York: Museum of the American Indian, 1921), 209–215.

10. Edgerton, "Christian Cross as Indigenous 'World Tree,' " 16.

11. Cécile Fromont, *The Art of Conversion: Christian Visual Culture in the Kingdom of Kongo* (Chapel Hill: University of North Carolina Press, 2014), esp. chap. 2, "Under the Sign of the Cross in the Kingdom of Kongo," 75–79 (with excellent references).

12. Tom Phillips, *Africa: The Art of a Continent; 100 Works of Power and Beauty* (New York: Guggenheim Museum Publications, 1996), 103.

13. Fromont, *Art of Conversion*, 65–108.

14. Ibid., 68–78.

15. See Chapter 3.

16. Fromont, *Art of Conversion*, 70–71.

17. Phillips, *Africa: The Art of a Continent*, 20.

18. See the exhibition catalogue from the Metropolitan Museum, *Kongo: Power and Majesty*, ed. Alisa LaGamma (New York: Metropolitan Museum of Art, 2015).

19. G. R. D. King, "Islam, Iconoclasm, and the Declaration of Doctrine," in *Late Antique and Medieval Art of the Mediterranean World*, ed. Eva R. Hoffman (Oxford: Blackwell, 2007), 213–226. Here, King mentions several cases in the eighth century when Muslim governors ordered that crosses be removed from public display in their territories.

20. Sidney Griffith, *The Church in the Shadow of the Mosque: Christians and Muslims in the World of Islam* (Princeton, NJ: Princeton University Press, 2008), 142–144.

21. Mahmoud Ayoub, "Towards an Islamic Christology II: The Death of Jesus; Reality or Delusion," *Muslim World* 70 (1980): 91–121; Michael Fonner, "Jesus' Death by Crucifixion in the Qur'an," *Journal of Ecumenical Studies* 29 (1992): 432–450; and, more recently and very thoroughly, Todd Lawson, *The Crucifixion and the Qur'ān: A Study in the History of Muslim Thought* (Oxford: Oneworld Publications, 2009).

22. This includes the commentary on the text by Abū Jafar Al-Tabarī (839–923) and a version in the *Gospel of Barnabas*, probably a fourteenth-century document written by a Christian convert to Islam.

23. See discussion in Chapter 2. Ramon Llull, a thirteen-century Franciscan missionary to Muslims, explained that their belief that Christ had not been crucified was intended to protect the honor of Jesus the prophet, not understanding that this form of death was intrinsic to Christian understanding of Jesus as savior. See Llull, *Libre del gentile e los tres savis* (Book of the Gentile and the Three Sages), art. 10, quoted in Richard Viladesau, *The Beauty of the Cross: The Passion of Christ in Theology and the Arts from the Catacombs to the Renaissance* (Oxford: Oxford University Press, 2006), 110.

24. Neal Robinson, *Christ in Islam and Christianity* (Albany: State University of New York Press, 1991), 56–57; and Kenneth Cragg, *The Call of the Minaret* (Oxford: Oneworld Publications, 2000), 224.

25. Gabriel Said Reynolds, "The Muslim Jesus: Dead or Alive?" *Bulletin of the School of Oriental and African Studies* 72 (2009): 237–258.

26. Tabarī 3.289, cited in Reynolds, "Muslim Jesus," 246n33.

27. See Holly Everett, *Roadside Crosses in Contemporary Memorial Culture* (Denton: University of North Texas Press, 2002).

28. Darius Liutikas and Alfonsas Motuzas, "The Pilgrimage to the Hill of Crosses: Devotional Practices and Identities," in *Redefining Pilgrimage: New Perspectives on Historical and Contemporary Pilgrimages*, ed. Antón M. Pazos (Burlington, VT: Ashgate, 2014), 104–126.

29. Barry Black, quoted in "What Are the Origins of Cross-Burning?" *Christian Science Monitor*, December 13, 2002.

30. Jeannine Bell, "O Say, Can You See: Free Expression by the Light of the Fiery Crosses," *Harvard Civil Rights-Civil Liberties Law Review* 39 (2004): 335–389.

31. James Cone, *The Cross and the Lynching Tree* (Maryknoll, NY: Orbis Books, 2011).

32. Genevieve Zubrzycki, *The Crosses of Auschwitz: Nationalism and Religion in Post-Communist Poland* (Chicago: University of Chicago Press, 2006).

33. See, e.g., Ian Johnson, "Chinese Christians Resist Government Plan to Remove Crosses," *New York Times*, August 10, 2015.

34. Carter Heyward and Beverly Harrison, "Pain and Pleasure: Avoiding the Confusions of Christian Tradition in Feminist Theology," in *Christianity, Patriarchy and Abuse: A Feminist Critique*, ed. Joanne Carlson Brown and Carole R. Bohn (New York: Pilgrim Press, 1989), 148–173.

35. The bibliography of feminist theology here is extensive. For an overview and useful bibliography, see Arnfridur Gudmundsdottir, *Meeting God on the Cross: Christ, the Cross, and the Feminist Critique* (Oxford: Oxford University Press, 2000); Elisabeth Moltmann-Wendel, "Is There a Feminist Theology of the Cross?" in *The Scandal of a Crucified World: Perspectives on the Cross and Suffering*, ed. Yacob Tesfai (Maryknoll, NY: Orbis Books, 1994), 87–98.

36. Again, the bibliography on the meaning of Jesus's suffering is extensive, but see Jon Sobrino, S.J. and Ignacio Ellacuria, S.J., eds., *Systematic Theology: Perspectives from Liberation Theology* (Maryknoll, NY: Orbis Books, 1996), esp. chap. 15, "The Crucified People," 257–278.

37. Kathryn Greene-McCreight, *Feminist Reconstructions of Christian Doctrine: Narrative Analysis and Appraisal* (Oxford: Oxford University Press, 2000), 83–84.

38. Elizabeth T. Vasko, "Redeeming Beauty? Christa and the Displacement of Women's Bodies in Theological Discourse," *Feminist Theology* 21 (2013): 195–208.

39. Stanley Peters to the Canadian Council of Catholic Bishops, November 29, 1999, http://www.cccb.ca/site/index2.php?option=com_content&task=emailform&id=805&itemid=180 (accessed January 5, 2016). See also Jaroslav Pelikan, *The Illustrated Jesus through the Ages* (New Haven, CT: Yale University Press, 1997), 241.

40. Steven C. Dubin, *Arresting Images: Impolitic Art and Uncivil Actions* (London: Routledge, 1992), 96–101.

Further Reading

1. *Scandalum Crucis*

Brown, Raymond E. *The Death of the Messiah*. 2 vols. New York: Doubleday, 1994.

Chapman, David. *Ancient Jewish and Christian Perspectives on Crucifixion*. Tübingen: Mohr Siebeck, 2008.

Cook, John Granger. *Crucifixion in the Mediterranean World*. Tübingen: Mohr Siebeck, 2014.

Hengel, Martin. *Crucifixion*. Philadelphia: Fortress Press, 1977.

Samuelsson, Gunnar. *Crucifixion in Antiquity*. Tübingen: Mohr Siebeck, 2011.

Sloyan, Gerald. *The Crucifixion of Jesus: History, Myth, Faith*. Minneapolis: Fortress Press, 1995.

Tzaferis, Vassilios. "Crucifixion: The Archaeological Evidence." *Biblical Archaeology Review* 11 (1985): 44–53.

Zias, Joseph, and Sekeles, Eliezar. "The Crucified Man at Giv'at ha-Mivtar: A Reappraisal." *Israel Exploration Journal* 35 (1985): 22–27.

2. *Signum Crucis*

Combs, Jason. "A Walking, Talking Cross: The Polymorphic Christology of the Gospel of Peter." *Early Christianity* 5 (2014): 198–219.

Crossan, John Dominic. *The Cross That Spoke: The Origins of the Passion Narrative*. San Francisco: Harper and Row, 1988.

Finegan, Jack. *The Archaeology of the New Testament*. Princeton, NJ: Princeton University Press, 1992.

Hurtado, Larry W. "The Staurogram in Early Christian Manuscripts: The Earliest Visual Reference to the Crucified Jesus?" In *New Testament Manuscripts: Their Texts and Their World*, edited by Thomas J. Kraus and Tobias Nicklas, 207–226. Leiden: Brill, 2006.

Irvine, Christopher. "The Iconography of the Cross as the Green Tree." In *The Edinburgh Companion to the Bible and the Arts,* edited by Stephen Prickett, 195–207. Edinburgh: Edinburgh University Press, 2014.

Ladner, Gerhard. "St. Gregory of Nyssa and St. Augustine on the Symbolism of the Cross." In *Images and Ideas in the Middle Ages: Selected Studies in History and Art,* 197–208. Rome: Edizioni di Storia e Letteratura, 1983.

Neuman de Vegvar, Carol. "In Hoc Signo: The Cross on Secular Objects and the Process of Conversion." In *Cross and Culture in Anglo-Saxon England,* edited by Karen Louise Jolly, Catherine E. Karkov, and Sarah Larratt Keefer, 79–117. Morgantown: West Virginia University Press, 2007.

Prieur, Jean-Marc. *Das Kreuz in der christlichen Literatur der Antike.* Bern: Peter Lang, 2006.

3. *Inventio Crucis*

Baert, Barbara. *A Heritage of Holy Wood: The Legend of the True Cross in Text and Image.* Translated by Lee Preedy. Leiden: Brill, 2004.

Borgehammar, Stephan. *How the Holy Cross Was Found.* Stockholm: Almquist and Wiksell, 1991.

De Blaauw, Sible. "Jerusalem in Rome and the Cult of the Cross." In *Pratum Romanum: Richard Krautheimer zum 100; Geburtstag,* edited by Renate Colella and Richard Krautheimer, 56–59. Wiesbaden: Dr. Ludwig Reichert Verlag, 1977.

Drijvers, Jan Willem. *Helena Augusta: The Mother of Constantine the Great and the Legend of Her Finding of the True Cross.* Leiden: Brill, 1992.

———. "The Power of the Cross: Celestial Cross Appearances in the Fourth Century." In *The Power of Religion in Late Antiquity,* edited by Andrew Cain and Noel Lenski, 237–248. Farnham, UK: Ashgate, 2009.

Frolow, A. *La relique de la Varie Croix: Recherches sur le développement d'un culte.* Paris: Institut français d'études byzantines, 1961.

Klein, Holger. "Constantine, Helena, and the Early Cult of the True Cross in Constantinople." In *Byzance et les reliques du Christ,* edited by Jannic Durand and Bernard Flusin, 31–59. Paris: Centre de recherche d'histoire et civilisation de Byzance, 2004.

Long, Jacqueline. "How to Read a Halo: Three (or More) Versions of Constantine's Vision." In *The Power of Religion in Late Antiquity,* edited by Andrew Cain and Noel Lenski, 226–235. Farnham, UK: Ashgate, 2009.

Weiss, Peter. "The Vision of Constantine." *Journal of Roman Archaeology* 16 (2003): 237–259.

Wilkinson, John. *Jerusalem Pilgrims before the Crusades.* Warminster, UK: Aris and Phillips, 2002.

Further Reading

4. *Crux Abscondita*

Corrigan, Kathleen. "Text and Image on an Icon of the Crucifixion at Mount Sinai." In *The Sacred Image East and West,* edited by Robert Ousterhout and Leslie Brubaker, 45–109. Urbana: University of Illinois Press, 1995.

Harley-McGowan, Felicity. "The Maskell Passion Ivories and Greco-Roman Art." In *Envisioning Christ on the Cross: Ireland and the Early Medieval West,* edited by Juliet Mullins, Jenifer Ni Ghrádaigh, and Richard Hawtee, 13–33. Dublin: Four Courts Press, 2013.

Jensen, Robin M. "The Passion in Early Christian Art." In *Perspectives on the Passion: Encountering the Bible through the Arts,* edited by Christine Joynes and Nancy Ann Macky, 53–84. London: T&T Clark, 2007.

Kartsonis, Anna. *Anastasis: The Making of an Image.* Princeton, NJ: Princeton University Press, 1986.

Scheckler, Allyson Everingham, and Mary Joan Winn Leith. "The Crucifixion Conundrum and the Santa Sabina Doors." *Harvard Theological Review* 103 (2010): 67–88.

Schiller, Gertrud. *Iconography of Christian Art.* Vol. 2, *The Passion of Christ.* Translated by J. Seligman. London: Lund Humphries, 1971.

Vikan, Gary. *Early Byzantine Pilgrimage Art.* Washington, DC: Dumbarton Oaks Research Library and Collection, 2010.

Viladesau, Richard. *The Beauty of the Cross: The Passion of Christ in Theology and the Arts from the Catacombs to the Eve of the Renaissance.* Oxford: Oxford University Press, 2006.

5. *Adoratio Crucis*

Baert, Barbara. *A Heritage of Holy Wood: The Legend of the True Cross in Text and Image.* Translated by Lee Preedy. Leiden: Brill, 2004.

Brubaker, Leslie. *Inventing Byzantine Iconoclasm.* London: Bristol Classical Press, 2012.

Cotsonis, John A. *Byzantine Figural Processional Crosses.* Washington, DC: Dumbarton Oaks Research Library and Collection, 1994.

Drijvers, Han J. W., and Jan Willem Drijvers. *The Finding of the True Cross and the Judas Kyriakos Legend in Syriac.* Louvain: Peeters, 1997.

Frolow, Anatole. *La relique de la varie croix: Recherches sur le développement d'un culte.* Paris: Institut français d'études byzantines, 1961.

Klein, Holger. "Constantine, Helena, and the Cult of the True Cross in Constantinople." In *Byzance et les reliques du Christ,* edited by Jannic Durand and Bernard Flusin, 31–59. Paris: Centre d'histoire et civilisation de Byzance, 2004.

Milner, Christine. "*'Lignum Vitae'* or *'Crux Gemmata'*? The Cross of Golgotha in the Early Byzantine Period." *Byzantine and Modern Greek Studies* 12 (1996): 77–99.

Regan, Patrick. "Veneration of the Cross." *Worship* 52 (1978): 2–12.

van Tongeren, Louis. *Exaltation of the Cross: Toward the Origins of the Feast of the Cross and the Meaning of the Cross in Early Medieval Liturgy*. Louvain: Peeters, 2000.

Wortley, John. "The Wood of the True Cross." In *Studies on the Cult of Relics in Byzantium up to 1204*, VI. 1–19. Farnham, UK: Ashgate, 2009.

6. *Carmina Crucis*

Anderson, Gary. *The Genesis of Perfection: Adam and Eve in Jewish and Christian Imagination*. Louisville, KY: Westminster John Knox, 2001.

Baert, Barbara. *A Heritage of Holy Wood: The Legend of the True Cross in Text and Image*. Translated by Lee Preedy. Leiden: Brill, 2004.

Cassiday, Brenden, ed. *The Ruthwell Cross: Papers from the Colloquium Sponsored by the Princeton Index of Christian Art, Princeton University, 8 December 1989*. Princeton, NJ: Princeton University Press, 1992.

Ghrádaigh, Jenifer Ní. "Towards an Emotive Christ? Changing Depictions of the Crucifixion on the Irish High Cross." In *Envisioning Christ on the Cross: Ireland and the Early Medieval West*, edited by Janet Mullins, Jenifer Ní Ghrádaigh, and Richard Hawtree, 262–285. Dublin: Four Courts Press, 2013.

Irvine, Christopher. "The Iconography of the Cross as the Green Tree." In *The Edinburgh Companion to the Bible and the Arts*, edited by Stephen Prickett, 195–207. Edinburgh: Edinburgh University Press, 2014.

Keefer, Sarah Larratt, Karen Louise Jolly, and Catherine E. Karkov, eds. *Cross and Cruciform in the Anglo-Saxon World: Studies to Honor the Memory of Timothy Reuter*. Morgantown: West Virginia University Press, 2010.

Kendall, Calvin B. "From Sign to Vision: The Ruthwell Cross and the Dream of the Rood." In *The Place of the Cross in Anglo-Saxon England*, edited by Catherine E. Karkov, Sarah Larratt Keefer, and Karen Louise Jolly, 129–144. Woodbridge, UK: Boydell Press, 2006.

Murdoch, Brian, and J. A. Tasioulas, eds. *The Apocryphal Lives of Adam and Eve*. Exeter: University of Exeter Press, 2002.

Ó Carragáin, Éamonn. *Ritual and the Rood: Liturgical Images and the Poems of the Dream of the Rood Tradition*. London: University of Toronto Press, 2005.

Stone, Michael. *A History of the Literature of Adam and Eve: Early Judaism and Its Literature*. Atlanta: Scholars Press, 1992.

Szövérffy, Joseph. *Hymns of the Holy Cross*. Leiden: Brill, 1976.

7. *Crux Patiens*

Chazelle, Celia. *The Crucified God in the Carolingian Era: Theology and Art of Christ's Passion*. Cambridge: University of Cambridge Press, 2001.

Constable, Giles. "The Cross of the Crusaders." In *Crusaders and Crusading in the Twelfth Century*, 67–79. Farnham, UK: Ashgate, 2008.

Derbes, Anne. *Picturing the Passion in Late Medieval Italy*. Cambridge: Cambridge University Press, 1996.

Marrow, James. "Inventing the Passion in the Late Middle Ages." In *The Passion Story: From Visual Representation to Social Drama*, edited by Marcia Kupfer, 23–52. University Park: Penn State University Press, 2008.

———. *Passion Iconography in Northern European Art of the Late Middle Ages and Early Renaissance*. Kortrijk: Van Gehemmert, 1979.

Marten, John R. "The Dead Christ on the Cross in Byzantine Art." In *Late Classical and Mediaeval Studies in Honor of Albert Mathias Friend, Jr.*, edited by Kurt Weitzmann, 189–196. Princeton, NJ: Princeton University Press, 1955.

Mitchell, Nathan. "The Cross That Spoke." In *The Cross in Christian Tradition: From Paul to Bonaventure*, edited by Elizabeth Dreyer, 72–92. New York: Paulist Press, 2000.

Neuman de Vegvar, Carol. "*In Hoc Signo:* The Cross on Secular Objects and the Process of Conversion." In *Cross and Culture in Anglo-Saxon England*, edited by Karen Louise Jolly, Catherine E. Karkov, and Sarah Larratt Keefer, 79–117. Morgantown: West Virginia University Press, 2007.

Noble, Thomas F. X. *Images, Iconoclasm, and the Carolingians*. Philadelphia: University of Pennsylvania Press, 2009.

Parker, Elizabeth C., and Charles T. Little, *The Cloisters Cross: Its Art and Meaning*. London: Harvey Miller, 1994.

Raw, Barbara. *Anglo-Saxon Crucifixion Iconography and the Art of the Monastic Revival*. Cambridge: Cambridge University Press, 1990.

Viladesau, Richard. *The Beauty of the Cross: The Passion of Christ in Theology and the Arts from the Catacombs to the Eve of the Renaissance*. Oxford: Oxford University Press, 2006.

8. *Crux Invicta*

Hall, Marcia B., and Tracy E. Cooper, eds. *The Sensuous in the Counter-Reformation*. Cambridge: Cambridge University Press, 2013.

Koerner, Joseph Leo. *The Reformation of the Image*. Chicago: University of Chicago Press, 2004.

Michalski, Sergiusz. *The Reformation in the Visual Arts: The Protestant Image Question in Western and Eastern Europe*. London: Routledge, 1993.

Palmer, Lee Wandel. *Voracious Idols and Violent Hands: Iconoclasm in Reformation Zurich, Strasbourg, and Basel*. Cambridge: Cambridge University Press, 1994.

Spraggon, Julie. *Puritan Iconoclasm in the English Civil War*. Woodbridge, UK: Boydell Press, 2003.

Viladesau, Richard. *The Triumph of the Cross: The Passion of Christ in Theology and the Arts from the Renaissance to the Counter-Reformation.* Oxford: Oxford University Press, 2008.

Watson, J. R. "Emblem and Irony: Passion Narrative in Post-Reformation Hymnody." In *Perspectives on the Passion: Encountering the Bible through the Arts,* edited by Christine E. Joynes, 122–138. London: T&T Clark, 2007.

9. *Crux Perdurans*

Cone, James. *The Cross and the Lynching Tree.* Maryknoll, NY: Orbis Books, 2011.

Dreyer, Elizabeth A. "Behold the One You Seek Has Been Lifted Up." In *The Cross in Christian Tradition: From Paul to Bonaventure,* edited by Elizabeth A. Dreyer. 192–253. Mahwah, NJ: Paulist Press, 2000.

Edgerton, Samuel Y. "Christian Cross as Indigenous 'World Tree' in Sixteenth-Century Mexico: The 'Atrio Cross' in the Frederick and Jan Mayer Collection." In *Exploring New World Imagery: Spanish Colonial Papers from the 2002 Mayer Center Symposium,* edited by Donna Pierce, 13–40. Denver: Denver Art Museum, 2005.

Fromont, Cécile. *Art of Conversion: Christian Visual Culture in the Kingdom of Kongo.* Chapel Hill: University of North Carolina Press, 2014.

Hughes, Jennifer Scheper. *Biography of a Mexican Crucifix: Lived Religion and Local Faith from the Conquest to the Present.* Oxford: Oxford University Press, 2010.

Lara, Jaime. *City, Temple, Stage: Eschatological Architecture and Liturgical Theatrics in New Spain.* Notre Dame, IN: University of Notre Dame Press, 2004.

Reynolds, Gabriel Said. "The Muslim Jesus: Dead or Alive?" *Bulletin of the School of Oriental and African Studies* 72 (2009): 237–258.

Young, Frances. *Construing the Cross: Type, Sign, Symbol, Word, Action.* Eugene, OR: Cascade Books, 2015.

Credits

1.1 Luigi Gregori, *Exaltation of the Holy Cross,* ceiling of the Lady Chapel, Basilica of the Sacred Heart, University of Notre Dame, ca. 1891. Photo: © Robin M. Jensen.

1.2 Bible from northeastern France, last quarter of the thirteenth century. Paul holding epistle from which Christ's cross emerges, beginning of Epistle to the Philippians. The Pierpont Morgan Library, New York. MS M.969, purchased on the Fellows Fund, 1976.

1.3 Heel bone (right calcaneum) with crucifixion nail from the first-century tomb of Yohanan after reconstruction, with mock-up. Photo: Courtesy of Joe Zias.

1.4 Crucifixion graffito, west wall, taberna 5, Puteoli. Image reproduced by special permission of the Ministero dei Beni e delle Attività Culturali e del Turismo. Photo supplied by Prof. G. Camodeca, Soprintendenza Speciale per i Beni Archeologici di Pozzuoli.

1.5 Alexamenos graffito, from the Palatine Hill area, Rome. Now in the Museo Nationale Romano (Terme di Diocleziano), Rome, Italy. Photo: Alinari / Art Resource, New York.

1.6 Leaf from a Beatus Manuscript: "The Lamb at the Foot of the Cross Flanked by Two Angels," ca. 1180, Spanish. The Metropolitan Museum of Art, New York (1991.232.1) (OASC). Purchase, the Cloisters Collection, Rogers and Harris Brisbane Dick Funds, and Joseph Pulitzer Bequest, 1991. www.metmuseum.org.

2.1 Moses raising the brazen serpent, Initial to Psalm 68, from Peter Lombard's *Commentaries on the Psalms and St. Paul.* Staats- und Universitätsbibliothek, Bremen. Ms. a. 244, fol. 113v.

2.2 *Ezekiel's Vision of the Sign "Tau."* Enamel plaque, mid-twelfth century, Flemish. The Walters Art Museum (44.616), Creative Commons (CC0 1.0).

2.3 Baptismal font from early Christian basilica, Bulla Regia, Tunisia, sixth century. Photo: © Robin M. Jensen.

2.4 *Tau rho* on African red slipware oil lamp, fourth century. From the collection of John Herrmann and Annewies van den Hoek. Photo: Courtesy of Annewies van den Hoek.

2.5 Fish and anchor gem from the Christian Schmidt collection, Munich. Photo: Courtesy of Jeffrey Spier.

Credits

2.6 Acrostic Rotas-Sator Square from Dura Europos, ca. 165–256 CE. Yale University Art Gallery (1933.298).

2.7 Sign of the Son of Man in Heaven, T'oros Roslin, Armenian (scribe), ca. 1262. The Walters Art Museum (W.539.104R), Creative Commons (CC0 1.0).

3.1 Piero della Francesca (ca. 1420–1492), "The Dream of Constantine," from the *Legend of the True Cross* fresco, Church of San Francesco, Arezza, Italy. Photo: Scala / Art Resource, New York.

3.2 Raphael (school of), *Apparition of the Cross to Constantine the Great*, Stanze di Raffaello, Vatican Palace, Vatican State. Photo: Scala / Art Resource, New York.

3.3 *The Legend of the Cross*, attributed to Antoniazzo Romano or Melozzo da Forli, late fifteenth century. Apse fresco from the Basilica of Santa Croce in Gerusalemme, Rome. Photo: © Robin M. Jensen.

3.4 Follis of Constantius II, ca. 350, minted in Siscia. Photo: CoinArchives Nomos AG, Obolos 4, auction lot 851 (February 21, 2016), courtesy of Yves Gunzenreiner, Nomos AG.

3.5 Statue of St. Helena by Andrea Bolgi, 1639. St. Peter's Basilica, Rome. Photo: © Robin M. Jensen.

3.6 Fourth-century sarcophagus with scenes of the Passion and empty cross. Museo Pio Cristiano, Vatican Museums, Vatican State. Photo: Vanni Archive / Art Resource, New York.

3.7 Fourth-century sarcophagus with Traditio Legis and Arrest of Peter. Museo Pio Cristiano, Vatican Museums, Vatican State. Photo: Vanni Archive / Art Resource, New York.

4.1 Scenes of Christ's Passion, relief from the Bresia Lipsanoteca (ivory casket), fourth century. Now in the Museo di Santa Giulia, Museo Civica Cristlano, Brescia. Photo: Gianni Dagli Orti / the Art Archive at Art Resource, New York.

4.2 Crucifixion on third- or fourth-century carnelian, the "Constanza Carnelian." The British Museum (1895, 1113.1). © The Trustees of the British Museum. All rights reserved.

4.3 Panel from an ivory reliquary box, the "Maskell Casket," ca. 420–430. The British Museum (1856, 0623.5). © The Trustees of the British Museum. All rights reserved.

4.4 Crucifixion on wooden panel from the door of Rome's Basilica of Santa Sabina, ca. 432. Photo: © Robin M. Jensen.

4.5 Crucifixion from the Rabbula Gospels, fol. 13a, ca. 586. Manuscript now in the Biblioteca Medicea Laurenziana, Florence. Photo: Scala / Art Resource, New York.

4.6 Pilgrimage ampulla with crucifixion and women at the empty tomb. © Dumbarton Oaks Research Library and Collection, Byzantine Collection, Washington, DC (BZ.1948.18).

4.7 Byzantine gold pectoral cross, sixth to seventh century. The British Museum (1949, 1203.1). © The Trustees of the British Museum. All rights reserved.

Credits

4.8 Crucifixion on panel, eighth century. Monastery of St. Catherine, Sinai, Egypt. Photo: Gianni Dagli Orti / The Art Archive at Art Resource, New York.

5.1 Coptic tapestry (curtain), fifth to sixth century, Egypt. Linen, wool; tapestry weave. Minneapolis Institute of Art (83.126). The Centennial Fund: Aimee Mott Butler Charitable Trust, Mr. and Mrs. John F. Donovan, Estate of Margaret B. Hawks, Eleanor Weld Reid.

5.2 Mosaic apse, Basilica of Santa Pudenziana, Rome, early fifth century. Photo: © Robin M. Jensen.

5.3 Mosaic from seventh-century chapel of Primus and Felicianus, San Stefano Rotondo, Rome. Photo: © Robin M. Jensen.

5.4 Apse mosaic, Basilica of Sant'Apollinare in Classe, ca. 540. Photo: © Robin M. Jensen.

5.5 Empty throne with gemmed cross, Arian Baptistery, Ravenna, late fifth century. Photo: © Robin M. Jensen.

5.6 Reliquary cross of Justin II (the Crux Vaticana), Constantinople, 568–574. Photo: Museum of the Treasury, St. Peter's Basilica, Vatican. Scala / Art Resource, New York.

5.7 *Saint Helena and Heraclius Taking the Holy Cross to Jerusalem*, Miguel Jiménez and Martin Bernat, Retable of the Holy Cross of Blosa, Museo de Zaragoza, Spain, 1481. Photo: Alfredo Dagli Orti / The Art Archive at Art Resource, New York.

5.8 Baptistery pavement, Benefensis (La Skhira, Tunisia), fifth century. Now in the Archeological Museum, Sfax. Photo: © Robin M. Jensen.

6.1 The Pérussis Altarpiece, circle of Nicolas Froment. Oil and gold on wood, ca. 1480. The Metropolitan Museum of Art, New York (54.195) (OASC). Purchase, Mary Wetmore Shively Bequest, in memory of her husband, Henry L. Shively, M.D., 1954. www.metmuseum.org.

6.2 *Tree of Life*, Pacino di Bonaguida, 1305–1310. Accademia Gallery, Florence, Italy. Photo: Alinari / Art Resource, New York.

6.3 *Te Igitur* page (fol. 15v) from the *Drogo Sacramentary*, Metz, ninth century. Now in the Bibliothèque Nationale de France (BnF). © BnF, Dist. RMN-Grand Palais / Art Resource, New York.

6.4 Armenian *khachkar*, Noraduz Cemetery, probably thirteenth century. Photo: Courtesy of Donnel O'Flynn.

6.5 Tree of Life, apse mosaic, Basilica of San Clemente, Rome. Photo: © Robin M. Jensen.

6.6 Muiredach's Cross, west side, tenth century, Monasterboice, Ireland. Photo: Andrea Jemolo / Scala / Art Resource, New York.

6.7 "The Tree Growing on Adam's Grave." Illumination from the *Hours of Catherine of Cleves*. Utrecht, the Netherlands, ca. 1440. The Pierpont Morgan Library, New York, MS M.917 / 945, p. 97. Purchased on the Belle da Costa Greene Fund and with the assistance of the Fellows, 1963. Image courtesy of Faksimile Verlag Luzern.

6.8 Apse mosaic, Basilica of St. John Lateran, Rome. Photo: © Robin M. Jensen.

Credits

7.1 Crucifixion, St. Gall Gospel Book, ca. 750. *Irish Evangelary from St. Gall (Quatuor Evangelia)*. Stiftsbibliothek,St. Gallen, Switzerland.

7.2 Crucifixion, mosaic, Monastery Church, Hosios Loukas, Greece, eleventh century. Photo: Hans A. Rosbach / Wikimedia Commons (CC-BY-SA-3.0).

7.3 Page from Hrabanus Maurus, *In honorem Sanctae Crucis,* ca. 1170. The British Library, Harley 3045, fol. 6v. © The British Library Board.

7.4 Crucifixion, ivory plaque from Metz, ca. 870. The Metropolitan Museum of Art, New York (1974.266) (The Cloisters Collection) and the Réunion des Musées Nationaux de France (Palais du Louvre), 1974. www.metmuseum.org.

7.5 Reliquary crucifix, found in Winchester but probably made in Germany or under German influence, ca. 900–1000. Enameled gold with walrus tusk ivory and wooden core. Victoria and Albert Museum, London. V&A Images / The Art Archive at Art Resource, New York.

7.6 Crucifix, Giunta Pisano (fl. 1236–1254), Basilica of San Domenico, Bologna, Italy. Photo: Scala / Art Resource, New York.

7.7 Emperor Frederick I, called Barbarossa, as crusader. Illuminated manuscript page. Biblioteca Apostolica Vaticana. Vatican Museums, Vatican State (Vat. Lat. 2001, fol. 1r). Photo: bpk, Bildagentur / Art Resource, New York.

7.8 Crucifixion, Matthias Grünewald, interior panel from the Isenheim Altarpiece, 1512–1516. Musée d'Unterlinden, Colmar, France. Wikimedia Commons (CC-PD-Mark).

8.1 Destruction of religious images in Zurich, 1524. Wikimedia Commons (CC-PD-Mark).

8.2 *Crucifixion,* Lucas Cranach the Elder, 1506–1520. Statens Museum for Kunst, Denmark, Copenhagen. Creative Commons (CC0 1.0).

8.3 *Luther Preaching,* Lucas Cranach the Elder, 1547. From the Wittenberg Altarpiece (predella). Stadtkirche, Wittenberg. bpk Bildagentur / Art Resource, New York.

8.4 *Klaus Hottinger and Party Take Down the Stadelhofen Crucifix*. Drawing attributed to Heinrich Thomann (1748–1794), from a copy of Heinrich Bullinger's *Reformationgeschichte*. Zentralbibliothek, Zurich (Ms B 316).

8.5 Francisco de Zurbarán, *Christ Crucified,* ca. 1665. Museu Nacional d'Art de Catalunya, Barcelona, Spain. Agustí Montal Bequest, 1966 (071676-000), www.museunacional.cat (CC BY-NC-SA 3.0).

8.6 Hieronymous Wierix, *Christ in the Wine Press,* before 1619. Engraving. The Metropolitan Museum of Art, New York 53.601.19(132). Harris Brisbane Dick Fund, 1953. www.metmuseum.org.

9.1 Atrial cross with Face of Christ, surmounting a small sepulcher attended by the Virgin Mary. Photo: Courtesy of Jaime Lara.

9.2 *Cruz de ánimas* with two carved kneeling figures, ca. 1820. The Snite Museum of Art, University of Notre Dame, Notre Dame, Indiana (2001.004.004). Acquired with funds provided by the Fritz and Milly Kaeser Endowment for Liturgical Art.

9.3 Brass crucifix, Angola, Republic of the Congo, sixteenth to seventeenth century. The Metropolitan Museum of Art, New York (1999.295.7) (OASC). Gift of Ernst Anspach, 1999. www.metmuseum.org.

9.4 *The Yellow Crucifixion,* Marc Chagall, 1942. Musée National d'Art Modern, Centre Georges Pompidou, Paris. © CNAC / MNAM / Dist. RMN-Grand Palais / Art Resource, New York. © 2016 Artists Rights Society (ARS), New York / ADAGP, Paris.

9.5 *Christa,* Edwina Sandys, 1975. Bronze sculpture. © Edwina Sandys / The American Rights Society.

Index

Index

Index

Index